MW00638200

the PHILLIES EXPERIENCE

A YEAR-BY-YEAR CHRONICLE OF
THE PHILADELPHIA PHILLIES

Tyler Kepner

MVP
BOOKS

First published in 2013 by MVP Books, an imprint of MBI Publishing Company,
400 First Avenue North, Suite 300, Minneapolis, MN 55401 USA

© 2013 MVP Books

Text compiled and edited by Facts That Matter Inc.
Contributing writers: David Aretha (editor), James Buckley Jr., Jim Gigliotti, Bruce Markusen, Matt
Silverman, Marty Strasen.

Photo copyrights as indicated on credits page.

All rights reserved. With the exception of quoting brief passages for the purposes of review, no part of this
publication may be reproduced without prior written permission from the Publisher.

The information in this book is true and complete to the best of our knowledge. All recommendations
are made without any guarantee on the part of the author or Publisher, who also disclaims any liability
incurred in connection with the use of this data or specific details.

We recognize, further, that some words, model names, and designations mentioned herein are the
property of the trademark holder. We use them for identification purposes only. This is not an official
publication.

MVP Books titles are also available at discounts in bulk quantity for industrial or sales-promotional use.
For details write to Special Sales Manager at MBI Publishing Company, 400 First Avenue North, Suite 300,
Minneapolis, MN 55401 USA.

To find out more about our books, visit us online at www.mvpbooks.com.

Library of Congress Cataloging-in-Publication Data

Kepner, Tyler.
 The Phillies experience : a year-by-year chronicle of the Philadelphia Phillies / Tyler Kepner.
   p. cm.
 Includes bibliographical references and index.
 ISBN 978-0-7603-4277-0 (hc : alk. paper)
 1. Philadelphia Phillies (Baseball team)--History--Chronology. I. Title.
 GV875.P45K47 2013
 796.357'640974811--dc23

                    2012042720

Editor: Josh Leventhal
Design manager: James Kegley
Layout: Laurie Young

Printed in China

CONTENTS

Introduction 6

The Nineteenth Century 8

1900–1919 14

1920s 44

1930s 60

1940s 76

1950s 92

1960s 110

1970s 126

1980s 146

1990s 166

2000s to Today 184

Photo Credits 218

Index 219

The World Series victory parade heads down
Broad Street on October 31, 2008.

INTRODUCTION
BITTER, SWEET MEMORIES

Relive the rags-to-riches story of the Philadelphia Phillies,
a perennial loser that became the envy of the baseball world.

Late in the evening of October 8, 1983, my father started driving down Broad Street
to our home in the suburbs. The Phillies had just won the National League pennant,
and we were too excited to find the ramp to the Schuylkill Expressway. We just kept
going, slicing through the heart of Philadelphia, pulled by the pulse of the city. I was in
the passenger seat, eight years old. It was the greatest moment of my childhood.

The Phillies had stomped the Los Angeles Dodgers, bursting to a lead in the first
inning and never letting go. My pitching hero, Steve Carlton, had recorded the win, and
my hitting hero, Mike Schmidt, had lifted Al Holland in his arms to start the celebration
at Veterans Stadium.

Up and down Broad Street, drivers honked the good news. World Series, here we come! My dad let me lean on the horn of his Chevette, and I was thrilled to do something that only made sense in the context of the one thing I cared most about in the world: the Phillies.

Nothing would ever be better, at least while I was a kid. A few days later, the Phillies won the opener of the World Series, in Baltimore, and then they lost four in a row.

We saw the last two games at the Vet, which was filled with people but not with faith. The Phillies led for one half of the 18 innings those two days, and by the end, enough fans had left that we shuffled down to the front row, against the tarp behind first base. We watched Scott McGregor and friends celebrate the Phillies' demise. I refused to utter the word *Orioles* for a year.

I had missed the better World Series of that era, in 1980, when the Phillies won their first championship. Born a bit too late, I guess. By the time the Phillies won another pennant, I was in college. By the time they won another title, I was covering the games as a reporter for *The New York Times*. No cheering in the press box.

But I think I grew up at precisely the right time to appreciate the spectrum of Phillies history. The first time I met a player—Bob Dernier, in 1982, at a car dealership in Flourtown—he signed a program bearing the slogan "Baseball's Best." That is what the Phillies called themselves in the heady days of Schmidt, Carlton, and Pete Rose. It did not last.

When the decade ended, the Phillies had tumbled to last place. That is right where they started in 1883, and where they have finished 31 times. In 2007, the Phillies became the first team in professional sports history to reach 10,000 losses.

Then something remarkable happened. The Phillies went on to win the National League East, and they quickly made it a habit. Players yearned for a chance to join the Phillies, and fans gobbled every ticket, every night. Citizens Bank Park became the hot place to be in Philadelphia. The Phillies began an unprecedented run of success.

In that spirit, *The Phillies Chronicle* shows just how far this franchise has come. The team that bumbled through 30 losing seasons in a 31-year span; that once tried to change its name to Blue Jays; that lagged behind every other NL team in integration; that traded Hall of Famers Ferguson Jenkins and Ryne Sandberg . . . somehow, *that* team would one day become the envy of baseball.

This book shows how it happened. It's all here, from the days that made you scream out your window in agony to the nights that made you lean on your car horn in joy.

—Tyler Kepner

Phillies yearbook, 1983.

BORN AS QUAKERS

Some of the most amazing events in Phillies history occurred during the nineteenth century, including a four-homer game, an outfield of three .400 hitters, and a pitcher who lost 48 games in one season.

O ne of the most famous pieces of trivia about the Philadelphia Phillies is only half correct. According to legend, the team is the oldest American pro sports franchise to play in the same hometown with the same nickname since its inception. In fact, they share that distinction. The Phillies were certainly born a long time ago, in 1883, but they were also known for their first seven years as the Quakers (named after the religious group that settled Pennsylvania). "Phillies" did not become the official team name until 1890, the same year that the Cincinnati Reds joined the National League.

The City of Brotherly Love's second pro baseball team, the Quakers came to be when the Worcester Ruby Legs folded in 1882. The National League, which had been formed in 1876, awarded the franchise to sporting goods magnate and former big-league outfielder Al Reach and his partner John Rogers. Reach picked "Phillies" as the nickname, but the team also used Quakers, picking up the name from a team that had played in the National Association.

For their first season, the Phillies owners hired as manager a man with one of the greatest nicknames in baseball history: former infielder Bob "Death to Flying Things" Ferguson. Under Ferguson, the club got off to such a bad start in 1883 that he handed the reins to Blondie Purcell. Together, the two managers would win only 17 of 98 games that year.

This postcard, published by Gordon Tindall as part of the "Great American Ballparks" series, depicts Philadelphia's Baker Bowl in its inaugural season of 1887.

The first Phillies were a collection of youngsters and gimpy oldsters. Ferguson himself, at 38, manned second base. Iron-armed, 20-year-old starting pitcher John Coleman took it on the chin day after day. He went 12–48, setting a still-standing major league record for losses in a season. In 538⅓ innings, Coleman gave up 772 hits while posting a 4.87 ERA. Other lowlights from that first season included the Phillies' 27 errors in a game against Providence; their 29–4 loss to Boston; and their 28–0 shutout loss to Providence, which, three centuries later, would stand as the worst shutout pasting of all time.

Reach and Rogers knew that the status quo wouldn't cut it, so in 1884 they brought in a manager with a proven pedigree. Harry Wright, a future Hall of Famer, had led the first-ever pro team, the Cincinnati Red Stockings, back in 1869. The British native had become one of the most respected men in the game, having turned his youthful skills as a cricket player into a long career in America's national pastime. As manager of the 1875 Boston Red Stockings of the National Association, he went 71–8.

Wright led the Phillies/Quakers to four straight winning seasons. A highlight was the 1886 campaign. Although they finished in fourth place, their .623 winning percentage would be the best by a Phillies club until 1976. In 1886, the Phillies attracted more fans than the crosstown-rival Athletics for the first time.

The Phillies got closer to the top of the league in 1887, finishing second. Overall, Wright proved his worth, only once leading the team to worse than a fourth-place finish.

Wright's last year as skipper, 1893, marked a turning point in both baseball and the team's talent level. The pitcher's mound was moved back, to its current location of 60 feet, 6 inches. Scores soared in 1894, and the Phillies benefitted along with everyone else. The team posted a .350 betting average, the highest ever for a major league team over a single season. The Phils were led by a Hall of Fame trio of outfielders who each topped .400. A fourth outfielder who spelled the regulars, Tuck Turner, hit .418.

That amazing outfield, still the only one in baseball history with three .400 hitters, is worth a closer look, as they were the best players of the decade for the Phillies franchise.

Center fielder "Sliding" Billy Hamilton led things off. His speed—four seasons with 100 or more stolen bases—and ability to get on base made him one of the best leadoff men ever. Hamilton led his league in walks five times, and he is one of a handful of players to average more than 1.0 runs per game over his career. He possessed more than pure speed; a dozen straight .300 campaigns contributed to his .344 lifetime average, seventh best in baseball history.

In right field, Sam Thompson was one of baseball's first true sluggers. A two-time NL home run leader, he averaged 0.93 RBI per game over his 15-year career, one of the best ratios of all time. He didn't join the Phillies until he was 29, but he had his best seasons with them, including 1895 when he led the league with 18 homers, 165 RBI, and a .654 slugging average. (That RBI total missed by one the number he had reached in 1887 with Detroit, which stood as the big-league standard until Babe Ruth plated 171 in 1921.) Thompson also had one of the strongest outfield arms in the game; six times he had more than 25 assists in a season. Reportedly, he was among the first to perfect the one-hop throw from his right-field position.

Bob "Death to Flying Things" Ferguson had been an outstanding manager with Hartford in the 1870s, but his tenure in Philadelphia was far from impressive. He went 4–13 with the inaugural Quakers in 1883.

PHILLIES PHACT

From 1885 to 1897, left-hand-throwing Jack Clements served primary backstop duties for Philadelphia, making him the last regular southpaw to work behind the dish.

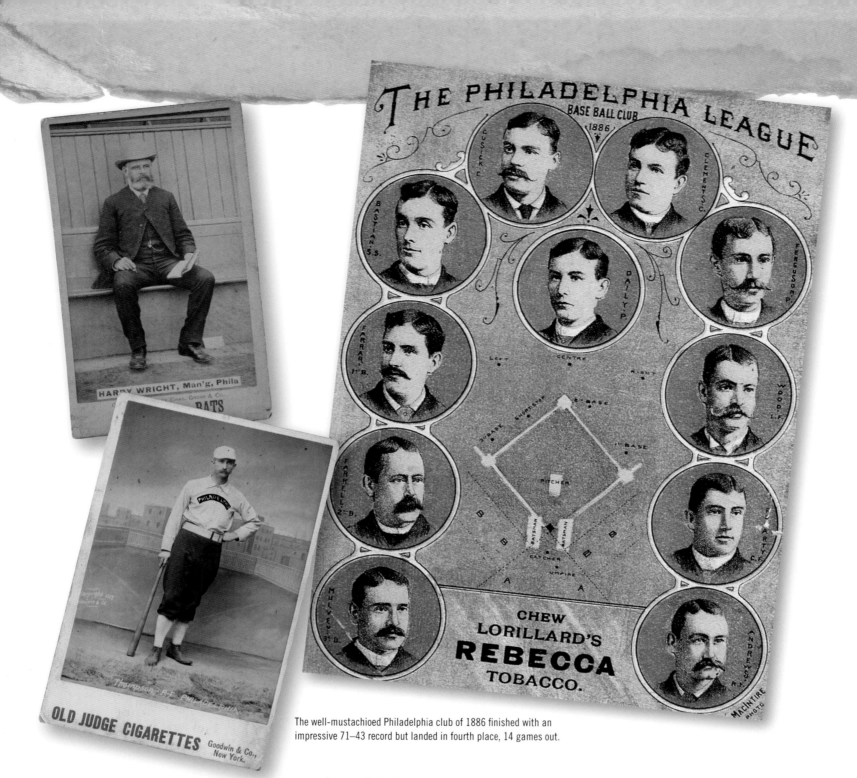

The well-mustachioed Philadelphia club of 1886 finished with an impressive 71–43 record but landed in fourth place, 14 games out.

Top: Harry Wright, a team leader for the 57–0 Cincinnati Red Stockings of 1869, proved adept as Philly's manager, posting a 636–566 record from 1884 to 1893.

Bottom: Sam Thompson packed quite a wallop for the Phillies in 1894 and 1895, when he averaged .402 while amassing 312 RBI—in just 221 games.

Over in left, "Big" Ed Delahanty was lighter than the 210-pound Thompson, but he was second to none in raw power. In 1896, Delahanty became the second player ever to hit four homers in one game. He led the NL twice in home runs while also pacing the league in doubles five times. A terrific all-around hitter, he posted three .400-plus seasons (all with the Phillies) on the way to a career average of .346, fifth best in history. He even stole an NL-best 58 bases in 1898. Delahanty played 13 of his 16 Hall of Fame seasons with the Phillies. Combine all that offensive firepower with terrific speed and great outfield play and you have a player whom some experts call the best all-around big-leaguer of the 1890s.

Though that trio of hitters brought plenty of thrills to Phillies fans, the men on the mound provided fewer reasons to cheer. Looking back on the Phillies' first decade-plus, you'll find the biggest highlights at the plate and on the base paths, not on the mound.

The Phillies' first standout pitcher was Charlie Ferguson, who won 99 games over his four seasons. In 1885, he also pitched the franchise's first no-hitter, a 1–0 win over the Providence Grays. He was such a good all-around player that he batted .337 one season while playing second base on his non-pitching days. Unfortunately, Ferguson died in 1888 of typhoid after going 22–10 in 1887. Ferguson's death cast a gloom over the team throughout that season, but it did lead indirectly to the acquisition of Delahanty, who was brought in to play second in place of Ferguson.

Kid Gleason had a couple of outstanding years on the mound for the Phillies. The part-time second baseman and future Chicago "Black Sox" manager won 38 games in 1890 and 24 in 1891 before moving to the Cardinals. He had a later stint with the Phils at the end of his career (1903–08) when he left the mound behind. In 1905, he led the NL with 699 at-bats at the age of 38.

Gus Weyhing earned the nickname "Rubber Arm" for topping 400 innings in five of his first seven seasons, including four with the Athletics and two with the Phillies. He had one outstanding season for the Phils in 1892, when he won 32 games with a 2.66 ERA. Left-hander Wiley Piatt had the only two good seasons of his career with the Phillies. In 1898 and 1899, he won 24 and 23 games.

> "You just want to shut your eyes, say a prayer, and chuck the ball [to Ed Delahanty]. The Lord only knows what'll happen after that."
>
> — National League pitcher Crazy Schmit

Delahanty's Big Day and Sad Demise

Big Ed Delahanty's biggest day came on July 13, 1896, in a game against the Chicago Colts (who would later become the Cubs). Pitcher Adonis Terry served up four pitches that Delahanty turned into homers. For many years, it was believed that all four were inside-the-park jobs in Chicago's capacious West Side Park, where the center-field fence was 560 feet from home plate. Recent baseball research robbed Big Ed of two of the inside-the-parkers, but he did in fact tally four homers in the game, becoming the first big-leaguer ever to do so.

Sadly, Delahanty's life ended early and his death remains shrouded in mystery. After leaving the Phillies for potentially richer pastures in the new American League in 1902, Delahanty's life unraveled. Beset by family medical problems, financial troubles due largely to gambling issues, and increased drinking, Delahanty bounced from team to team. While with the Washington Senators in 1903, he found himself on a train bound from Detroit to New York. At one point, a drunken, abusive Delahanty was kicked off the train near a bridge over the Niagara River. Accounts vary from this point, but the end result was that Delahanty either jumped or fell off the bridge to his death. It was a dramatic and tragic end for one of the Phillies' greatest heroes.

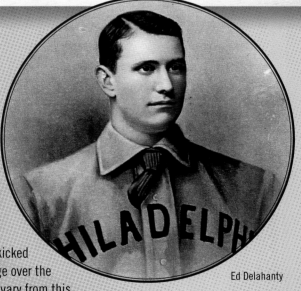
Ed Delahanty

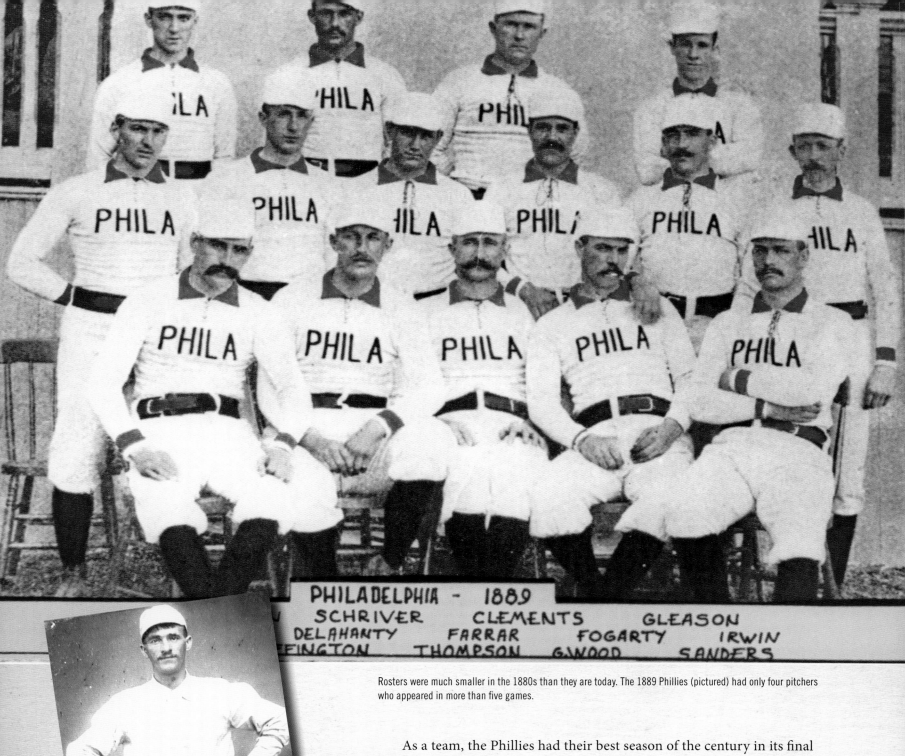

PHILADELPHIA – 1889
SCHRIVER   CLEMENTS   GLEASON
DELAHANTY   FARRAR   FOGARTY   IRWIN
FINGTON   THOMPSON   G.WOOD   SANDERS

Rosters were much smaller in the 1880s than they are today. The 1889 Phillies (pictured) had only four pitchers who appeared in more than five games.

As a team, the Phillies had their best season of the century in its final year. The team won 94 games in 1899, a win total they would not match until 1976. Delahanty was continuing his powerful hitting. At 31 and in the prime of his career, he led the NL in batting (.410) as well as hits, doubles, total bases, and RBI. A youngster named Nap Lajoie, who would go on to greater fame with the Athletics and Indians, hit .378 in limited action. Future Hall of Famer Elmer Flick chipped in with a .342 average. Even with all that firepower, however, they still finished nine games behind the Brooklyn Superbas in the NL pennant race.

With a team of talented young hitters and with the game set to explode in the new century, the Phillies and their fans looked forward to a fantastic future. Little did they know that their first championship was 80 years in the distance.

A part-time outfielder when he first came to Philadelphia in 1887, Charlie Buffinton was dominant as a full-time pitcher in 1888, going 28–17 with a 1.91 ERA.

Early Phillies Homes

So, where did all these bounteous batters and marvelous moundsmen from Philadelphia ply their trades? The Phillies first played at the public Recreation Park. In 1887, the team moved to what would be its home for more than four decades, a site bounded by four streets: Broad, Lehigh, 15th, and Huntingdon. The first version of the ballpark was known as Huntingdon Grounds. It was one of the finest ballparks yet built: the first to have an entirely brick exterior and the first to have pavilions. A crowd of 20,000 packed the place on Opening Day 1887. However, a fire in August 1894 destroyed much of that original structure.

By the start of the 1895 season, a new baseball palace was built on the same site. (Just try getting a ballpark built that fast today!) Named the Philadelphia Baseball Grounds,

it would be renamed Baker Bowl after owner William Baker during the World War I era. The ballpark looked more like a serving platter than a bowl. A strange bulge in the outfield, the result of an underground train tunnel, gave the place an enduring nickname: The Hump.

The design of Baker Bowl, however, was groundbreaking. It was the first ballpark built with cantilevered supports, which eliminated many of the obstructed view seats that pillar-supported second decks created. It also boasted a right-field wall that towered over the playing surface. It was, to pitchers' dismay, only 272 feet to the right-field corner. Not surprisingly, hitters loved the "Band Box," as it was known (a term that would become part of baseball lore for any small, intimate ballpark).

The Phillies played their first four seasons (1883–1886) at Recreation Park, which hosted its first ballgame in 1860.

DEADBALL DRAMA

In the early years of the century, the Phillies endured financial hardship, roster raids, and a horrific tragedy. But in 1915, Pete Alexander took them all the way to the World Series.

One of baseball's enduring charms is its continuity, the way it is passed through generations, with history the connective tissue. In Philadelphia, that history is unbroken. We can tell young fans at Citizens Bank Park that the team they are watching has existed for more than a century. Then, as now, the game had nine innings, nine fielders per side, 90 feet between bases—one, two, three strikes, you're out.

But the old ball game has seen overwhelming changes, of course, not only in the obvious ways—integrated rosters, specialized bullpens, media coverage, on and on and on—but in the background stories that make up each season. And over the first two decades of the twentieth century, baseball's Deadball Era, the Phillies weathered the kind of drama that would seem outrageous today.

Some of their best players, including Nap Lajoie, a five-time batting champion and future Hall of Famer, ditched the Phillies to jump to the newly created American League in 1901. The Phillies were so strapped for cash in 1902 that they needed a loan from the owner of the Pirates to keep the team afloat.

The bleachers at Baker Bowl collapsed in 1903, killing 12 fans. In 1909, the Phillies endured two ownership changes in one year. The 1910 Phillies wore uniforms highlighted in green. There was another team in town, Connie Mack's Athletics of the American League, and it won three World Series and played in five before the Phillies even won their first pennant.

There was one other important difference between the Phillies of this era and the teams of so many years to follow: These Phillies were actually pretty good. They finished with a winning record in 11 of the century's first 20 seasons, and they captured the first pennant in team history in 1915.

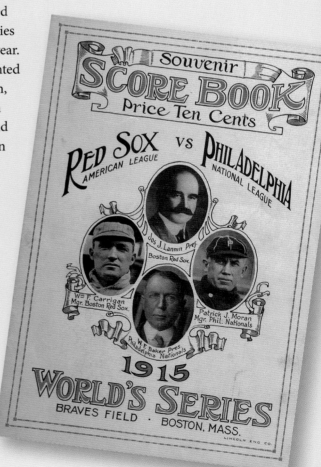

After winning the opener of the 1915 World Series over Boston, the Phillies wouldn't win another game in the Fall Classic for 65 years.

Thirty-one wins from pitcher Pete Alexander (left) and strong leadership by manager Pat Moran (right) helped lead the Phillies to their first National League pennant in 1915.

The Phillies never sustained success for very long, but by their standards, even a three-year streak of winning seasons (1915–17) was a notable achievement. The team would not post a winning record in three successive seasons again until the 1960s.

A stalwart of the early years was outfielder Sherry Magee, who signed with the Phillies at age 19 in 1904 and was ready for the majors immediately. At age 22, he paced the circuit in RBI with 85. In 1910, he led the league in runs scored (110), RBI (123), and batting average (.331). Yet Magee was an ornery sort who brawled with teammates and even once slugged an umpire in the mouth. He was traded to the Boston Braves after the 1914 season and thus missed the Phillies' trip to the 1915 World Series.

The Phillies went 90–62 that season, seven games better than Magee's second-place Braves. The hitting star was Gavvy Cravath, who led the league in homers (24) and RBI (115), and the pitching great was Grover Cleveland "Pete" Alexander, who was 31–10 with a 1.22 ERA and led the league in every important pitching category.

Signed off the Syracuse roster of the New York State League for $750 in 1910, Alexander led the NL in victories five times from 1911 to 1917, averaging 27 per year. He registered the only World Series victory for the Phillies when he beat the Red Sox in Game One in 1915.

But Alexander lost Game Three, and another future Hall of Famer, Eppa Rixey, dropped the Game Five finale. The Phillies stayed strong the next two years, finishing second both times, before trading Alexander and embarking on three decades of misery.

Highlights

January 1: The Phillies begin the twentieth century as one of eight National League teams. The others are the Pittsburgh Pirates, New York Giants, Brooklyn Superbas (Dodgers), Boston Beaneaters (Braves), St. Louis Cardinals, Cincinnati Reds, and Chicago Orphans (Cubs). The NL is the sole major league.

April 19: The Phillies win their first game of the century, a 19–17 thriller against Boston.

April 28: The Phils rout the Giants 19–1.

May 11: The Phillies take care of Cincinnati 20–11.

July 12: Noodles Hahn of Cincinnati no-hits the Phillies.

July 13: A day after going hitless, the Phils crush Pittsburgh 23–8.

September 6: The Phillies beat the Cubs 20–5.

NOTES

Outfielder **Elmer Flick** (.367–11–110) leads an offense that boasts six .300 hitters.

First baseman **Ed Delahanty** bats .323 with 109 RBI.

Second baseman **Nap Lajoie** raps .337, and outfielder **Roy Thomas** (.316) amasses 37 steals and a NL-high 132 runs.

Red Donahue, Chick Fraser, and **Bill Bernhard** tie for the team lead in wins (15).

SIMPLY ELECTRIC

Phillies Pull Out All the Stops in New Century

The Phillies didn't "ring in" a new century of baseball. According to the Cincinnati Reds, they "buzzed" their way into it. And according to some—including those Reds—it was electronic espionage that helped Philadelphia to a 45–23 home record while going 30–40 on the road.

In September, Reds shortstop Tommy Corcoran started digging his spikes into the third-base coaching box, to the wonderment of fans at Philadelphia Baseball Grounds (later Baker Bowl). What he found, allegedly, was a metal box buried beneath the ground with protruding electric wires—a rudimentary "buzzing device" that was operated from the home clubhouse in center field.

From there, it was purported that backup catcher Morgan Murphy used a telescope to steal signs from opposing catchers. Murphy would relay the calls to third-base coach Petie Chiles through a series of buzzes that Chiles, standing atop the device, could feel. Chiles (who was arrested and sentenced to two years of hard labor in Texas after the season for his involvement in a con scheme) would allegedly shout verbal cues to assist his Philadelphia batters.

"He had an unusual twitch in his leg at times," baseball historian Joe Ditmarr wrote of Chiles, "and often stood in one position, right in the middle of a perpetual wet spot in the corner of the coach's box."

Nothing much was made of the late-season "discovery," which came as the Phillies finished third in the eight-team National League (scaled back from 12 teams). There were stories that Pittsburgh did the same thing in its home park.

However they did it, these Phillies were a stellar hitting club. Their .290 team average was second in the league, just three points behind that of champion Brooklyn. Outfielder Elmer Flick finished second to Pittsburgh's Honus Wagner in the batting race with a .367 average and led the NL with 110 RBI. With better pitching and defense, Philadelphia might have made a run at the pennant.

A slick hitter with quick feet, Elmer Flick batted .338 in four years with the Phillies before jumping to the crosstown Athletics in 1902.

A GAME OF "WHAT IF"

Without Their "Nap," Phils Settle for Second

The arrival of the American League in 1901 meant a bitter departure for the Philadelphia Phillies. Nap Lajoie, the club's emerging star second baseman, had been told before the season by owner John Rogers that he would be paid the same salary as teammate Ed Delahanty. However, it soon came to Lajoie's attention that Delahanty was raking in $3,000—$400 more than Lajoie was earning. "I saw the checks," an irate Lajoie noted.

Now that Philadelphia hosted a team in the new American League—Connie Mack's Athletics—Lajoie had an option. He and three Phils pitchers jumped to the Athletics despite Rogers' efforts to block the deal, and Lajoie enjoyed one of the greatest seasons in major league history. He gave the AL its first Triple Crown winner with a .426 average, 14 home runs, and 125 RBI.

Rogers eventually won the injunction he sought to keep Lajoie from playing for the A's when the case went all the way to the Pennsylvania Supreme Court. However, the ruling was not made until one day into the 1902 season, at which point Lajoie was prevented from playing for a Pennsylvania team other than the Phillies. He wound up starring for Cleveland.

Even without Lajoie, the Phillies were formidable in 1901. Delahanty was a force offensively, and the club's 2.87 team ERA ranked second in the National League behind only pennant-winning Pittsburgh. A terrific second half that included a 10-game winning streak in August and September helped the Phillies notch an 83–57 record. They finished 7½ games behind the Pirates.

Still, Philadelphia's NL fans had to wonder "what if." The loss of four regulars, including one of the greatest hitters and second sackers in the history of the game, had contributed to a rocky start from which their club could never make it all the way back. And now, there was a new team in town to compete with not only for talent, but also for the town's sports-loving fans.

Slugger Ed Delahanty not only jumped to the American League after his 1901 season, he also encouraged many of his teammates to take the upstart league's money.

Highlights

March: Phillies hit machine Nap Lajoie jumps to the Philadelphia Athletics of the American League, which begins its first season as a major league circuit.

April 18: Brooklyn beats the Phillies 12–7 on Opening Day. It is the first game in the National or American League this year, and is thus the first game in modern major league history.

May 8: The New York Giants defeat the Phillies 9–8 when Giants first baseman John Ganzel uses the hidden-ball trick to tag out Harry Wolverton to end the game.

June 24: The Phillies blow out Cincinnati 19–1 and 8–0 in a doubleheader sweep.

September 7: Philly beats Pittsburgh 4–1 for the club's tenth consecutive victory.

October 5: The team closes 50–27 to finish with 83 victories, which ties for the second most in the majors.

NOTES

Red Donahue, Bill Duggleby, and **Al Orth** all finish with exactly 20 wins.

Ed Delahanty leads the NL in doubles (38) and ranks second in batting (.354) and RBI (108).

Nap Lajoie hits .426 for the rival Athletics. It will be the highest MLB batting average in the twentieth century.

▸ 56-81   7th ◂

Highlights

April 21: The Pennsylvania Supreme Court rules that Nap Lajoie had violated his contract with the Phillies and that the team could "restrain him from playing for another club." Despite this bizarre ruling, Lajoie continues his Hall of Fame career in Cleveland.

May 13: A year after losing to the Phillies 19–1, Cincinnati beats them 24–2.

October 3: The Phillies close the season just like they began it, with a 7–0 shutout defeat. It marked the team's 16th scoreless outing of the season.

NOTES

Granted, it's **the Deadball Era,** but the Phillies belt only five home runs all year, fewest in the majors. Only one starting player hits a home run.

Outfielder Shad Barry leads the team in batting (.287), homers (3), RBI (58), and doubles (20).

Outfielder Roy Thomas leads the club in steals (17) and runs (89).

Doc White (16–20, 2.53) is the team's winningest pitcher.

The Athletics, who win the American League pennant, outdraw their cross-town rivals 420,078 to 112,066.

TURN FOR THE WORSE

Exodus Extends from Players to Fans

One day into the 1902 season, the Pennsylvania Supreme Court ruled in favor of the Phillies in their quest to stop Nap Lajoie, their turn-of-the-century star, from playing for the crosstown rival Athletics. It was a hollow victory, however, as the Athletics and the American League continued to pilfer their best players, setting the stage for a stretch of Phillies' futility that would last for more than a decade.

Elmer Flick, the team's top run scorer during a second-place finish in 1901, joined Connie Mack's A's before the season, as did 20-game winner Bill Duggleby and shortstop Monte Cross. Red Donahue, a 20-game winner the previous summer, jumped to St. Louis. And the Washington Senators swiped four players, including 20-game winner Al Orth and left fielder Ed Delahanty, who went on to lead the majors with 43 doubles in 1902.

Just as Philadelphia's top National League players found greener pastures, so did the club's fans. After drawing nearly 235,000 fans the previous year, the Phillies attracted less than half that many in 1902. The City of Brotherly Love's baseball lovers didn't have to travel far to find their fix. Across town, the Athletics beat the Phillies at the gate by a margin of almost four to one.

While Lajoie was winning fans in Cleveland and Delahanty was batting .376 in Washington, the Phils won 27 fewer games than they had the previous season, hitting a mere .247 as a team and shaving opponents' ERAs throughout the league. Shad Barry, 23 and in his first full season, accounted for 60 percent of the team's home run total with a mere *three* long balls.

By the time it was over—thankfully, according to fans, and only with the help of a generous late-season loan from Pirates owner Barney Dreyfuss that helped keep the team operable—the Phillies resided in seventh place among eight teams and knew they had a long climb ahead.

Outfielder Shad Barry's 20 doubles and 3 homers in 1902 might not seem like much, but he ranked in the top 10 in the NL in both categories.

TRAGIC COLLAPSE

Disaster Abounds as Phillies Change Hands

Seasons don't get much worse than the one the Phillies weathered in 1903. It began with the sale of the franchise in February. Jimmy Potter, a wealthy and well-connected man in social circles, bought the club for $170,000 from Al Reach and John Rogers. Potter was not a baseball man; that much was clear. In his defense, however, not even Harry Houdini could have rescued the Phillies from the events of this season.

The losing was bad enough, and Philadelphia did plenty of it. New manager Chief Zimmer—installed (believe it or not) by Pirates owner Barney Dreyfuss as part of his financial loan to the Phils to keep the team afloat—guided the team to 86 setbacks, the most in its history. The Phillies' earned run average of 3.96 was not only last in the National League but also downright embarrassing in the Deadball Era.

Then things went from bad to worse. One week into August, an altercation on 15th Street prompted hundreds of fans to rush to the top of the left-field stands. The wooden structure could not support the weight, and the bleachers collapsed. It was a horrific scene that cost 12 fans their lives and injured 232 others.

The Phillies were forced to play their next few homestands at Columbia Park, home of the Athletics, and a stretch of steady rain forced nine consecutive postponements. Even Mother Nature seemed to be conspiring against the Phillies.

The team did enjoy Chick Fraser's September 18 no-hit victory against the Cubs, but that milestone moment was a silver lining on an otherwise dark and dreary cloud. In fact, Zimmer could take no more. The former catcher retired from managing after his one and only major league season and became—of all things—an umpire.

Highlights

January 9–10: Representatives of the National and American Leagues lay out a framework that both leagues can live with. Teams agree to stop raiding each other's rosters, and the champions of each league will play each other in a postseason series—which will be called the World Series.

July 2: Former Phillies star Ed Delahanty dies when he jumps or falls off the International Bridge into Niagara Falls.

August 8: The left-field bleachers at Baker Bowl collapse, killing 12 people and injuring 232.

August 27: Phillies pitchers walk 17 Brooklyn batters.

August 31: "Iron Man" Joe McGinnity of the Giants pitches both games of a doubleheader against Philadelphia, winning both.

September 18: Chick Fraser no-hits the Cubs, winning 10–0.

NOTES

Phillies owners John Reach and Al Rogers sell the team to socialite Jimmy Potter.

Roy Thomas leads the club in batting at .327, and outfielder **Bill Keister** strokes .320.

Bill Duggleby (13–16) leads the team in wins, as no pitcher posts a winning record.

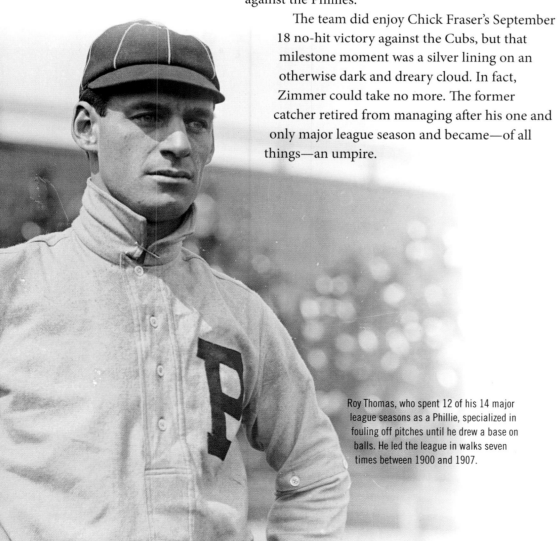

Roy Thomas, who spent 12 of his 14 major league seasons as a Phillie, specialized in fouling off pitches until he drew a base on balls. He led the league in walks seven times between 1900 and 1907.

The Baker Bowl Collapse

The 1903 season was not going well. On August 8 it turned into a disaster. Literally.

The last-place Phillies dropped the first game of the Saturday doubleheader to the Boston Braves. Yet there was a good crowd of approximately 10,000 at the ballpark, which later would be called the Baker Bowl but was then commonly known as Philadelphia Baseball Grounds.

The second game was tied in the fourth inning when a few fans turned their attention away from the contest between sixth-place Boston and the eighth-place home club to focus on a disturbance on 15th Street below the left-field bleachers. Reports differ about whether it was a fight between two drunken men or a woman yelling in distress. Whatever it was, a throng of patrons quickly crammed onto the narrow metal walkway far above the street. The weight was too much, and the support beams gave way.

Body fell upon body by the dozens, until hundreds lay in piles as others frantically tried to help. More than 200 were injured. Twelve died.

The Star of Wilmington, Delaware, reported: "In every direction the wounded were being borne upon stretchers, or mattresses borrowed from nearby dwellings, while others lay moaning with pain upon the baseball diamond awaiting assistance."

Following the tragedy, the Phillies finished the season at new Columbia Park, where they shared the ballpark with the hated Philadelphia Athletics.

Yet the worst crowd disaster in baseball history was neither the first nor the last such incident at the ballpark on West Huntingdon and Broad streets. Seven years after it was built, an August 6, 1894, fire engulfed the grandstand, the bleachers, a train shed, and nearby stables (the horses were rescued). Fortunately, the morning blaze began after the team had just left on a road trip.

The replacement was a modern marvel of the day. The ballpark's grandstand was reinforced with iron, the first of its kind. Still, it could not prevent the disastrous collapse nine years later.

By 1927, the ballpark was renamed Baker Bowl after the team's owner, but tragedy found it once more. One person died and 50 were hurt in a stampede that resulted after the stands along first base crumpled under the weight of people seeking shelter from a rainstorm.

Never has one ballpark endured so many catastrophes. Hopefully, none ever will again.

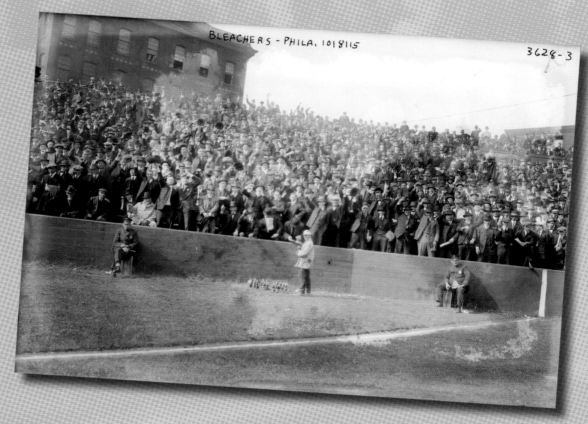

On the day of the disaster in 1903, a swarm of fans climbed to the top of the left field bleachers, causing them to collapse. Things were a bit calmer at the 1915 World Series, shown here.

Bottoms Up

Phillies Descend to Last Place in 100-Loss Season

Hugh Duffy was an Irish New Englander with enormous pride. Any swagger in his step came well earned during a brilliant career as a star outfielder for the Boston Beaneaters. His debut as a player/manager—a 48–89 struggle with Milwaukee in 1901—was not what he had hoped for, but those days began to look like a beacon of light after what Duffy experienced as Phillies manager in 1904. It could only be called a nightmare.

Overseeing a club with little in the way of veteran talent, Duffy dropped 26 of his first 31 decisions as a National League skipper. Having participated in luring NL stars to the American League while in Milwaukee, he could not have been shocked at his club's ineptitude. In the previous three years, many of the top Phillies stars had left for American League clubs. Still, the magnitude of the Phillies' struggles was far worse than he had expected.

PHILLIES PHACT

On August 21, the Phillies reach their lowest depths of the season, if not the history of the franchise, as their eighth straight defeat drops them to 27–79.

They were outscored by a staggering 213 runs. Separate losing streaks of 7, 8, 9, and 12 games put the club 58 games out of first place at one stage and 54 games under .500 by mid-September. They averaged 2.6 errors per game. They became the first team in franchise history to lose 100 games in a year, and their last-place finish was the club's first since its inaugural season in 1883.

Duffy himself hit .283 in 18 games as an outfielder, but the brightest light in his first season in Philadelphia was an outfielder some 18 years his junior. Sherry Magee, a 19-year-old sensation, thrilled his manager with both his play in the field and his promise at the plate. The scrappy Pennsylvania native became an immediate favorite with fans, ripping 101 hits in just 95 games—a dozen of them triples—and giving fans at least one reason to come out to the park.

After the season, owner Jimmy Potter—who had no baseball acumen—handed the club presidency duties over to Billy Shettsline.

Highlights

April 14: Hugh Duffy, a .326 lifetime hitter and future Hall of Famer, begins his tenure as the Phillies' new manager.

May 5: The team's ninth straight loss puts the Phils at 2–12.

May 30: The Phillies drop their twelfth straight, 15–4 to the Giants, and are now 5–26.

October 3: The Phillies' 16–4 loss to Pittsburgh is their 100th defeat of the season—a first for the franchise.

NOTES

Outfielder John Titus leads the team in batting (.294).

Outfielder Sherry Magee, a promising 19-year-old rookie, hits .277 with a team-best 57 RBI.

Chick Fraser (14–24) leads the staff in wins and losses.

Tully Sparks is the most effective pitcher (2.65 ERA) but finishes only 7–16.

Shortstop Rudy Hulswitt commits 56 errors (down from a league-high 81 in 1903).

The Phillies commit 401 errors, 48 more than any other team. Their fielding average is .937.

The team averages fewer than 2,000 fans per game.

1905

Highlights

June 11: The vastly improved Phillies claim their 11th win in 12 games—all on the road—to up their record to 28–17.

June 30: An eighth straight victory puts the Phils at 39–24.

July 16: Pitcher Kid Nichols, a seven-time 30-game winner in the 1890s, is claimed off waivers from St. Louis.

August 24: Cubs pitcher Ed Reulbach goes all the way in a 2–1, 20-inning victory over the Phillies.

October 14: The Philadelphia Athletics, in the World Series for the first time, lose in five games to the Giants.

NOTES

With three new infielders, **the Phillies** commit 126 fewer errors than the year before.

Roy Thomas ranks in the league's top five in batting (.317), hits (178), and runs scored (118).

Sherry Magee leads the team in RBI (98), scores 100 runs, and steals 48 bases.

John Titus ranks eighth in the league in batting (.308) and second in doubles (36).

Newly acquired **Togie Pittinger** posts a 23–14 record and leads the staff in victories.

Hall of Famer Kid Nichols goes 10–6, 2.27 in his 17 outings with the team.

ONE GIANT LEAP

Young Phillies Race to 31-Win Improvement

From top to bottom, the 1905 Philadelphia Phillies were new and improved. It started in the front office, where struggling owner Jimmy Potter gave up the presidency of the club to Billy Shettsline. Throw in a rejuvenated roster that featured better pitchers, stronger fielders, and more potent hitters, and Hugh Duffy's club was poised to make big strides. It did.

Fans noticed. A club-record 317,000-plus spun the Baker Bowl turnstiles to watch the Phillies make a 31-game improvement in the standings. They did not make a pennant run by any means, finishing fourth in the National League and 21½ games behind the Giants, but the team was competitive—and a dramatic improvement over the previous year's squad.

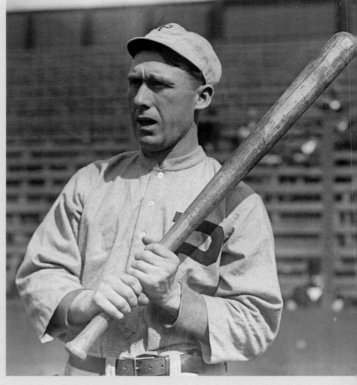

"Silent" John Titus swung a loud bat in 1905, batting .308 and ranking among the NL's top five in slugging (.436), doubles (36), and RBI (89).

Philadelphia's outfield was among the very best in baseball, featuring Sherry Magee (.299), John Titus (.308), and Roy Thomas (.317). That trio was dangerous at the plate and graceful roaming the lawn, helping the Phillies reduce their error total from 401 the previous year to 275.

Shettsline made some key moves that sparked the Phillies' resurgence in 1905. The midseason acquisition of 35-year-old Kid Nichols gave the Phillies more than a veteran presence on the hill and in the clubhouse. It helped the club produce five double-digit winners in the rotation, none more effective than Charles "Togie" Pittinger.

Pittinger had been brought in from Boston before the season for pitcher Chick Fraser and third baseman Harry Wolverton—another Shettsline decision that reaped immediate dividends. The veteran right-hander went 23–14, topping the Phillies in wins, in a major league–leading 46 outings.

The Phillies were 19 games over .500 in early August after a doubleheader sweep of the Cardinals set their record at 57–38. However, even at that high-water mark for the year, they stood 11 games behind the Giants in what became a one-sided chase for the NL pennant. No NL club stood within nine games of New York by season's end.

FISTICUFFS AND FIRSTS

Brawl with Giants, Lush No-Hitter Highlight Season

Philadelphia's 1906 season featured good guys and bad guys, and it took less than one series for the tone to be set. That first homestand saw the defending National League champion New York Giants visit town, and there was no one the Phillies despised more than Giants skipper John McGraw. It showed.

McGraw's swagger riled up Paul Sentell more than anyone, and the Phillies backup infielder vented his feelings in a fistfight at Baker Bowl. While cooler heads ultimately prevailed on the field, the same could not be said in the stands. A group of Phillies fans swarmed Giants players on 15th Street after the game, and what began as a fierce rivalry was officially a bitter one.

Watching much of the commotion on that day was one of the true "good guys." Johnny Lush, a former scholar-athlete at Philadelphia's Girard College for fatherless boys, frequently visited his old school and gave its students free tickets to come watch the Phillies play weekend games. It was during a weekday outing on May 1 that Lush—a left-hander with a baffling curveball—penned his name in the history books.

Lush threw a no-hitter that afternoon at Brooklyn in a 6–0 victory against the Superbas. At 20 years old, Lush became the youngest major-leaguer ever to throw a no-hitter, and it would be an amazing 8,945 games before another Phillies pitcher would no-hit an opposing team.

It was a rare bright spot in a season that quickly turned south for a club that had looked promising for much of the previous year. With their pitching, hitting, and defense slipping, the Phillies never saw the plus side of .500 after mid-July. The team lost 13 more games than it had the previous season and wound up 45½ games behind the Tinker-to-Evers-to-Chance Chicago Cubs in the standings.

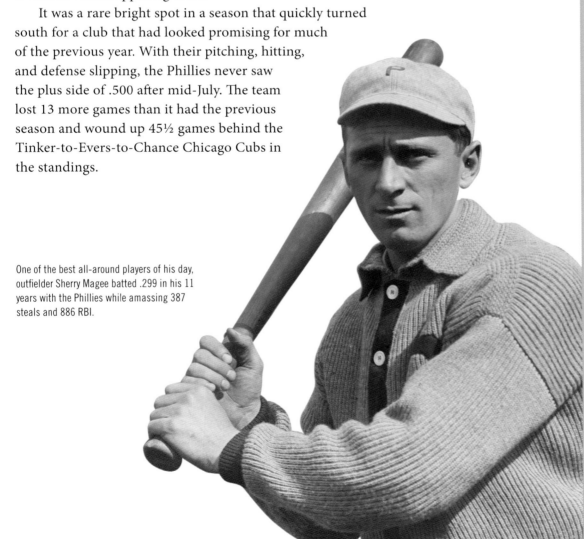

One of the best all-around players of his day, outfielder Sherry Magee batted .299 in his 11 years with the Phillies while amassing 387 steals and 886 RBI.

Highlights

April 21: Against Boston, the Phillies score a season-high 18 runs.

May 1: Johnny Lush throws a no-hitter against the Brooklyn Superbas.

May 31: The Phils defeat the Giants 5–1 to improve to 26–18, just three games out of first place.

August 31: Three months later, the Phillies are 35½ games out of first.

October 1: With one of the most dominating staffs in history (1.75 ERA), the Cubs shut out the Phillies for the sixth time this season.

NOTES

Now the team's unquestioned star, **Sherry Magee** leads the club in batting (.282), doubles (36), triples (8), homers (6), RBI (67), and steals (55).

Roy Thomas leads the league in walks (107) for the sixth time in seven years.

Shortstop **Mickey Doolan** tops the NL in errors with 66, although he also records more assists than any player in the league.

Tully Sparks (19–16) leads the team in wins and ERA (2.16).

Johnny Lush also shines on the hill, going 18–15 with a 2.37 ERA.

Highlights

April 11: The Phillies, who open the season with new manager Billy Murray, win the first game by forfeit over the Giants. It is the only time all year that they'll be in first place.

September 23: The Cubs beat the Phillies 4–1 on a day in which they turn a triple play and clinch the pennant.

October 2: Third baseman Eddie Grant goes 7-for-7 in a doubleheader despite facing Giants pitching greats Rube Marquard and Christy Mathewson.

October 5: The Phillies close the season strong, winning their last seven games.

NOTES

Sherry Magee tops the NL in RBI (85) and finishes second in batting (.328). He ranks among the league's top five in numerous other categories.

John Titus (.275, 63 RBI) is the only other force in the lineup.

Tully Sparks (22–8, 2.00) is the staff's big winner.

Rookie pitchers **George McQuillan** and **Harry Coveleski** go a combined 5–0 with a 0.44 ERA in 61 innings.

The Phillies rank third in the NL in attendance (341,216), but the Athletics are still the top draw in the city and the AL (625,581).

A NEW DIRECTION

Murray Steps In, Manages Phillies to Third Place

Hugh Duffy, weary after a disappointing season and after watching the crosstown Athletics dominate the Philadelphia baseball scene year after year, left for the International League after the 1906 season. Up from the minors to take over as Phillies manager was laid-back New Englander Billy Murray, a farm system winner with a keen eye for talent.

His big-league debut, and first victory, was a most memorable one. Frank Corridon pitched a one-hitter through eight innings at the Polo Grounds. But Giants fans, who hated the Phillies in one of the National League's most heated rivalries, swarmed the diamond and refused to leave, with their team trailing 8–0. So the game went into the books as a forfeit win for Philly.

The remainder of the season was—by and large—more conventional, and it included encouraging signs from Murray's boys. They jumped 10 games over .500 in early June and stayed double digits above .500 for much of the season. A strong finish put them close to 20 games over by year's end, and their 83–64 record was a dozen wins more than the previous season's tally.

Perhaps even more encouraging was the team's success at the gate. More than 340,000 fans came out to cheer Sherry Magee to a runner-up finish in the National League batting chase. His .328 average trailed only Honus Wagner's .350 mark. The attendance total was an improvement of nearly 50,000 over the previous slate, although the Philadelphia Athletics were still spinning the turnstiles at the much quicker pace.

Murray showed his scouting chops late in the season, when the club bought a pair of pitchers who made an immediate impact. George McQuillan went 4–0 with a 0.66 ERA in 41 innings, including 25 straight scoreless frames. And Harry Coveleski did not allow an earned run in 20 innings over four late-season games.

An electrician in the offseason, pitcher George McQuillan electrified Philadelphia in his first two big-league seasons (1907–1908), going a combined 27–17 with a 1.44 ERA.

GIANT KILLER

Coveleski, Phillies Spoil New York's Pennant Plans

Harry Coveleski hardened his muscles, and his resolve, while working the coal mines of his native Pennsylvania as a young man. So when the pitcher was sent down to Lancaster to begin the 1908 season in the minors despite having made an impressive major league debut the year before, he was not about to complain. Instead, he worked on refining his motion, switching to an overhand delivery that would cause angst for hitters over the next decade.

The left-hander was dominating farmhands when he heard news of an Independence Day no-hitter thrown by the Giants' Hooks Wiltse against the Phillies. When he got his chance, he thought, he would show those New Yorkers a thing or two.

That time arrived in late September of a season in which the Phillies were good, but far from great. George McQuillan, Tully Sparks, and Frank Corridon combined for 53 victories toward an 83–71 record and fourth-place National League finish. But it was Coveleski who earned the nickname "Giant Killer" and put a lasting stamp on the Phillies' 1908 season.

The Giants were tied for first place on September 29 when Coveleski shut them out at the Polo Grounds 7–0. Two afternoons later in Philadelphia, he held them to four hits in a 6–2 win. That's when things got interesting. Phillies manager Billy Murray offered his southpaw a $50 bonus if he would take the hill again on October 3. Coveleski probably would have done it for nothing.

The 22-year-old knocked New York into third place with a 3–2 win, retiring the side with the bases loaded in the ninth inning. The Giants lost the pennant by a single game to the Cubs, and they were irate about the manner in which it played out.

"It was a lousy trick," Giants manager John McGraw said, "pitching that young left-hander out of turn in his efforts to beat us out of a pennant."

Murray countered: "In this game, you're out to win ball games."

Slick-fielding first baseman Kitty Bransfield was one of only five NL hitters to top .300 in 1908.

Highlights

July 4: Hooks Wiltse of the Giants throws a 10-inning no-hitter against the Phillies in the morning game of a doubleheader. Wiltse misses a perfect game only because he hits the twenty-seventh batter he faces.

July 28: The Phillies shut out St. Louis 1–0 for their 14th win in 15 games.

August 1: The Phillies shut out the Reds for the third game in a row.

October 3: Rookie pitcher Harry Coveleski beats New York for the third time in six games, ultimately costing the Giants the pennant.

NOTES

First baseman Kitty Bransfield leads the team in batting (.304), homers (3), and RBI (71). He is one of only five .300 hitters in the NL.

Sherry Magee hits .283 and ranks second in the NL in doubles (30) and triples (16).

Six Phillies steal 20 or more bases, headed by **Magee** with 40.

George McQuillan (23–7) emerges as the staff ace, finishing fourth in the NL in wins and third in ERA (1.53).

The Phillies lead the league in earned run average at 2.10, although every team's ERA is below 2.80.

The City Series

The Phillies and Athletics have never met in more than a century's worth of World Series. Yet those two clubs met regularly in the fall—and spring—when they were located only a couple of miles from each other in Philadelphia. The games never counted in the standings, but they meant plenty.

The City Series was an annual exhibition series held in Philadelphia between the Phillies and A's during the half century they shared the city. Their early relationship in Philadelphia certainly did not engender brotherly love.

A founding team in the American League in 1901, the A's boasted the heavy-hitting Napoleon Lajoie, who led the fledgling league in nearly every category that year. In fact, his .426 average has never been equaled in the AL. Lajoie had been Phillies property, batting .345 over 492 games, until he was signed by Connie Mack in 1901. A court order forbade Lajoie from playing in Pennsylvania, so Mack sent him to Cleveland. The rancor made for a tense relationship while the leagues feuded over players and turf. When peace was declared in 1903, however, the newly minted exhibition contests in Philadelphia fueled an instant rivalry.

The Phillies won the inaugural contest, 6–5 in 10 innings, on April 9, 1903. The Phils won four of the five games played that spring, but they dropped four of seven in the fall, with all games played at Columbia Park because of a fatal walkway collapse at Baker Bowl. The teams continued the tradition of spring and fall exhibitions, though in years when one team played in the World Series—the A's appeared eight times and the Phillies twice—no fall City Series was held. In most years, bragging rights in the head-to-head match-ups served to carry fans into the spring, when the City Series began again on the eve of a new season.

By the time the A's moved to Kansas City after the 1954 season, the two teams had played more than 200 exhibitions. One hundred years after the first City Series, the Oakland A's journeyed to Philadelphia in 2003 in interleague play. Though these games counted in the standings, no bragging rights were involved—but the city's honored past was recalled. The Phillies invited former Philadelphia A's Ed Joost and Gus Zernial to attend the game, while former U.S. senator Connie Mack, grandson of the Philadelphia A's manager and owner, threw out the first pitch.

The Phillies and Athletics shared a city for more than half a century and faced off against one another for most of those years.

TORRID TURNOVER

Phillies Get New Owners, Another Skipper

The Phillies changed ownership twice in 1909. Four months after purchasing the club from Jimmy Potter in February, majority owner Israel Durham—a force in Philadelphia politics—died. The surviving members of his ownership group held on to the club for the remainder of the season, but that was it. In November, after a dreary 74–79 campaign, they sold the franchise to sportswriter Horace Fogel, who promptly did something most sportswriters only get the opportunity to report about. He fired the manager, Billy Murray.

Murray's downfall was the season's first half. The Phillies stumbled out of the gate with a 33–42 record, rendering their 41–37 second half too little and too late. Top hitter Sherry Magee slumped, hitting just .270, and the club even entertained thoughts of trading the outfielder to the Giants for Mike Donlin. Murray, however, nixed the idea. "That deal will be made over my dead body," the manager said.

While the Phillies had trouble getting their offense going, they also struggled to keep opponents off the scoreboard. Three starting pitchers posted double-digit victories and winning records. But Tully Sparks (6–11) floundered after winning 16 games the summer before, and George McQuillan (13–16) was reportedly enjoying the Philadelphia nightlife far more than he was enjoying his starts. Perhaps just as troubling were trends taking place off the field, and that's not even accounting for McQuillan. While the Athletics celebrated the opening of Shibe Park by finishing second in the American League and drawing nearly 675,000 fans, the Phils were having a hard time coaxing Philadelphians out for an afternoon at Baker Bowl. Attendance was down 28 percent from the previous season—a trend that new ownership and a new manager would have to contend with.

> "That deal will be made over my dead body."
>
> —Manager Billy Murray

With 40 wins over the two seasons, Earl Moore was the Phillies' ace in 1909 and 1910. He was nicknamed "Crossfire" for his wicked sidearm delivery.

Highlights

February 26: A syndicate headed by Israel Durham, a big political boss in Philadelphia, buys the Phillies from Jimmy Potter.

April 12: The Athletics begin play at Shibe Park, baseball's first concrete and steel ballpark, just six blocks from the Phillies' home at Baker Bowl.

June 9: The Phillies lose their eighth straight game, dropping from four games out of first place to 12½ games out.

June 28: Durham dies, leaving team ownership in the hands of James McNichol and Clarence Wolf.

November 26: Sportswriter and former big-league manager Horace Fogel buys the Phillies. He receives financial backing from Charles P. Taft, brother of current U.S. president William Taft.

NOTES

Sherry Magee leads the team in RBI (66) and ranks second in the NL in doubles (33) and triples (14).

Earl Moore (18–12, 2.10) leads the staff in wins.

The Phillies' attendance drops by 28 percent to 303,177—less than half of what the Athletics draw in their new home.

Highlights

April 14: The Phillies begin the season with Charles Dooin taking charge behind the plate as player/manager.

June 2: The Phils suffer their 10th straight loss and their 14th in 15 games, dropping them from first place to 10 ½ back.

October 6: Boston bombs the Phillies 20–6.

October 23: The Athletics become the first Philadelphia team to win a World Series, as they oust the Cubs in five games.

Late October: Without owner Horace Fogel's approval, Dooin orchestrates a multiplayer deal with Cincinnati. The trade ends up going through.

NOTES

Sherry Magee leads the league in batting (.331), OBP (.445), slugging (.507), RBI (123), and runs (110). He ranks second in doubles (39) and triples (17) and fourth in SBs (49).

Outfielder Johnny Bates ranks seventh in the NL in batting (.305).

Every **Phillies regular** records double digits in steals.

Earl Moore goes 22–15 and leads the NL in strikeouts (185).

George McQuillan finishes 9–6 and leads the league in ERA (1.60). He twice is suspended by the Phillies for violating team rules.

SECOND FIDDLE

Phillies Can't Compete with World Series Champs

Philadelphia celebrated its initial World Series championship in 1910. Unfortunately for Phillies fans, it was across town at Shibe Park, where Connie Mack was managing the Athletics to powerhouse status in the American League. Meanwhile, over at the sparsely populated Baker Bowl, catcher Charlie "Red" Dooin was serving as player/manager and trying to turn around a team—now clad in green and white jerseys in a change that would last only one season—that had fallen on hard times in 1909. By and large, the popular backstop did a fine job in that regard. He couldn't keep the club within an arm's length of Chicago as the Cubs ran off with the National League pennant, but he guided the Phillies back above .500 with a 78–75 record. Meanwhile, Sherry Magee captured the NL batting title with a stellar comeback season.

Magee had struggled through back-to-back sub-.300 campaigns, but in 1910 he rediscovered his hitting stroke. His .331 average allowed him to edge Pittsburgh's Vin Campbell (.326) for the batting crown. He also led the league in RBI, runs, on-base percentage, slugging, and total bases, and he swiped 49 bags.

> **PHILLIES PHACT**
>
> For 1910, the Phillies wear green and white uniforms, but they are ditched after the season.

The rejuvenated offense carried the Phillies to seven victories in their first eight games. By early June, they had slipped nine games under .500, but a strong second half produced a winning record and a fourth-place finish in the NL.

Magee's resurgence wasn't the only boost to the offense. Johnny Bates came over from Boston and hit .305 with 31 steals. Had the Phils boasted more consistent pitching, they almost certainly would have made an even bigger jump in the standings. George McQuillan was suspended twice—once by Dooin and later by team president Horace Fogel—for rules violations, putting a damper on his 1.60 ERA. Earl Moore was suspended along with McQuillan the first time, but he came back on good behavior and put together his best season—22 wins against 15 defeats.

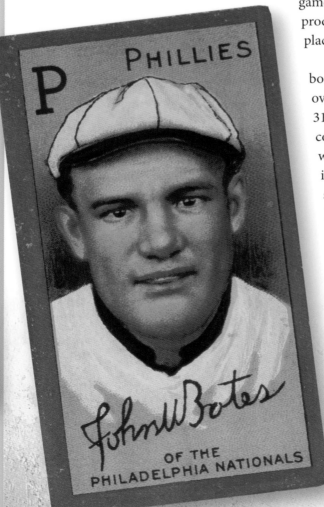

With Sherry Magee and little Johnny Bates (pictured), the Phillies had two of the most productive outfielders in the league in 1910.

This was the perspective from behind Baker Bowl's home plate. The "dead" balls of the era kept fly balls in the park.

Highlights

April 15: Pitcher Grover Cleveland "Pete" Alexander makes his MLB debut.

May 15: With a 21–5 rout of the Reds, the Phillies have a 21–6 record and a four-game lead in the NL.

July 10: After being ejected from a game, Sherry Magee punches umpire Bill Finneran, breaking his jaw. Magee will be suspended for the rest of the season, although the suspension will be commuted after 36 days.

July 21: The Phillies (52–32) hold first place for the last time.

September 7: Alexander defeats Boston ace Cy Young 1–0 in a game that lasts just 87 minutes.

September 21: Alexander tosses his fourth consecutive shutout.

NOTES

Rookie Pete Alexander leads the NL in wins (28–13), innings (367), complete games (31), and shutouts (7).

Catcher/manager Red Dooin leads the team in batting (.328) but breaks his leg in midseason.

First baseman Fred Luderus raps .301 with team highs in homers (16) and RBI (99).

Sherry Magee, the player who slugged an umpire, ranks fifth in the NL in slugging average (.483).

NEW LOOK, SAME FINISH

Trade Revamps Phillies, but They Again Place Fourth

The Phillies took drastic measures toward changing their fate before the 1911 season, and they went well beyond switching back to the red and white uniforms after a one-year move to green and white. High-maintenance, rule-breaking, party-loving pitcher George McQuillan was among those sent to Cincinnati in a four-for-four trade that gave Philadelphia the services of hitters Hans Lobert and Dode Paskert and pitchers Jack Rowan and Fred Beebe. After the somewhat controversial deal was completed, team president Horace Fogel truly felt the pieces were coming together for a pennant run, and fans were inclined to agree. The club's attendance of 416,000 barely missed setting a franchise record.

On July 15, 1911, rugged first baseman Fred Luderus became the first Phillie ever to hit two over-the-fence home runs in one game.

For much of the year, those patrons watched first-place baseball. The Phillies spent 58 calendar days atop the National League through late July. The former Reds on the roster made an impact, but none matched the contributions of a 24-year-old rookie from Nebraska. Grover Cleveland "Pete" Alexander debuted by leading the majors with 28 victories—nearly twice the total of his closest teammate—and seven shutouts, including four consecutively. The right-hander with pinpoint accuracy paced the NL with 367 innings.

Still, Red Dooin's team finished the season in fourth place, no better than it had the previous year despite a slightly better record. Dooin himself hit .328, but he broke his leg in July—one of a handful of costly injuries to the club—and his team gave up more runs than it scored for the season. Making matters worse, Sherry Magee earned a suspension for hitting an umpire.

Seven-game slumps in August and October made it impossible for the Phillies to keep pace with the pennant-winning Giants. Fogel's wheeling and dealing might have finally put Philadelphia in a position to compete, but it would take some time.

After the season, the Phillies played nine exhibition games in Cuba against top Havana-area clubs, honing their skills for what Fogel was certain would be better years to come.

SWAN SONG FOR FOGEL

Controversial Owner Makes a Noisy Exit

The disappointment of the Phillies' 1912 season went far beyond their 73 wins against 79 losses. The team that Horace Fogel had crafted to make a run at the top spot in the National League sagged under the weight of injuries, expectations, and erratic front-office leadership.

Sherry Magee broke his wrist in the very last preseason game, an omen to be sure. Pete Alexander, who had led the majors in victories as a rookie in 1911, slumped to a 19–17 sophomore season. The team's .267 batting average ranked seventh in the NL. One of the few bright spots was the acquisition of big-hitting outfielder Gavvy Cravath, who at age 31 led the club with 11 home runs in his first full year in the majors.

By season's end, it became painfully obvious to Phillies fans—who were showing up in fewer numbers at the gate—that their team was well out of the race. However, there was some end-of-the-year drama.

Fogel, his loyalty bound to the Chicago Cubs for their prior assistance in keeping the Phillies afloat, accused NL President Thomas Lynch of having games fixed so that the New York Giants would win the pennant. Lynch did not take such accusations quietly. He fought back after the 1912 season, charging Fogel with improper conduct. At a November gathering in New York City, the owners voted to expel Fogel "forever from the National League."

"I will sell or represent as I please the Philadelphia club in the National League as long as I feel inclined to do so," Fogel offered defiantly after the decision was made, "and no one can disturb me from doing so."

Fogel was wrong about that. A syndicate led by former Pirates executive and respected baseball man William H. Locke took ownership of the Phillies a few months later.

Highlights

May 14: After getting shut out by the Cubs, the Phillies are 7–13, 9½ games out of first place. They won't get any closer.

July 18: Gavvy Cravath steals home in the eleventh inning to beat the Cubs.

September 6: Jeff Tesreau throws a no-hitter against the Phillies.

November 27: National League owners vote to expel Phillies owner Horace Fogel from the league after Fogel accused league officials and umpires of "fixing" the pennant race so that the Giants would win. Ironically, Giants owner John T. Brush died on November 26.

NOTES

A rash of injuries and ailments plague the team all season, including a preseason broken wrist by star hitter **Sherry Magee.**

Gavvy Cravath hits .284 with 11 homers and 70 RBI in his first full big-league season.

Third baseman Hans Lobert leads the team with a .327 average.

Outfielder Dode Paskert strokes .315, while Magee hits .306 and **Fred Luderus** knocks in 69 runs.

Pitcher Pete Alexander slumps to 19–17 with a 2.81 ERA, but he leads the NL in innings (310⅓) and strikeouts (195).

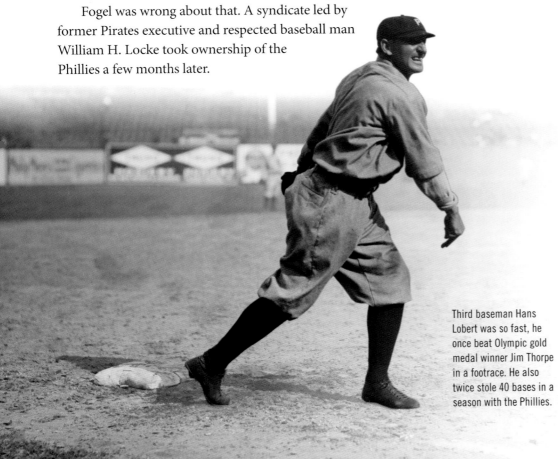

Third baseman Hans Lobert was so fast, he once beat Olympic gold medal winner Jim Thorpe in a footrace. He also twice stole 40 bases in a season with the Phillies.

Highlights

January 15: It is announced that a syndicate headed by William H. Locke, a former front-office official with the Pirates, has purchased the Phillies. William F. Baker, a former New York police commissioner, is part of the syndicate.

June 10: With a record of 29–12, the Phillies hold a six-game lead in the NL.

July 3: The Giants complete a four-game sweep of the Phils and wrest first place from them for good.

July: With the death of Locke, Baker assumes control of the Phillies.

NOTES

Gavvy Cravath hits .341 and leads the NL in HRs (19), RBI (128), hits (179), total bases (298), and slugging (.568).

Fred Luderus ranks second in the NL in HRs (18).

Defensive specialist **Bill Killefer** takes over the regular catching duties from his manager, Red Dooin.

Second-year **pitcher Tom Seaton** leads the league in wins (27–12) and strikeouts (168).

Pete Alexander finishes 22–8.

The Phillies set a team attendance record (470,000).

STARS EMERGE

Phillies Overtaken by Giants During Record-Setting Season

While the Philadelphia Athletics were winning their third World Series championship in four years in 1913, across town the Phillies were showing fans that the City of Brotherly Love was no one-team town. A new attendance record (470,000), a second-place finish, and a franchise-best 88 victories provided ample evidence of that.

The Phils' .265 batting average ranked third in the National League. Their pitching staff, led by Tom Seaton (NL-best 27 victories) and Pete Alexander, paced the league in strikeouts. And their fielding percentage was also tops.

For a while, that terrific trifecta looked to be the stuff of a pennant-winner. However, the New York Giants blew past the first-place Phillies down the stretch, leaving Philadelphia's NL club to celebrate its emerging talent—and its future. Gavvy Cravath, picked up just the year before, broke out with 19 home runs and 128 RBI. He led the majors in both categories while hitting .341. Bill Killefer earned rank as perhaps the best backstop in the NL, while Sherry Magee and Hans Lobert each hit .300.

And no one could approach the Phillies for raw power. Behind Cravath, Fred Luderus (18 homers), and Magee (11), Philadelphia had three of the top four home run hitters in the NL. The club launched 73 home runs on the season, 14 more than its nearest competitor.

One major setback did strike the Phillies during 1913, one year before World War I and the emergence of the Federal League. The summer death of respected baseball man William Locke put William F. Baker, a former New York police commissioner, in charge of the team's new ownership group. Baker did not possess the baseball savvy of Locke, but Phillies fans had to be thinking that would hardly matter. After this season, the key pieces seemed to be in place for a legitimate pennant run.

Tom Seaton's best season (27–12 in 1913) on the field was his worst year off of it, as he lost his child and nearly his wife during childbirth.

TURBULENT TIMES

As War Erupts in Europe, Federal League Raids Rosters

Calling 1914 a year of turmoil in the Phillies organization would be like calling the Atlantic Ocean a little wet. Across that body of water, war was breaking out. In Philadelphia's National League baseball world, it was more of a series of battles—with a new league, with the team's own players, and with a controversial managerial change.

It all began when the Federal League, which had begun operations in 1913, declared itself a major league and began offering big salaries to AL and NL players. While no team was located in Philadelphia, Federal League clubs plucked several Phillies players— among them top pitcher Tom Seaton, fellow hurlers Ad Brennan and Howie Camnitz, infielders Otto Knabe and Mickey Doolan, and utility man Jimmy Walsh. The Phillies simply would not make the lucrative offers required to keep them.

One player they did rescue was star catcher Bill Killefer. Originally signing with Chicago's Federal League team for nearly double his $3,000 annual salary, Killefer changed his mind 12 days later when the Phillies upped the ante. The case went to court, where a judge declared both teams to have "unclean hands" and allowed Killefer to return to Philadelphia.

It was a mixed blessing, considering Killefer was rejoining a team that drew less than 140,000 fans. And with its depleted lineup, the Phillies were overmatched against those NL teams that did more to keep the Feds from raiding their talent.

Pete Alexander and Erskine Mayer accounted for more than half of the team's victories. Only one regular, Beals Becker, hit .300. Utility man Sherry Magee hit .314, but he earned more attention for his bid to become the manager who would replace the fired Red Dooin. Hans Lobert and Pat Moran also wanted the job. Moran won out.

"It's all off with the Philadelphia club," Seaton remarked from his new club, the Brooklyn Tip-Tops. "Trouble is bound to follow."

On the last point, Seaton missed his mark.

Erskine Mayer, whose father composed an opera in Hebrew, won 21 games for the Phillies in 1914 and again in 1915.

Highlights

April 13: Having declared itself a third major league, the Federal League begins play. Star pitcher Tom Seaton is one of several Phillies who have jumped to the new circuit.

July 14: With a loss to Cincinnati, the Phils drop below .500 for good.

September 9: The Phils are no-hit by Boston's George Davis, a Harvard Law School student.

October 20: Owner William Baker fires manager Red Dooin, replacing him with former Phillies catcher Pat Moran.

December 24: The Phils trade Sherry Magee to the Boston Braves.

NOTES

Gavvy Cravath leads the league in homers (19) and ranks second in RBI (100).

Sherry Magee bats .314 and leads the NL in RBI (103), hits (171), total bases (277), doubles (39), and slugging (.509) in his final season as a Phillie.

Outfielder Beals Becker ranks second in the league in batting (.325).

Pete Alexander leads the league in wins (27–15), complete games (32), and strikeouts (214).

Erskine Mayer finishes with a 21–19 record.

Phillies attendance plummets to 138,474, or 1,775 fans per game.

Highlights

April 23: Showing lots of hustle under new manager Pat Moran, and getting great pitching, the Phillies open the season at 8–0.

July 13: With an 8–0 win over St. Louis, the Phillies move into first place for good.

September 29: Pete Alexander throws a one-hit shutout over Boston for his 31st victory. Winners of 18 of the last 22, the Phils are up eight games with six games to go.

October 8: Behind Alexander, the Phillies defeat the Boston Red Sox 3–1 in Game One of the World Series.

October 9 and 11: Boston takes 2–1 victories, each with a run in the ninth inning, in Games Two and Three.

October 13: After another 2–1 win in Game Four, the Red Sox win Game Five—and the series—5–4 on a Harry Hooper solo homer in the top of the ninth.

NOTES

Gavvy Cravath leads the NL in HRs (24), RBI (115), runs (89), OBP (.393), and slugging (.510).

Pete Alexander paces the league in wins (31–10), ERA (1.22), complete games (36), strikeouts (241), and shutouts (12).

PENNANT FEVER

Manager Moran Guides Phillies to First NL Flag

Out with the old, in with the new. And welcome, Philadelphia Phillies, to the top. For the first time since the turn of the century, a manager with no major league experience took over an established club and led it to a pennant. That Pat Moran, a former Phillies backup catcher who paid close attention to the nuances of the game from his position on the bench, did it with a team that finished in sixth place the year before was a testament to his abilities.

"This is not a sixth-place ball club," Moran told sportswriters at the team's spring training camp in St. Petersburg, Florida, six months before managing the team to its first National League pennant.

The two other Phillies who had vied for Moran's managerial position the year before were shipped elsewhere before the season. Longtime outfield star Sherry Magee was sent to Boston for Possum Whitted. And third baseman Hans Lobert was traded to the Giants for third sacker Milt Stock and pitcher Al Demaree. Demaree would contribute 14 wins—behind only Pete Alexander (31) and Erskine Mayer (21)—to the championship cause.

Red Dooin, the outgoing player/manager, was traded to Cincinnati for second baseman Bert Niehoff. Moran and owner William F. Baker made another sharp move in signing 24-year-old shortstop Dave Bancroft. While Bancroft didn't hit major league pitching particularly well in the early

Phillies catcher Pat Moran, shown here with his son, was promoted to manager in October 1914. His savvy trades and strict discipline resulted in an instant pennant in 1915.

When the Phillies took on the Red Sox for the championship cup, Boston's pitching was so dominant that Babe Ruth (18–8) didn't get a chance to start in the World Series.

going, he was brilliant defensively and went on to enjoy a Hall of Fame career.

The Phillies emerged from camp with a new commitment to discipline and details. Moran demanded it. They promptly won their first 8 games and 11 of their first 12. Alexander was almost unhittable at times—and frequently unbeatable. First baseman Fred Luderus was stroking the ball all over the field, and home run king Gavvy Cravath was driving in runs like no one in baseball.

The Phillies' first pennant was, in fact, a runaway after they recovered from a late-June/early-July hitting slump. They never fell below second place, took over first for good by mid-July, and outpaced the Boston Braves by seven games for the pennant.

Another Boston team, however, would prove to be a formidable foe once the Phillies reached their first World Series. It was also the initial World Series for a young Red Sox pitcher named Babe Ruth. The 20-year-old had won 18 games during the regular season but did not take the mound against the NL champs. He did get to the plate for the first time in a World Series game, grounding out as a pinch hitter in the ninth inning of the opener.

The Phillies' 3–1 victory behind Alexander in that game sent the home fans racing onto the field, where they carried players on their shoulders and celebrated as if the championship was sealed. That, unbeknownst to any of the revelers, would be the last World Series game the Phillies would win for 65 years.

The Red Sox won each of the next three games—one in Philadelphia in front of 20,000 and two in Boston in front of 40,000—by identical 2–1 scores. The Red Sox used Braves Field because it held more fans than Fenway Park. Baker refused a similar offer from the Philadelphia Athletics, turning down the chance to put an extra 10,000 or so fans in the seats.

The Red Sox clinched the crown with a 5–4 road win in Game Five. Luderus batted .438 for the Series and hit his club's only home run. His teammates struggled at the plate, though. The NL champs were doomed by a .182 team average.

PHILLIES PHACT

In the opening game of the World Series, Pete Alexander retired a young Babe Ruth, who was making his first World Series appearance, in the ninth inning.

"Outside of Alexander, I do not think any of the Philly pitchers compare with my men."

—Manager Bill Carrigan of the Red Sox, who dropped the World Series opener to Alexander and then took the next four

1916

▶ 91-62   2nd ◀

Highlights

May 6: At quirky Ebbets Field, Brooklyn beats Philly in the eleventh inning when a George Cutshaw blast bounces in front of, onto, and over the fence.

September 9: Swept by the Giants in a doubleheader, the Phillies fall out of first place in a tight four-team race.

September 23: Pete Alexander pitches and wins both games of a doubleheader against Cincinnati.

October 2: Against Boston, Alexander records his sixteenth shutout to put the Phillies in a tie for first place, but they will drop out of first for good with a loss in the nightcap of the day's doubleheader.

NOTES

Gavvy Cravath leads the team with a .283 average, 11 homers, and 70 RBI.

Pete Alexander leads the NL in victories with 33—the most by a Phillies pitcher in the twentieth or twenty-first century. He is also tops in 1916 in ERA (1.55), complete games (38), shutouts (16), and strikeouts (167).

Eppa Rixey shines with a 22–10 record and 1.85 ERA.

The Phillies post a 2.36 ERA and lead the league with 25 shutouts.

The Phils draw a franchise-record 515,365 fans.

REPEAT NOT IN CARDS

Despite One More Win, Phils Fall Short in Pennant Bid

Staying at the top, the adage goes, can be tougher than getting there in the first place. The 1916 Phillies probably would not have argued, despite the effort that went into climbing to a pennant the season before.

One year after claiming their first National League flag, the Phillies made a valiant run at a second straight. Their 91–62 record, in fact, was one game better than the pennant-winning mark of the year before. However, it was 2½ games shy of Brooklyn's record in the NL standings, keeping the Phillies from a chance to avenge their 1915 World Series setback to the Red Sox. Boston repeated in 1916, defeating Brooklyn in five games thanks in part to Babe Ruth's 14-inning, complete-game victory on the mound in Game Two.

> **PHILLIES PHACT**
>
> Pete Alexander records 16 shutouts, setting a modern MLB record that still stands and quite likely will never be broken.

It was no fault of Pete Alexander's that the Phillies came up short in the tight, four-team NL race. The dominant right-hander led the majors for the second straight year in victories, shutouts, and ERA, and he won his third successive NL strikeout title.

At the plate, five of the eight regulars in the lineup batted at least .279. The Phillies led the NL in doubles and finished second in home runs. An eight-game winning streak gave them a game-and-a-half lead on September 7, but two days later they were knocked from their perch during a doubleheader loss to the Giants.

A basketball player at the University of Virginia, 6-foot-5 Eppa Rixey (left) enjoyed the first great season of his Hall of Fame pitching career in 1916.

Alexander was sometimes used in both games of doubleheaders, as even with a tired arm he was better than almost any pitcher in the game. His 2–0, three-hit win over the Braves in the opener of an October 2 doubleheader—his 33rd victory of the year—put the Phillies back in first place. A loss in the nightcap, though, dropped them behind Brooklyn, and a doubleheader loss to the Braves the next day in the season finale sealed their second-place fate.

Some pointed to Erskine Mayer's demise as the main reason for the Phillies' failure to repeat. True, the man who had won 21 games during the pennant-winning season dropped to 7 wins in 1916. However, defense was at least equally to blame. Philadelphia struggled up the middle, with Dave Bancroft making 60 errors at shortstop and Bert Niehoff 49 at second base. Both led the league in miscues at their positions, as did Fred Luderus with 28 errors at first base. The Philadelphia infield was a dangerous place to be during the 1916 campaign.

All in all, however, it was a strong season for the Phillies. Their bid for a second flag required a great season from Brooklyn to be thwarted. The Phils posted their top record of the century up to that point. They were also a popular attraction at the box office as they came off their first pennant. A record 515,365 fans attended games at Baker Bowl, a figure that would not be topped by Phillies fans for three decades.

The owner of this ticket to Baker Bowl on May 27, 1916, saw the Phillies get swept by Brooklyn in a doubleheader. Philly ranked second in the NL in attendance that year.

Home Run King

Gavvy Cravath earned the nickname "Cactus" for his prickly personality. He liked playing practical jokes on teammates, and he enjoyed needling Eppa Rixey, a Southerner, about the Civil War—which undoubtedly got on the pitcher's nerves. But the Phillies were willing to put up Cravath. After all, he was the Babe Ruth of the Deadball Era.

After several unimpressive seasons in the American League, Cravath found a home in Philadelphia in 1912 at age 31. From 1913 through 1919, this Phillies outfielder led the National League in home runs six times. His 24 long balls in 1915 led the major leagues by 11 and helped power the Phillies to their first World Series. He also was a tremendous run producer, topping the NL in RBI in 1913 (128) and 1915 (115). Twice he batted .341 in a season.

While some left-handed power hitters were able to pull the ball over Baker Bowl's short right-field fence, Cravath did not have that advantage; he batted right-handed. Nevertheless, he was a skilled enough batsman, and had enough power, to reach that short fence from the right-handed batter's box.

Gavvy Cravath was a six-time home run champ in the waning years of the Deadball Era.

1917

Highlights

April 6: The United States enters the Great War. The conflict will not have much of an effect on Major League Baseball in 1917.

June 26: The Phillies hold onto first place for the last time this season.

August 5: The Phils move from third to second place, which they will hold for the rest of the season (but they will never come close to catching the Giants).

September 3: Pete Alexander records two complete-game victories against Brooklyn, including a 5–0 shutout in the first game of the doubleheader.

December 11: Owner William Baker confounds Phillies fans when he trades Alexander and catcher Bill Killefer to the Cubs for pitcher Mike Prendergast (3–6 in 1917), catcher Pickles Dillhoefer (.126 batting average in 1917), and cash.

NOTES

Gavvy Cravath hits .280–12–83, leading the team in each category and the league in home runs.

Pete Alexander leads the NL in wins (30–13), complete games (34), shutouts (8), and strikeouts (200). His 1.83 ERA is good enough for second best in the league.

Eppa Rixey goes 16–21 despite a 2.27 ERA.

SELLING THEIR SOUL

Phils Trade Alexander for Two Nobodies and Cash

There was a time when the Phillies, and their fans, would have been thrilled with a second-place showing in the National League. But after winning the 1915 NL pennant and making an inspired run the following year, their runner-up finish in 1917 was not celebrated by players or fans.

The New York Giants ran off with the pennant by 10 games. While the Phillies were their closest competitors in the final standings, it was never really a race during the second half of the season. That was largely because Pete Alexander was virtually a one-man show on the mound for Pat Moran's club, and baseball championships are won by teams—not individuals.

Alexander led the NL in most significant pitching categories, winning 30—his age—for the third consecutive year. His closest teammate was Eppa Rixey with 16 victories, but Rixey also dropped a whopping 21 decisions.

At the plate, Philadelphia was again one of the best power-hitting teams in the game. Outfielders Possum Whitted and Gavvy Cravath led the club with matching .280 averages, while the Phillies cut down on their errors from the previous year.

Away from the field, tensions were high as the United States entered the Great War right around the time the baseball season was starting. No one was sure what the impact on baseball might be. Some cities allowed servicemen into the games for free. Attendance was down in many cities, Philadelphia among them. Owners were concerned.

Phillies owner William F. Baker later admitted that the war was not his main concern when he angered fans by trading Alexander to the Cubs after the season. He dealt his dominating ace for three-win pitcher Mike Prendergast and light-hitting catcher William "Pickles" Dillhoefer.

"I needed the money," said Baker, who also confounded just about everyone when he pointed out that "there is no reason for believing that [Alexander] would be better next year."

It was a turning point in Phillies history.

PHILLIES PHACT

On May 23, Pete Alexander throws a two-hitter against the Reds while cracking three hits himself, including a home run, in a 5–1 victory.

Alexander the Great

Grover Cleveland "Pete" Alexander is often overlooked today. He bridged the era between the dead ball and the lively ball, and he excelled in both periods. But it wasn't just opposing hitters he had to contend with; Alexander the Great came of age in one of the best hitter's parks in history.

Baker Bowl, with its 280-foot fence in right field—and a 300-foot power alley—was a boon to hitters of any era.

As a 24-year-old rookie in 1911, Alexander led the league in wins (28), innings (367), and shutouts (7). He completed 31 of 37 starts while finishing 11 games in relief. He won 68 games over the next three years, but Alexander was just warming up.

From 1915 to 1917, he won at least 30 games per season—the last such trifecta in history. In fact, only four pitchers since Alexander have won 30 games even once. Alexander led the Phillies to their first pennant, in 1915. His microscopic 1.22 ERA that season resulted in 12 shutouts and 31 wins. The next year, he claimed the pitching Triple Crown for the second straight year—33 wins, 1.55 ERA, and 167 strikeouts—while tying the all-time mark with 16 shutouts. He led the National League in wins and strikeouts for the fourth straight year in 1917, recording 30 and 200 exactly.

Alexander's three-year dynasty included a record of 94–35, 1,531$\frac{1}{3}$ innings, a 1.54 ERA, 108 complete games, and 36 shutouts. And even in the Deadball Era, allowing just 13 homers over three years is astounding—especially when you consider that Baker Bowl was his home park.

So how did the Phillies reward the pitcher who had logged 190 wins for them in just seven seasons? They sent him packing. Alexander and his catcher, Bill Killefer, were shipped to Chicago for the low-watt battery of Mike Prendergast and Pickles Dillhoefer, plus $55,000. With America at war and the future uncertain, the Phillies had said goodbye to a player whom *The New York Times* called "the greatest pitcher in the game at the present time."

Alexander wound up winning just twice in 1918 for the Cubs before serving in an artillery division during the final months of the Great War, in which he lost much of his hearing and becoming epileptic. He already had a drinking problem and had suffered severe headaches for years from being hit in the head.

Despite all that going against him, he won 181 more times in the majors and still had enough left to be a World Series hero at 39. His 373 career victories are the third most in big-league history.

Since 1915, an MLB pitcher has reached 30 wins in a season seven times—three of them were by Pete Alexander (1915–17).

May 9: After opening at 8–2, the Phillies lose their ninth straight game (six to New York) and are now 10 games behind the 18–1 Giants.

July 7: The Cubs beat the Phillies 2–1 in 21 innings, with pitcher John "Mule" Watson going all the way for the Phils.

September 2: Due to the war, the AL and NL decide to end the regular season on this date.

NOTES

Gavvy Cravath leads the NL in home runs with eight.

First baseman Fred Luderus leads the team in batting (.288) and RBI (67).

Catcher Pickles Dillhoefer goes 1-for-11 in his sole season in Philadelphia.

Mike Prendergast (13–14) and **Brad Hogg** (13–13) lead the team in victories.

The Phillies draw only 122,266 fans, although they play only 56 home games (67 on the road).

FREE FALLING

Without Their Ace, Phils Tumble to Sixth Place

With the United States entering the war in Europe, the government called for baseball's 1918 regular season to end on Labor Day. For the Philadelphia Phillies, the early finish could not have arrived soon enough.

Having traded dominant starter Pete Alexander to the Cubs and watched Eppa Rixey join the military, the Phils were without an ace. It showed. Mike Prendergast, obtained in the unpopular Alexander trade, and Brad Hogg tied for the club lead with 13 victories. Neither one, however, posted a winning record. The team's 3.15 ERA ranked dead last in the National League, as opponents routinely teed off on Philadelphia's young hurlers. Not a single member of the starting rotation had celebrated his 30th birthday.

PHILLIES PHACT

Star pitcher Eppa Rixey misses the season due to military service. Former ace Pete Alexander plays only three games for the Cubs before going off to war, where he will suffer debilitating injuries.

So after three straight years making their home in the top two of the NL standings, the Phillies were reduced to the also-ran status they had held for much of the first decade and a half of the twentieth century, finishing sixth. They won six of their first seven games, but a nine-game losing streak that started in late April began a slide that lasted through most of the summer.

The shortened schedule actually hurt the Phillies more than it did most teams, as the loss of September home dates meant they played 11 more games on the road than at home. And away from Baker Bowl, they finished 11 games under .500. Even fate, it seemed, did not care to shine on Philadelphia.

By the time the Red Sox were defeating the Cubs in the World Series—the "Summer Classic," as it were—the Phils were pondering their future. It would be a future without the manager who had sparked the greatest run of success in franchise history. Pat Moran had won a pennant and achieved two runner-up finishes in four seasons as manager when he was relieved of his duties. It was a move that gave him a chance to win a World Series crown the following year in Cincinnati.

A BAD FIX

Only the "Black Sox" Are Sorrier than Last-Place Phillies

The 1919 season will forever loom as a black eye for Major League Baseball. It was, of course, the year Shoeless Joe Jackson and the unbeatable White Sox were upset in the World Series by Cincinnati, only to have a stunned nation later learn that no less than eight Chicago regulars had been "on the take," having conspired with gamblers to lose games on purpose. Those players were banned from the game for life.

The victorious Reds were managed by Pat Moran, who had guided the Phillies to a National League pennant in 1915 and second-place finishes the following two years. Moran had been replaced in Philadelphia by Jack Coombs, but it quickly became obvious that no skipper could have saved the Phillies' ship from sinking.

With the worst pitching, second worst batting average, and third worst fielding percentage in the NL, Philadelphia finished right where one might have expected: dead last. Coombs, who had absorbed enough misery, was fired after an 18–44 start. Home run champion Gavvy Cravath took his place, but he fared only slightly better at 29–46 (although he did post the team's top batting mark). Each of the two skippers suffered through a 13-game losing skid, and neither was able to win more than five games in a row.

Perhaps the most curious development of the Phillies' 1919 season was their attendance, which doubled over the previous season's mark. To be fair, some of the increase had to do with the fact that the 1918 season had been shortened due to U.S. involvement in the Great War. The decline of the Philadelphia Athletics—losers of 104 games—was also a contributing factor.

Were it not for the A's and that infamous Chicago "Black Sox" scandal, the Phillies might have been the laughingstock of baseball. As it was, they were simply a team with a long way to go.

Outfielder Irish Meusel batted .300 for the Phillies three years in a row before becoming a centerpiece of the New York Giants dynasty in the 1920s.

Highlights

April 30: Philly and Brooklyn play to a 9–9, 20-inning tie. Joe Oeschger goes the distance for the Phillies.

May 20: The Phillies score six runs in the bottom of the ninth to beat St. Louis 8–7.

June 1: The Phils defeat Brooklyn 10–9 in 18 innings.

June 20: The Phillies lose their thirteenth consecutive game; all are on the road.

July 7: The Phillies steal eight bases in the ninth inning against the Giants, who win 10–5.

July 8: Gavvy Cravath replaces Jack Coombs as manager.

July 9: The team suffers another thirteenth consecutive loss.

August 2: Fred Luderus sets an MLB record by playing in his 479th consecutive game.

September 28: The Giants defeat the Phillies 6–1 in the shortest MLB game ever: 51 minutes.

NOTES

Gavvy Cravath wins his sixth and final home run crown (12).

Outfielder Irish Meusel leads the club in batting (.305) and steals (24).

Lee Meadows (8–10) tops the staff in wins, ERA (2.33), and strikeouts (88).

41

1900-1919 Record Book

Team Leaders

Batting
1900: Elmer Flick, .367
1901: Ed Delahanty, .354
1902: Shad Barry, .287
1903: Roy Thomas, .327
1904: John Titus, .294
1905: Roy Thomas, .317
1906: Sherry Magee, .282
1907: Sherry Magee, .328
1908: Kitty Bransfield, .304
1909: Johnny Bates, .293
1910: Johnny Bates, .305
1911: Fred Luderus, .301
1912: Hans Lobert, .327
1913: Gavvy Cravath, .341
1914: Beals Becker, .325
1915: Fred Luderus, .315
1916: Gavvy Cravath, .283
1917: Gavvy Cravath, .280
1918: Fred Luderus, .288
1919: Irish Meusel, .305

Home Runs
1900: Elmer Flick, 11
1901: Ed Delahanty, 8;
  Elmer Flick, 8
1902: Shad Barry, 3
1903: Bill Keister, 3
1904: Red Dooin, 6
1905: Sherry Magee, 5
1906: Sherry Magee, 6
1907: Sherry Magee, 4
1908: Kitty Bransfield, 3
1909: John Titus, 3
1910: Sherry Magee, 6
1911: Fred Luderus, 16
1912: Gavvy Cravath, 11
1913: Gavvy Cravath, 19
1914: Gavvy Cravath, 19
1915: Gavvy Cravath, 24
1916: Gavvy Cravath, 11
1917: Gavvy Cravath, 12
1918: Gavvy Cravath, 8
1919: Gavvy Cravath, 12

RBI
1900: Elmer Flick, 110
1901: Ed Delahanty, 108
1902: Shad Barry, 58
1903: Bill Keister, 63
1904: Sherry Magee, 57
1905: Sherry Magee, 98
1906: Sherry Magee, 67
1907: Sherry Magee, 85
1908: Kitty Bransfield, 81
1909: Sherry Magee, 66
1910: Sherry Magee, 123
1911: Fred Luderus, 99
1912: Gavvy Cravath, 70
1913: Gavvy Cravath, 128
1914: Sherry Magee, 103
1915: Gavvy Cravath, 115
1916: Gavvy Cravath, 70
1917: Gavvy Cravath, 83
1918: Fred Luderus, 67
1919: Irish Meusel, 59

Wins
1900: Red Donahue, 15–10;
  Chick Fraser, 15–9;
  Bill Bernhard, 15–10
1901: Red Donahue, 20–13;
  Bill Duggleby, 20–12;
  Al Orth, 20–12
1902: Doc White, 16–20
1903: Bill Duggleby, 13–16
1904: Chick Fraser, 14–24
1905: Togie Pittinger, 23–14
1906: Tully Sparks, 19–16
1907: Tully Sparks, 22–8
1908: George McQuillan, 23–17
1909: Earl Moore, 18–12
1910: Earl Moore, 22–15
1911: Pete Alexander, 28–13
1912: Pete Alexander, 19–17
1913: Tom Seaton, 27–12
1914: Pete Alexander, 27–15
1915: Pete Alexander, 31–10
1916: Pete Alexander, 33–12
1917: Pete Alexander, 30–13
1918: Brad Hogg, 13–13;
  Mike Prendergast, 13–14
1919: Lee Meadows 8–10

ERA
1900: Chick Fraser, 3.14
1901: Al Orth, 2.27
1902: Doc White, 2.53
1903: Tully Sparks, 2.72
1904: Tully Sparks, 2.65
1905: Tully Sparks, 2.18
1906: Tully Sparks, 2.16
1907: Tully Sparks, 2.00
1908: George McQuillan, 1.53
1909: Earl Moore, 2.10

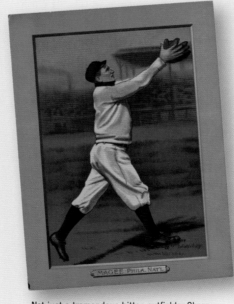

Not just a tremendous hitter, outfielder Sherry Magee possessed an accurate arm and made spectacular catches.

1910: George McQuillan, 1.60
1911: Pete Alexander, 2.57
1912: Eppa Rixey, 2.50
1913: Ad Brennan, 2.39
1914: Pete Alexander, 2.38
1915: Pete Alexander, 1.22
1916: Pete Alexander, 1.55
1917: Pete Alexander, 1.83
1918: Brad Hogg, 2.53
1919: Lee Meadows, 2.33

Strikeouts

1900: Al Orth, 68
1901: Doc White, 132
1902: Doc White, 185
1903: Chick Fraser, 104
1904: Chick Fraser, 127
1905: Togie Pittinger, 136
1906: Johnny Lush, 151
1907: Frank Corridon, 131
1908: George McQuillan, 114
1909: Earl Moore, 173
1910: Earl Moore, 185
1911: Pete Alexander, 227
1912: Pete Alexander, 195
1913: Tom Seaton, 168
1914: Pete Alexander, 214
1915: Pete Alexander, 241
1916: Pete Alexander, 167
1917: Pete Alexander, 200
1918: Brad Hogg, 81
1919: Lee Meadows, 80

NL Leaders

1900: Runs—Roy Thomas, 132;
　　　RBI—Elmer Flick, 110
1901: Doubles—Ed Delahanty, 38;
　　　Shutouts—Al Orth, 6
1907: RBI—Sherry Magee, 85
1910: Batting Average—Magee, .331;
　　　Runs—Magee, 110;

RBI—Magee, 123;
　　　Strikeouts—Earl Moore, 185;
　　　Shutouts—Moore, 6
1911: Hits—Gavvy Cravath, 179;
　　　Home Runs—Cravath, 19;
　　　RBI—Cravath, 128;
　　　Wins—Pete Alexander, 28;
　　　Complete Games—Alexander, 31;
　　　Shutouts—Alexander, 7
1912: Strikeouts—Alexander, 195
1913: Wins—Tom Seaton, 27;
　　　Strikeouts—Seaton, 168;
　　　Shutouts—Alexander, 9
1914: Hits—Magee, 171;
　　　Doubles—Magee, 39;
　　　Home Runs—Cravath, 19;
　　　RBI—Magee, 103;
　　　Wins—Alexander, 27;
　　　Strikeouts—Alexander, 214;
　　　Complete Games—Alexander, 32
1915: Runs—Cravath, 89;
　　　Home Runs—Cravath, 24;
　　　RBI—Cravath, 115;
　　　Wins—Alexander, 31;
　　　ERA—Alexander, 1.22;
　　　Strikeouts—Alexander, 241;
　　　Complete Games—Alexander, 36;
　　　Shutouts—Alexander, 12
1916: Wins—Alexander, 33;
　　　ERA—Alexander, 1.55;
　　　Strikeouts—Alexander, 167;
　　　Complete Games—Alexander, 38;
　　　Shutouts—Alexander, 16
1917: Wins—Alexander, 30;
　　　ERA—Alexander, 1.44;
　　　Strikeouts—Alexander, 200;
　　　Complete Games—Alexander, 34;
　　　Shutouts—Alexander, 8
1918: Home Runs—Cravath, 8;
　　　RBI—Magee, 76
1919: Home Runs—Cravath, 12

A career .240 hitter, Charles "Red" Dooin caught more than 1,100 games for the Phillies, second to only Mike Lieberthal on the all-time franchise list.

PHILLIES 1900–1919 All-Decade Team

1B	FRED LUDERUS
2B	OTTO KNABE
SS	DAVE BANCROFT
3B	HANS LOBERT
C	RED DOOIN
OF	ROY THOMAS
OF	GAVVY CRAVATH
OF	SHERRY MAGEE
SP	PETE ALEXANDER
SP	TULLY SPARKS

HALF-BAKED

Phillies owner William F. Baker has short arms and deep pockets.
The result is 10 losing seasons during the decade.

The Phillies' home ballpark was originally known as the Philadelphia Baseball Grounds. Owner William F. Baker renamed it after himself, a gesture that spoke to the ego of a man who never capitalized on the 1915 pennant—and, in fact, never really tried.

The Phillies had finished the teens in a sorry state, with a 47–90, last-place finish in 1919. Under Baker's tightfisted control, things only got worse. Every other decade in team history has included at least one winning season. But not the 1920s.

Four times in the decade, the Phillies lost at least 103 games. Their best record was 71–82, good for fifth place in 1929, the year before Baker died. His stewardship in the last decade of his life was marked by transparent trades, like the one in 1920 that sent future Hall of Fame shortstop Dave Bancroft to the New York Giants for two players—and $100,000. Baker kept the cash, while the Giants won the pennant the next three years.

Baker was notoriously impatient with his managers. In a six-year stretch, from 1918 through 1923, the Phillies used a different manager every year. Only one, Kaiser Wilhelm, could lift the team out of last place—in 1922, by a mere four games.

Art Fletcher lasted four seasons before Stuffy McInnis and the 1927 team dropped 103 games. Baker replaced McInnis with Burt Shotton, and the team promptly got worse, losing 109 games in 1928. Only the 1941 club, with 111 defeats, has ever lost more.

The Phillies had one major star through the decade, outfielder Cy Williams, who led the league in home runs in 1920, 1923, and 1927. Williams hit 202 home runs in the 1920s to rank third in the majors for the decade, trailing only Babe Ruth and Rogers Hornsby.

Yet without much of a team around Williams, few Philadelphians seemed to notice. The Phillies drew 330,998 fans in 1920, and they never topped that figure for the rest of the decade (indeed, not until 1943). The Athletics, meanwhile, ascended to the top of the game at the end of the 1920s. The A's drew more than 839,000 fans to Shibe Park in their championship season of 1929. That same year, just 281,200 fans watched the Phillies at Baker Bowl, where two sections of stands had collapsed during a game two years earlier, causing $40,000 in damages and dozens of injuries.

The '29 Phillies, at least, were showing signs that they could

Fresco Thompson started at the keystone position for the Phillies in the late 1920s and posted a .300 average in his four seasons with the team.

Johnny Mokan reaches first base safely during the 1927 season opener against the Giants at Baker Bowl. It was the first of 103 losses for the Phillies that year, beginning one of four 100-loss seasons of the decade.

hit. Williams was nearing the end, but other left-handed hitters like him were starting to take aim at Baker Bowl's right-field wall. In 1929, first baseman Don Hurst and outfielders Chuck Klein and Lefty O'Doul combined to smash 106 home runs, and the Phillies hit .309 as a team.

Yet the offensive firepower did not help the team on the whole. The Phillies scored 897 runs that season, but their pitchers allowed 1,032. They finished 27½ games out of first place. It added up to a fifth-place finish, the best of a brutal decade.

Highlights

April 20: Player/manager Gavvy Cravath inserts himself as a pinch hitter and belts a three-run homer to beat the Giants 3–0. It is his last career home run.

June 7: The Phillies trade future Hall of Fame shortstop Dave Bancroft to the Giants for two players and $100,000.

June 24: From this day until season's end, the Phillies and A's will both be in last place.

June 28: Bancroft goes 6-for-6 against his old team as the Giants crush the Phils 18–3.

September 14: The Phils rout the Reds 21–10.

NOTES

The Phillies lead the NL in home runs with 64. They are the only major league team to out-homer Yankees slugger Babe Ruth (54).

Outfielder Cy Williams hits .325 and leads the league in home runs with 15.

Irish Meusel (.309–14–69) is the club's second best hitter.

Colorful Casey Stengel, acquired from the Pirates prior to the season, contributes a .292 average as a full-time outfielder.

Lee Meadows (16–14, 2.84) leads the club in wins and ERA, while Eppa Rixey (11–22, 3.48) leads the NL in losses.

OUTBASHED

Hitters Can't Make Up for Weak Pitching

Slugger/manager Gavvy Cravath insisted during spring training that his 1920 Philadelphia Phillies were no last-place club. He was wrong by a half-game margin, although his troops did collect 15 more victories than they had the previous season.

As news of the 1919 "Black Sox" scandal was surfacing, along with reports that the Phillies had actually won a game that was "thrown" by the Chicago Cubs, Cravath was trying to coax wins out of a team that was largely overmatched against its National League foes. The Phillies could knock balls out of the park, once again leading the NL in home runs, but their pitching staff recorded the highest ERA in the league.

The 1920 season marked the end of the Deadball Era in baseball. Babe Ruth, now with the Yankees, shattered the single-season home run record with a staggering 54 dingers. The Phils hit 64 as a *team,* and they were the *only* team in the majors to out-homer Ruth. The Babe broke his own record of 29 home runs, set the year before. Before that, any twentieth century player who socked even 10 balls over the fences was considered a slugger.

The Phillies' greatest stumble of 1920 was a June trade in which they dealt shortstop Dave Bancroft to the Giants for shortstop Art Fletcher, pitcher Bill Hubbell, and $100,000. "Just how the Phillies benefit from this remarkable transaction is hard to imagine," the *Philadelphia Inquirer* wondered.

Bancroft went on to punish the Phillies as an opponent on his way to the Hall of Fame. Hubbell would register just one winning season in a Philadelphia uniform, and Fletcher would play only one more year beyond the 1920 campaign.

The Phillies did have one of the top hitting outfields in the majors, with Cy Williams, Irish Meusel, and the newly acquired Casey Stengel batting a collective .310 with 38 total home runs and 191 RBI.

Shown here in 1917, Dave "Beauty" Bancroft was one of the smoothest fielding shortstops of his era, but the Phillies traded him in 1920 for two players and much-needed cash.

LONG BALLS GALORE

Last-Place Phillies, Yankees' Ruth Set Homer Marks

Baseballs were getting livelier in the 1920s, and fans were digging the long ball—particularly in New York City.

One year after spitballs were banned from baseball, Babe Ruth of the Yankees walloped 59 home runs in 1921, breaking his own major league record for the second consecutive year. New York fans were coming out to the ballpark in droves (more than 1.2 million paid) to watch the "Sultan of Swat" forever change the game.

In Philadelphia, however, the Phillies' new National League record of 88 home runs in one season did not have the same impact. Less than 274,000 fans showed up to watch the club—a last-place attendance mark for a last-place team. And it wasn't even close in the standings. The Phillies were 13½ games behind the seventh-place team while under the reign (for most of the year) of Philadelphia native, longtime major league pitcher, and former Yankees manager "Wild" Bill Donovan, who had replaced Gavvy Cravath during the offseason.

As was the case during the 1920 season, it was no fault of the Phillies outfielders. Irish Meusel and Cy Williams hit .353 and .320, respectively, while 24-year-old Bevo LeBourveau chipped in with a .295 average. Williams and Meusel also combined for 30 home runs.

The pitching staff, however, could hardly have been more generous to opposing hitters. Its 4.48 ERA was easily the highest in the league, and its 333 strikeouts were the fewest. Imagine how many homers the Phillies might have launched had they been allowed to bat against their own pitchers.

Donovan lasted 87 games, and he would never manage in the majors again. Owner William F. Baker fired him with this statement: "Donovan's activities with the Philadelphia National League club for the balance of the season will be limited to the endorsement of his pay check every two weeks." His replacement, Kaiser Wilhelm, went 26–41 down the stretch.

As a dead-pull, left-handed hitter, Cy Williams was a perfect fit for Baker Bowl, where he cracked 138 of his 211 career home runs.

Highlights

March: MLB bars Phillies first baseman Gene Paulette for life for complicity in fixing games.

April 13: The Phils open the season with new manager Wild Bill Donovan.

July 4: A 4–24 skid puts the team at 19–49.

July 7: Phillies pitcher George Smith allows 15 runs and 20 hits to St. Louis in a 15–2 loss.

July 24: With the team at 25–62, owner William Baker replaces Donovan with Kaiser Wilhelm.

July 25: The club trades Irish Meusel, who is hitting .353, to the Giants for two players and cash.

July 31: Rookie third baseman Goldie Rapp goes hitless after beginning his stint in Philly with a 23-game hitting streak.

August 5: KDKA in Pittsburgh stages the first broadcast of an MLB game, the Pirates over the Phillies 8–5.

August 12: Smith throws a 12-hit shutout against the Braves.

NOTES

Cy Williams (.320–18–75) swings the biggest bat in the lineup after Meusel's departure.

First baseman Ed Konetchy strokes .321 with 59 RBI.

Righty George Smith posts the worst numbers (4–20, 4.76) on the league's worst pitching staff.

The close right-field fence was a tempting home-run target, but the towering wall with the Lifebuoy ad helped prevent even more fly balls from leaving the yard.

Home Run Haven

Once new baseballs were put into play more frequently—after Cleveland's Ray Chapman was killed by a discolored ball in 1920—balls started soaring out of parks like never before. Nowhere did the balls fly out like they did at Baker Bowl.

Starting in 1918, the Phillies had the highest earned run average in the National League for an astounding 17 consecutive years. The team's ERA stayed at 5.00 or higher from 1925 to 1930, including two seasons north of 6.00. Philly's 6.71 ERA in 1930 is the highest ever by a major league team. Baker Bowl was also where the Giants, in 1923, became the first NL team to score in every inning. A 28 spot put up by the 1929 Cardinals marked the most runs by an NL team in the twentieth century.

Right field at Baker Bowl was just 280 feet from home plate, with right-center a mere 300 feet. The cause for the short field was an adjoining rail yard, whose tunnel underneath the outfield created a bump known as "The Hump." To make the short poke more challenging, the fence in right stood 40 feet high. But as more and more batters cleared the fence, a 20-foot screen was added. Philly's tall wall made for the perfect

Lifebuoy soap billboard, which led to the familiar joke: "The Phillies use Lifebuoy and they still stink."

While the short fence didn't help Phillies pitchers, the team led the league in homers for four straight years (1919–23). Cy Williams won three home run crowns for the Phils in the 1920s. The lefty center fielder was such a dead-pull hitter that he inspired managers to move their infields to the right when he batted—the first "Williams Shift" two decades before Ted. Cy Williams clubbed an NL-record 41 homers in 1923, and he also held the league's career home run mark with 251 until Rogers Hornsby passed him in 1929.

Though anxious to vacate Baker Bowl, the Phillies were kept there by a 99-year lease signed in 1912. It took until 1938 for the Phils to negotiate a move down the road to Shibe Park, which they shared with the Athletics. Unlike decrepit Baker Bowl, which had been the first ballpark to be reinforced with steel in 1894, Shibe Park—later renamed Connie Mack Stadium—was considered ahead of its time when it was opened in 1909. It remained a respected major league facility until Veterans Stadium opened in 1971.

Same Old Song

History Repeats Itself on Numerous Counts

The Phillies were becoming adept at producing carbon copies of their previous failures. It was, as many a sportswriter was quick to point out, among the few things they were good at.

Just as they did during their miserable 1921 season, the 1922 Phils racked up the following mixed bag:

- set a modern National League home run record (116)
- attracted less than 275,000 patrons to their home games
- handed the ball to the worst pitching staff in the National League
- fielded a hot-hitting outfield (Curt Walker, Cliff Lee, and Cy Williams all topped .300)
- took instructions from a skipper who would never again manage in the majors

This time, that last distinction came in the form of Kaiser Wilhelm. An early-century pitcher with Pittsburgh, Boston, Brooklyn, and Baltimore, Wilhelm had been owner William F. Baker's choice to replace Wild Bill Donovan midway through the previous season and had bettered Donovan's winning percentage by a pretty good margin down the stretch.

In his only full season as a major league skipper, one can say this much about the Ohio native—he did keep the Phillies out of last place. By winning 57 games against 96 defeats, Philadelphia finished four games better than the 100-loss Boston Braves. And that was the end of his managerial career.

Five of the club's regular eight position players socked 12 or more home runs, which furthered the Phillies' reputation as a big-hitting, poor-pitching organization. No game was more telling on that front than the "shootout in Chicago," in which the Phillies and Cubs accounted for a major league record 49 runs in one game. After just four innings, Philadelphia trailed 25–6 in that contest before staging an inspired comeback.

After Wilhelm was relieved of his duties at season's end, a dramatic comeback—in the big picture—was precisely what the Phillies would continue to search for year after year.

> ### PHILLIES PHACT
> In the highest scoring MLB game of the century, the Chicago Cubs defeat the Phillies 26–23 at Wrigley Field on August 25.

Highlights

May 7: Jesse Barnes of the Giants no-hits the Phillies.

May 15: A 19–7 loss to St. Louis begins a 12-game losing streak that will bury the team in basement.

May 25: A line drive by Brooklyn's Tommy Griffith fractures the skull of pitcher Bill Hubbell.

August 25: In losing to the Cubs 26–23, the Phillies give up 10 runs in the second and 14 in the fourth.

September 15: Against St. Louis, catcher Butch Henline becomes the first NL player in the century to hit three homers in a game.

November 7: Manager Kaiser Wilhelm is fired.

NOTES

Philadelphia leads the NL in home runs with 116.

The Phils' 4.64 ERA is the highest in the league. They gave up 10 straight hits in one game and 46 hits in a doubleheader.

Cy Williams bats .308 and leads the team in homers (26) and RBI (92).

Other big hitters include outfielder **Curt Walker** (.337–12–89), outfielder **Cliff Lee** (.322–17–77), **Butch Henline** (.316–14–64), and second baseman **Frank Parkinson** (.275–15–70).

Lee Meadows and **Jimmy Ring**, both 12–18, lead the team in wins.

Highlights

May 11: Cy Williams belts three homers and plates seven as his Phils beat St. Louis 20–14. The teams combine for 10 home runs at the Baker Bowl.

May 27: A 2–18 skid drops the team's record to 8–25. On this day, Williams blasts his fifteenth homer of the month.

May 29: Williams knocks in a run against the Braves, giving him 44 RBI for the month—a mark that will remain a twentieth-century MLB record for May.

June 1: The Giants rout the Phillies 22–8.

July 13: The Reds feast on Phillies pitching, winning 21–7.

NOTES

Cy Williams leads the NL in homers with a team-record 41 and ranks second in RBI (114).

Five regulars hit above .300, including **Butch Henline** (.324) and **Cliff Lee** (.321).

Jimmy Ring (18–16) is the only pitcher with a winning record.

Bill Hubbell goes 1–6 with a 8.35 ERA while yielding 102 hits in 55 innings.

The Phillies give up a league-high 6.5 runs a game, including 8.0 runs per contest in tiny Baker Bowl.

WORK OF "ART"

Fletcher Takes Over as Skipper, but Phils' Woes Persist

If Phillies owner William F. Baker didn't get the best end of the deal on the playing field in sending Dave Bancroft to the Giants for Art Fletcher, Bill Hubbell, and cash in 1920, he had a chance to redeem himself by handing the leadership of his club to a resource he acquired in the unpopular trade. Actually, Baker was a huge Fletcher fan, and before the 1923 season he installed the veteran shortstop as the team's new manager, replacing Kaiser Wilhelm.

Fletcher had been a member of one of the greatest infields of the Deadball Era while with the Giants, and his fiery nature and will to win were famous among baseball fans. "If there be one among the gamesters of baseball," wrote sportswriter Frank Graham, "that man be Fletcher."

Unfortunately for Baker, Fletcher, and Phillies faithful, an ultra-competitive streak would not necessarily help a man whose team was forced to rely on a subpar pitching staff in a launching pad of a ballpark. And such was the fate of Fletcher's 1923 Phillies.

Jimmy Ring gave the Phillies five straight years of double-digit wins in the 1920s, including a career-high 18 in 1923.

Their 5.34 team ERA was more than a full run higher than that of any other National League team. And unlike the previous few clubs, this one struggled at the plate, too. The Phillies used their short fences to once again lead the NL in home runs, but their .278 average was next to last in the league. Without the ability to keep opponents from lighting up the scoreboard or a way to consistently outscore them with the bats, the Phils were in a world of hurt.

Hard to believe, but Fletcher's 1923 club never won more than three games in a row all season. The Phillies' 50–104 record was its worst of the twentieth century, and it was the worst mark in Philadelphia NL history since the lowly Quakers went 17–81–1 in 1883.

Slow Climb

Fletcher's Phillies Claw Out of NL Basement

There must have been some level of satisfaction for owner William F. Baker—even as his Art Fletcher–led club lost 96 games—in that the 1924 Phillies beat out Dave Bancroft's Boston Braves for seventh place in the National League. After all, Bancroft and Fletcher were the key cogs in a 1920 trade between Philadelphia and New York that favored the Giants. At least in the managerial department, as it pertained to 1924, the Phillies finally got a leg up.

The other elements of the season, however, were all too familiar to Philadelphia fans.

For the second straight year, their club posted the highest ERA in the NL by a wide margin. While they continued driving balls out of the miniature Baker Bowl at a rapid pace, their opponents did the same, outscoring the Phillies by 173 runs. Philadelphia played 35 games decided by five or more runs, dropping 26 of them.

Perhaps strangely, then, this was the season in which a member of the first-place Giants asked a Phillies player to actually help lose a game *on purpose.*

Rookie Jimmy O'Connell reportedly asked Philadelphia shortstop Heinie Sand to hold back during a September game during a heated pennant race between the Giants and Brooklyn. "It will be worth $500 to you," O'Connell muttered to Sand, "if you don't bear down too hard."

Sand made it clear to O'Connell that he would do no such thing, and he told Fletcher about the incident immediately. It prompted an investigation by MLB Commissioner Kenesaw Mountain Landis, who heard from O'Connell that it was Giants coach Cozy Dolan who had put him up to the weak bribery attempt. O'Connell also implicated three teammates—future Hall of Famers Ross Youngs, George Kelly, and Frankie Frisch. After digging into the matter, Landis ultimately exonerated that trio while banning O'Connell and Dolan from the game for life.

Besides his good-guy role in a 1924 gambling scandal, Heinie Sand was a pretty good shortstop, garnering NL MVP votes in 1925.

Highlights

July 8: The Reds nip the Phillies 2–1 in 16 innings.

July 25: George Harper cracks an inside-the-park grand slam against the Cubs.

July 28: The Phillies play 25 innings of a doubleheader without an error, an example of their outstanding defense throughout the season.

August 15: The Phillies lose their tenth straight game.

September 1–3: Brooklyn defeats the Phils six times in three days.

September 27: Phillies shortstop Heinie Sand tells manager Art Fletcher that Giants outfielder Jimmy O'Connell offered him $500 to throw this day's game. MLB Commissioner Kenesaw Mountain Landis will investigate.

NOTES

Cy Williams leads the team with a .328 average, 24 homers, and 93 RBI.

Third baseman Russ Wrightstone bats .307, and **first baseman Walter Holke** cracks .300.

Jimmy Ring (10–12) and **Bill Hubbell** (10–9) tie for the team high in wins.

Phillies pitchers again have the league's highest ERA (4.87).

The Phils go 19–34 in one-run games and 7–17 in extra-inning contests.

Highlights

May 12: Pitcher Jimmy Ring belts a grand slam en route to an 8–5 win over the Pirates.

June 17: After starting the season at 21–21, the Phillies lose their eleventh straight game.

July 18: With his team down 7–2 to the Cubs in the bottom of the tenth, Cy Williams hits a grand slam—but the Phils lose 7–6.

August 19: The Phillies defeat Pete Donohue of the Reds, ending the pitcher's 20-game winning streak against the team.

August 28–September 1: The Pirates win five straight games in Philly, scoring 10 runs or more in each game.

September 13: Dazzy Vance of Brooklyn no-hits the Phillies, winning 10–1.

NOTES

Outfielder George Harper ranks sixth in the NL in hitting at .349. He also leads the team in homers (18), RBI (97), runs (86), and doubles (35).

Cy Williams raps .331 with 13 homers.

Catcher Jimmie Wilson (.328) and **first baseman Chicken Hawks** (.322) contribute to a team that bats .295 overall.

Jimmy Ring (14–16) leads the team in wins but also tops the league in walks allowed for the fourth straight season.

PROGRESS AT THE PLATE

Hot-Hitting Phillies Manage a Sixth-Place Tie

If hope springs eternal in the human breast, as Alexander Pope once penned, then the 1925 season was a good example for Philadelphia Phillies fans. Hope, at least for a while, seemed to be returning to the City of Brotherly Love. Attendance climbed back over the meager 300,000 mark, though the club still ranked last in the National League at the box office. One week into June, the Phillies were playing .500 ball. After dropping an average of 100 games over the previous two seasons, that was progress indeed.

The greatest strides came at the plate. This club could hit like neither of Art Fletcher's previous two could. Four starters—George Harper, Cy Williams, Jimmie Wilson, and Chicken Hawks—eclipsed .320 for the season. Only two NL teams could top the Phillies' .354 on-base percentage or their .425 slugging percentage.

> ### PHILLIES PHACT
>
> On September 2, New York Giants hitters go 30-for-58 in a 24–9 win at the pitching nightmare that is the Baker Bowl.

However, a familiar gloom hung over the overmatched pitching staff. Philadelphia was the only team in the NL to register an ERA of more than 5.00, and it allowed 15 more home runs than the Chicago Cubs—the next-worst team in the league in that category. Not a single regular in the starting rotation compiled a winning record for the year. Only so much blame could be attributed to the small size of Baker Bowl, their home park. After all, Phillies opponents had no trouble winning there.

As it happened, the season turned south during a long June road trip. The Phillies were 20–20 and in fourth place—the NL's upper division—entering a massive 23-game road trip that began in Pittsburgh. During that stretch of games away from home, the Phils managed to drop 11 in a row. They returned home from the jaunt in sixth place.

The Phillies slipped to last entering the final weekend of the season, but a doubleheader sweep of the Giants on the final day vaulted them into a tie for sixth with the Brooklyn Robins.

Opposite: Sometimes referred to as the "Cigar Box" for its tiny dimensions, Baker Bowl also featured a hill that ascended to the center field wall, an added challenge for outfielders.

1926

▶ 58-93   8th ◀

Highlights

June 11: Russ Wrightstone cracks two doubles, a triple, and a homer and drives in seven runs as his Phillies defeat Pittsburgh 13–11.

June 24: Jack Knight enters the game as a reliever for Philly and hits two home runs at New York.

August 11: The Reds rout the Phillies 21–3.

September 8: Cy Williams clouts a walk-off grand slam in the ninth inning to defeat Brooklyn 8–4.

NOTES

Cy Williams ranks fourth in the NL in batting (.345), third in homers (18), and first in slugging (.568).

Outfielder Freddy Leach rips .329 and leads the team in RBI (71).

Infielder **Russ Wrightstone** (.307), catcher **Jimmie Wilson** (.305), and outfielder **Johnny Mokan** (.303) also hit over .300.

Hal Carlson (17–12, 3.23) emerges as the staff ace.

The remaining rotation regulars go a combined 36–67, and the team's ERA is a league-worst 5.03.

The Phillies go 15–7 against seventh-place Brooklyn but have great trouble with every other team.

FAREWELL, FLETCH

Manager's Reign Ends as Team Sinks to the Cellar

Art Fletcher accomplished something as skipper of the Philadelphia Phillies. Having served four seasons in the dugout, he outlasted each of William F. Baker's managerial selections since Pat Moran had led three of his four teams to top-two finishes in the National League. Considering that Fletcher never wound up in the upper division, his four-year tenure could be considered somewhat miraculous.

The 1926 slate served as his swan song, and it was not a pretty one. The Phillies, who had raised hopes (at least marginally) by tying for sixth place in 1925 with one of the more potent offenses in the league, tumbled back into the basement. They won 10 fewer games than they had the previous season, and they finished 7½ games behind seventh-place Boston.

As was the case through much of the decade, their outfield was stellar, with Cy Williams, Freddy Leach, and Johnny Mokan each topping .300. Catcher Jimmie Wilson, just 25 years old, hit .305.

Once again, the crux of the team's problems could be attributed

Russ Wrightstone batted over .300 five times for the Phillies from 1922 through 1927, including a high of .346 in 1925.

to the arms delivering the ball to Wilson when he crouched behind the plate. It was difficult to imagine Philadelphia's pitching getting any worse than it had been over the previous few seasons, but that was the case.

The Phillies' 5.03 ERA was more than a full run higher than the next-worst average in the league. It's a good thing that Hal Carlson enjoyed the best season of his career, because without the 17-win veteran the Phillies' pitching woes might have been record setting. No one else in the rotation was remotely close to the .500 mark.

An argument with umpire Bill Klem in September earned Fletcher an indefinite suspension from NL President John Heydler, and that's how his four-year managerial run came to an end. It was decided during that suspension that Fletcher would not return. The next year, he began a 19-year run as a Yankees coach that netted him nine World Series titles.

A Year of Disasters

Pitching and Hitting Collapse, as Does a Grandstand

The summer of 1927 was a memorable one for baseball. It produced one of the legendary numbers in the history of sports. Sixty. Babe Ruth hit that many balls over major league fences in 1927, besting his previous single-season record by one. Ruth's epic 1927 mark would stand for more than three decades.

For the Philadelphia Phillies, 1927 held no such magic. In fact, it was one of the more disastrous seasons in franchise history. William F. Baker enlisted former Philadelphia Athletics first baseman Stuffy McInnis with piloting his club out of last place. Burdened with the worst pitching staff in baseball, McInnis could do no such thing.

Philadelphia's 5.36 ERA was more than a run higher than any other in the National League. No other club in either league had one as high as 5.00. With that kind of pitching, it's no wonder the Phillies finished nine games behind Boston's Braves in their effort to climb out of the cellar.

Between the collapse of a Baker Bowl grandstand in May (one man died of a heart attack and dozens were injured), the move of several games across town to Shibe Park, and a 14-game skid in September, the 1927 Phillies were simply an ugly wreck in front of 305,420 witnesses.

Offensively, they weren't even knocking balls out of the park like they had been. In previous seasons, the one thing fans could count on was a home run derby when the Phillies took the field. Though Cy Williams led the NL with 30 taters in 1927, his teammates combined for just 27—a far cry from the days when the team would lead the NL in that category.

To no one's surprise, the 1927 campaign marked the beginning and the end of the McInnis era. Baker relieved him of his managerial job after the 51–103 season.

In 1927, second baseman Fresco Thompson ranked among the NL leaders in hits (181), doubles (32), triples (14), and steals (19) while batting .303.

Highlights

May 14: A Russ Wrightstone grand slam causes so much foot stomping at Baker Bowl that a grandstand collapses, injuring dozens of fans. One person dies of a heart attack.

May 20: After a 15–2 rout of the Reds, the Phillies possess a 14–11 record. They will go 37–92 the rest of the way.

May 22: Brooklyn clocks the Phils 20–4.

June 19: Jack Scott pitches two complete games for Philadelphia in a doubleheader split with Cincinnati.

August 5: Cy Williams hits for the cycle and drives in six runs against Pittsburgh.

September 24: A 10–2 loss to the Cubs marks the Phillies' fourteenth consecutive defeat.

NOTES

Cy Williams leads the NL in home runs with 30 and drives in 98 runs.

Russ Wrightstone, second baseman **Fresco Thompson,** and third baseman **Freddy Leach** all top .300 and drive in at least 70 runs.

Jack Scott (9–21) paces the staff in both wins and losses.

Dutch Ulrich is by far the most effective pitcher (3.17 ERA), but he still goes 8–11.

Burt Shotton is named the new manager after the season.

Highlights

June 6: The Phillies open the season at 7–34.

July 20: The Phils lose their twelfth consecutive game.

August 2: The pitching staff gives up 18 runs for the second straight game, against St. Louis and then Pittsburgh.

August 4: The Phillies conclude a five-game losing streak in which they give up 75 runs.

September 24: The team again loses a twelfth straight game.

October 29: The Phils trade outfielder Freddy Leach to the Giants for outfielder Lefty O'Doul and cash.

NOTES

The club's **109 losses** set a team record. **The Phillies** go 2–20 against St. Louis, go 3–22 in May, and are 16–35 in one-run games.

Third baseman Pinky Whitney bats .301 with a team-best 103 RBI, while **Freddy Leach** rips .304 with 96 RBI.

First baseman Don Hurst sets a Phillies rookie record with 19 home runs.

Rookie Chuck Klein bashes .360 with 11 homers in 64 games.

On a team with a league-high 5.61 ERA, **Ray Benge** is the "ace" of the staff at 8–18.

Jimmy Ring is 4–17, **Les Sweetland** goes 3–15, and **Russ Miller** is 0–12.

Next Up: Shotton

Change at the Helm Doesn't Change Philly's Fortunes

Former major league outfielder and minor league manager Burt Shotton won two National League pennants as a manager. Unfortunately for the Phillies, those came in the 1940s when he was leading Jackie Robinson and the mighty Brooklyn Dodgers. Shotton accepted his first big-league managing job with Philadelphia in 1928, and it was a rude welcome to say the least.

Coming off a 51–103 season and suiting up a shaky pitching staff, the outlook was not promising. After losing 34 of the season's first 41 games, it grew even worse. Two 12-game losing streaks plagued a squad that finished the year with a miserable 5.61 ERA. All but one other team in the NL registered ERAs lower than 4.00, putting the Phillies in a position of being thoroughly overmatched almost every time they took the field, home or away.

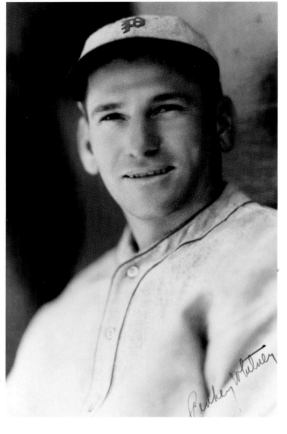

As a rookie in 1928, third baseman Arthur "Pinky" Whitney rapped .301–10–103, his first of four 100-RBI seasons with the Phillies.

Their 43–109 record was not only the worst in the majors, it was 51 games behind the NL-pennant-winning St. Louis Cardinals. The Phillies needed a telescope even to see the 103-loss, seventh-place Boston Braves.

The good news for Shotton, and Phillies fans, could be found on several players' birth certificates. That is, some of the top members of the 1928 club were young, which held promise for the future. First baseman Don Hurst, 22, launched 19 home runs. Third baseman Pinky Whitney, 23, hit .301 as a rookie. And 23-year-old outfielder Chuck Klein was bought in midseason from Fort Wayne to add more pop to the offense.

"All right, Klein, get in uniform," Shotton reportedly told the youngster. "They tell me you can hit. Goodness knows, we need hitters." Then, as the story goes, Shotton turned and mumbled to himself, "We need everything."

Among those needs was a fan base. Only 182,168 patrons came out to watch baseball's worst team during the 1928 season. Shotton could hardly blame the no-shows.

SCREEN SHOTS

Baker Bowl Altered for "Public Safety"

A 15-foot-high screen, added to the top of Baker Bowl's right-field wall in the middle of the 1929 season, did not keep the Phillies from making a considerable jump in the standings. A year after losing a staggering 109 games, a revamped Philadelphia club made a dramatic turnaround, claiming 71 wins against 82 defeats.

The screen, conspiracy theorists thought, was ordered by owner William F. Baker to keep Phillies slugger Chuck Klein from making a run at Babe Ruth's hallowed home run record (and subsequently demanding a fat raise). The official word, however, was that home runs were flying out of the miniature Baker Bowl at such a rapid pace that automobiles and pedestrians on Broad Street were in constant danger during Phillies games. It was a matter, Baker maintained, of public safety.

Broad Street *was* under siege from soaring baseballs, whether it was the Phillies batting or pitching. The club made a terrific trade that brought Lefty O'Doul to the outfield. He fell just two points shy of the .400 mark and set a National League record with 254 hits while also belting 32 homers and driving in 122 runs. And while Klein did not threaten Ruth's record of 60 home runs, he did claim the NL home run crown with 43 in his first full big league season. The Phillies hit a sizzling .309 as a team, topping the league in that category as well as in homers.

It's a good thing their offense became so potent, because Phillies hurlers were easily the most generous in baseball. Though Claude Willoughby and Les Sweetland notched winning marks at the top of the rotation, they pitched for a staff that posted an abysmal 6.13 ERA. No other NL staff came within a run of that mark, making the Phillies' ascent from last to fifth place somewhat miraculous.

Burt Shotton's club was, quite literally, pounding its way to victories. And as the stock market crashed and the nation sank into the Great Depression following the 1929 season, it would soon become clear that an all-hitting, no-pitching approach was no recipe for sustained success.

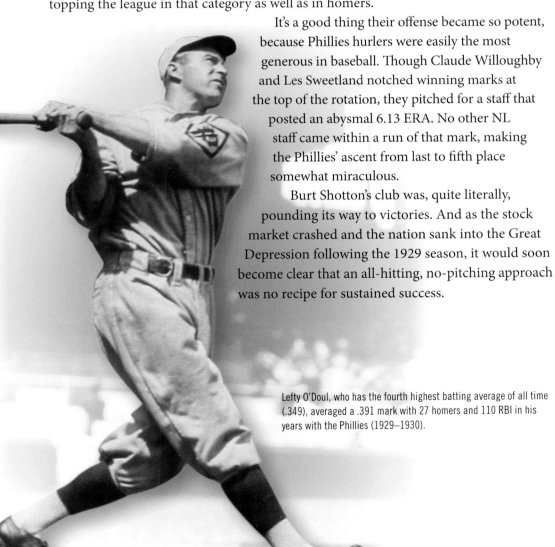

Lefty O'Doul, who has the fourth highest batting average of all time (.349), averaged a .391 mark with 27 homers and 110 RBI in his years with the Phillies (1929–1930).

Highlights

May 18: Brooklyn and Philly combine for 50 runs in a doubleheader, with the Robins taking the first game 20–16.

June 6: Ray Benge shuts out Cincinnati to improve the Phillies' record to 21–20. A 2–16 stretch will follow.

July 6: The visiting Cardinals score 10 in the first and 10 in the fifth, and they go on to defeat the Phillies 28–6 on 28 hits.

October 5: Phillies pitchers semi-intentionally walk Giants slugger Mel Ott (42 homers) five times so that Chuck Klein (43 homers) will win the home run crown, which he does.

NOTES

Lefty O'Doul leads the NL with a .398 average and 254 hits, which will stand as a twentieth-century NL record. He also amasses 32 homers, 122 RBI, and 152 runs.

Chuck Klein hits .356 with 43 homers, 145 RBI, and 219 hits.

First baseman Don Hurst cracks .304–31–125.

Part-time catcher **Spud Davis** bashes .342, **Pinky Whitney** hits .327 with 200 hits, and **Fresco Thompson** goes for .324 with 202 hits.

O'Doul, Klein, Thompson, and **Whitney** become the first—and to date only—NL quartet of teammates to knock 200 or more hits in the same season.

Claude Willoughby leads the staff in wins (15–14).

THE 1920s RECORD BOOK

Team Leaders

Batting
1920: Cy Williams, .325
1921: Irish Meusel, .353
1922: Curt Walker, .337
1923: Butch Henline, .324
1924: Cy Williams, .328
1925: George Harper, .349
1926: Cy Williams, .345
1927: Freddy Leach, .306
1928: Freddy Leach, .304
1929: Lefty O'Doul, .398

Home Runs
1920: Cy Williams, 15
1921: Cy Williams, 18
1922: Cy Williams, 26
1923: Cy Williams, 41
1924: Cy Williams, 24
1925: George Harper, 18
1926: Cy Williams, 18
1927: Cy Williams, 30
1928: Don Hurst, 19
1929: Chuck Klein, 43

RBI
1920: Cy Williams, 72
1921: Cy Williams, 75
1922: Cy Williams, 92
1923: Cy Williams, 114
1924: Cy Williams, 93
1925: George Harper, 97
1926: Freddy Leach, 71
1927: Cy Williams, 98
1928: Pinky Whitney, 103
1929: Chuck Klein, 145

Runs
1920: Cy Williams, 88
1921: Cy Williams, 67
1922: Curt Walker, 102
1923: Cy Williams, 98
1924: Cy Williams, 101
1925: George Harper, 86
1926: Heinie Sand, 99
1927: Heinie Sand, 87
1928: Fresco Thompson, 99
1929: Lefty O'Doul, 152

Stolen Bases
1920: Cy Williams, 18
1921: Irish Meusel, 8
1922: Curt Walker, 11;
Cy Williams, 11
1923: Curt Walker, 12
1924: George Harper, 10
1925: George Harper, 10
1926: Clarence Huber, 9
1927: Fresco Thompson, 19
1928: Fresco Thompson, 19
1929: Fresco Thompson, 16

Doubles
1920: Cy Williams, 36
1921: Cy Williams, 28
1922: Curt Walker, 36
1923: Walter Holke, 31;
Cotton Tierney, 31
1924: Cy Williams, 31
1925: George Harper, 35
1926: Heinie Sand, 30
1927: Fresco Thompson, 32
1928: Freddy Leach, 36
1929: Chuck Klein, 45

Triples
1920: Cy Williams, 10
1921: Irish Meusel, 7
1922: Curt Walker, 11
1923: Russ Wrightstone, 7
1924: Cy Williams, 11
1925: George Harper, 7;
Heinie Sand, 7
1926: Freddy Leach 7,
Clarence Huber, 7
1927: Fresco Thompson, 14
1928: Freddy Leach, 11;
Fresco Thompson, 11
1929: Pinky Whitney, 14

Wins
1920: Lee Meadows, 16–14
1921: Lee Meadows, 11–16
1922: Jimmy Ring, 12–18;
Lee Meadows, 12–18
1923: Jimmy Ring, 18–16
1924: Jimmy Ring, 10–12;
Bill Hubbell, 10–9
1925: Jimmy Ring, 14–16
1926: Hal Carlson, 17–12
1927: Jack Scott, 9–21
1928: Ray Benge, 8–18
1929: Claude Willoughby, 15–14

Phillies outfielder Curt Walker was one of the league's top sluggers in 1922, rapping .337 while scoring 102 runs and driving in 89.

ERA

1920: Lee Meadows, 2.84
1921: Jimmy Ring, 4.24
1922: Lefty Weinert, 3.40
1923: Jimmy Ring, 3.87
1924: Jimmy Ring, 3.97
1925: Hal Carlson, 4.23
1926: Hal Carlson, 3.23
1927: Dutch Ulrich, 3.17
1928: Ray Benge, 4.55
1929: Claude Willoughby, 4.99

Strikeouts

1920: Eppa Rixey, 109
1921: Jimmy Ring, 88
1922: Jimmy Ring, 116
1923: Jimmy Ring, 112
1924: Jimmy Ring, 72
1925: Jimmy Ring, 93
1926: Hal Carlson, 55
1927: Hub Pruett, 90
1928: Jimmy Ring, 70
1929: Ray Benge, 78

NL Leaders

1920: Home Runs—Cy Williams, 15
1923: Home Runs—Cy Williams, 41
1925: Shutouts—Hal Carlson, 4
1927: Home Runs—Cy Williams, 30
1929: Batting Average—
   Lefty O'Doul, .398;
   Hits—O'Doul, 254;
   Home Runs—Chuck Klein, 43

NL Awards

NL MVP Voting

1929: Lefty O'Doul, 2nd

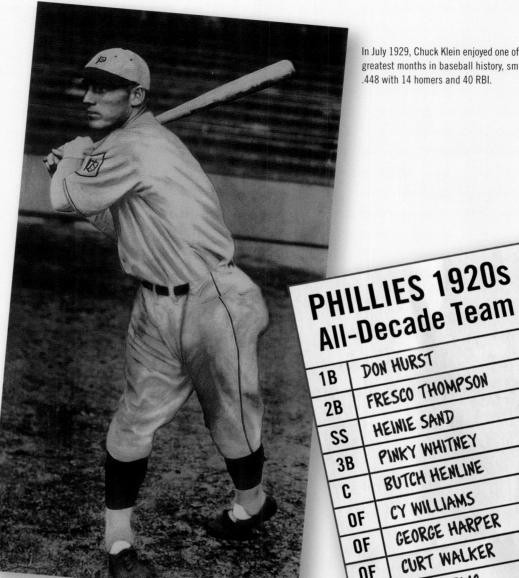

In July 1929, Chuck Klein enjoyed one of the greatest months in baseball history, smashing .448 with 14 homers and 40 RBI.

PHILLIES 1920s All-Decade Team

1B	DON HURST
2B	FRESCO THOMPSON
SS	HEINIE SAND
3B	PINKY WHITNEY
C	BUTCH HENLINE
OF	CY WILLIAMS
OF	GEORGE HARPER
OF	CURT WALKER
SP	JIMMY RING
SP	LEE MEADOWS
RP	PHIL COLLINS

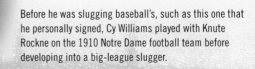

Before he was slugging baseball's, such as this one that he personally signed, Cy Williams played with Knute Rockne on the 1910 Notre Dame football team before developing into a big-league slugger.

DEPRESSION ERA

The Phillies put up some big numbers in the 1930s, such as 170 RBI by Chuck Klein and a 6.71 team ERA. The net result is one winning season and a sea of empty seats.

Imagine a decade in which a 78–76 season qualifies as the overwhelming highlight. Welcome to 1930s baseball, Phillies style. The Depression era yielded a thoroughly depressing team.

The Phillies did not deserve the support of their fans in this decade, and they did not get it. With discretionary funds in short supply, Philadelphians saved what little money they had and stayed away from Baker Bowl. Why waste money on consistently sorry baseball? The Phillies ranked last in the National League in attendance in every season of the '30s, except for 1931, when they ranked sixth of eight.

That season represented a marginal improvement from the first team of the decade, the 1930 bunch that won just 52 games. The 1931 squad won 66, moving up to sixth place, before the leap to 78 wins and a fourth-place finish in 1932.

Through 1933, at least, the Phillies boasted one of baseball's elite hitters: future Hall of Famer Chuck Klein, who took full advantage of the cozy Baker Bowl. For his career, Klein slugged at a .705 rate in that bandbox. Nowhere else was his slugging percentage higher than .553.

Klein's left-handed power terrorized pitchers, and he led the league in total bases in each of the first four years of the decade. He was MVP of the league in 1932, and he captured the Triple Crown in 1933 with a .368 average, 28 homers, and 120 runs batted in. Yet just as they would many years later with Ferguson Jenkins and Ryne Sandberg, the Phillies traded a player bound for Cooperstown to the Chicago Cubs.

In any case, starting in 1933, the Phillies would begin a streak of 13 consecutive seasons in which they finished seventh or eighth in the eight-team National League. Managers Burt Shotton and Jimmie Wilson could not rouse the team to any real success.

The Phillies played their final game at Baker Bowl on June 30, 1938, moving to Shibe Park, where they would play through 1970. They also wore unusual uniforms that season, with a giant block-letter "P"—in yellow—on the home jersey.

But change brought only more of the same, no matter

F. O'DONNELL HURST *Phi-N 1b*

First baseman Don Hurst, pictured on this Big League Collectibles card, averaged 109 RBI for the Phils from 1929 through 1932, with a league- and career-high 143 in 1932.

where the team played or what it was wearing. The 1938 Phillies finished last, at 45–105, and Wilson gave way to James "Doc" Prothro—a dentist in the offseason—for 1939. That team played one more game (a loss, naturally), giving it the worst record of the decade: 45–106.

The 1939 Phillies were outscored by more than 300 runs for the season. No player reached double digits in home runs or stolen bases, and no pitcher recorded more than 10 victories. The team's ERA was 5.17, which looks atrocious except when compared to the ERA at the start of the decade: 6.71 in 1930.

So the pitching had made progress, on paper anyway, but at least that 1930 team could boast a brawny offense, with Klein and Lefty O'Doul hitting above .380, Pinky Whitney driving in 117 runs, and Klein plating 170, a club record that still stands. By the end of the decade, the Phillies were awful on the mound and at the plate, and the standings told the same familiar, discouraging story: last place.

Dick Bartell comes charging home against Cubs catcher Gabby Hartnett in 1932 action. The shortstop scored more than 100 runs in two of his four season with Philadelphia and twice batted over .300.

1930

52-102   8th

Highlights

April 20: Forty-three-year-old Pete Alexander, reacquired by the Phillies in a trade, loses to the Giants 2–1 in his first game of the year. He won't last the season.

June 6: Phillies outfielder Denny Sothern collects five hits, including four doubles, against Cincinnati.

June 17: Chuck Klein beats Pittsburgh with a walk-off hit, extending his hitting streak to a team-record 26 games. He'll go hitless the next game.

August 3: Klein's second 26-game hitting streak comes to an end.

September 6: Brooklyn defeats Philly 22–8.

September 16: The Phillies score five in the ninth and five in the tenth to beat Pittsburgh 15–14.

October 14: The Phillies trade Lefty O'Doul and Fresco Thompson to Brooklyn for lesser players and cash.

NOTES

Chuck Klein bashes .386–40–170 with 250 hits and NL highs in doubles (59), total bases (445), and runs (158).

Lefty O'Doul bats .383, knocks 22 homers, and drives in 97 runs while scoring 122.

Pinky Whitney hits a career-high .342, good enough for third-best on his own team. He also contributes 8 homers and 117 RBI.

The Phillies set a dubious MLB record with a 6.71 ERA.

BAT RICH, ARM POOR
Phillies Fall Back to Basement Despite Torrid Hitting

There may never be another season like 1930. For that, Phillies fans can be thankful. Their club set twentieth-century franchise records, some of which still stand, for hits, doubles, total bases, and runs. They finished second in the National League with a .315 batting average and 345 doubles. Outfield mates Chuck Klein and Lefty O'Doul each topped .380—yet finished third and fourth in the NL batting race that year—and the duo crossed the plate 280 times between them. Klein set a franchise record by driving in 170 runs.

Those numbers, backing even an average pitching staff, might have been good enough to propel a team squarely into a pennant race. Or at least to a winning record.

The Phillies, however, had nothing resembling an average pitching staff. Their 6.71 ERA set a (still-standing) major league record, although it should be noted that the Baker Bowl was a launching pad and that 1930 has gone down in baseball history as the "Year of the Hitter." Nevertheless, the Phillies bumbled to a 52–102 record and last place in the NL.

Philadelphia sportswriter Jimmy Isaminger, describing the plight of his town's NL franchise, wrote, "Nine runs are a whopping lot, but mean nothing when cotton-armed pitchers give the opponents 16!"

So desperate was manager Burt Shotton to find someone—anyone—who could get batters out, he brought back 43-year-old former Phillies ace Pete Alexander for one last shot. It was yet another of the team's 1930 pitching failures, as Alexander went 0–3 in nine games while yielding almost two hits per inning and finishing with a 9.14 ERA.

The 1930 Phillies never won more than three games in a row, and they typically found themselves on the short end of lopsided outcomes. Their attendance of less than 300,000 ranked last in the National League.

And on December 4, the club found itself in the market for a new leader when owner William F. Baker died in Montreal. It was the end of an era. Thankfully, some might say.

Chuck Klein posted phenomenal numbers with 40 homers, 170 RBI, and a .386 average in 1930—and didn't lead the league in any of those categories, although he was tops in the NL in runs (158) and doubles (59).

New Beginning

Front-Office Changes Precede Jump in Standings

Charlie Ruch, a William F. Baker colleague, was named president of the Phillies on January 5, 1931—one month after Baker died of a heart attack. Business manager Gerald P. "Gerry" Nugent, however, would be the man largely responsible for running the club.

Business considerations played no small factor in keeping franchises afloat during the Great Depression. American families were struggling to survive, and their great American game served as a welcome distraction. During his reign, Nugent would make any deal he could (i.e., selling away his stars) to keep his team afloat.

By and large, the 1931 Phillies did a fine job giving their fans a reason to cheer. Baker had brought in two key players in trades just before he died. Pitcher Jumbo Elliott arrived from the Brooklyn Dodgers, and shortstop Dick Bartell was obtained from the Pittsburgh Pirates. The Phils lost outfielder Lefty O'Doul in the Elliott deal, but turning around their shoddy pitching was of foremost importance.

They made tremendous strides in that regard. One year after posting a 6.71 ERA—worst in major league history—the Phillies managed a 4.58 mark. Make no mistake, they were still the worst in the National League in that department. But the difference of better than two runs and the addition of Elliott (19–14) at the front of the rotation gave the club a legitimate chance to win games. The year before, that was not the case.

The offense took a step back after its torrid 1930 campaign, resulting in lower scoring but more competitive games. Chuck Klein remained a monster in the heart of the batting order. By his side in the outfield was Buzz Arlett, who hit .313 with 18 home runs in his only big-league season.

While many fans could not afford to spend their savings on baseball during these dark economic times, those who did come out to the Baker Bowl witnessed 40 wins against 36 defeats, as the Phillies climbed to sixth place in the NL.

After the season, the National League loaned the Phillies money so that the team could stay afloat during the Depression.

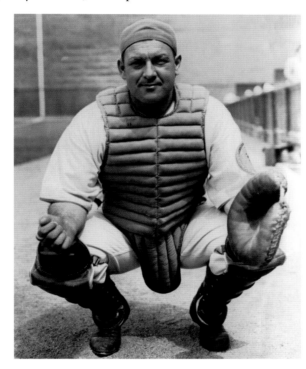

Spud Davis, who holds one of the highest career averages in history for a catcher (.308), smashed .321 in his eight years with the Phillies.

Highlights

July 1: Chuck Klein hits for the cycle, and the Phillies turn a triple play, in an 11–6 home win over the Cubs.

July 11: Phillies pitcher Dutch Schesler gives up 22 hits and 16 runs as the Giants win 23–5.

September 16: St. Louis finishes a six-game sweep of the Phillies, who have now gone 5–51 against the Cardinals since 1927.

NOTES

Chuck Klein hits .337 and leads the league in homers (31), RBI (121), runs (121), and slugging (.584). Frankie Frisch of the Cardinals edges Klein in the balloting for the first-ever NL MVP Award.

Four starters besides Klein hit over .300, including catcher **Spud Davis** (.326), outfielder **Buzz Arlett** (.313), second baseman **Les Mallon** (.309), and first baseman **Don Hurst** (.305).

Pitcher Jumbo Elliott leads the staff in wins (19–14).

Ray Benge is 14–18 but with an impressive 3.17 ERA.

1932

▸ 78-76 4th ◂

Highlights

April 12: Pitcher "Fidgety" Phil Collins cracks four hits and defeats the Giants 13–5 on Opening Day.

June 30: Chuck Klein hits two home runs, giving him 24 on the season.

July 6: Shortly after the Phillies lose in Chicago, Cubs shortstop Bill Jurges is shot twice (but not fatally) by his spurned girlfriend, Violet Popovich Valli, in his hotel room.

August 1: The Phillies rout the Pirates 18–5.

NOTES

The team leads the league in runs with 844.

Chuck Klein paces the NL in homers (38), runs (152), hits (226), total bases (420), slugging (.646), and steals (20).

Don Hurst (143), **Chuck Klein** (137), and **Pinky Whitney** (124) finish first, second, and third in the NL in RBI.

Six starters bat over .300, led by Klein (.348), Hurst (.339), and Spud Davis (.336).

Klein becomes the first Phillie to win the NL MVP Award.

Phil Collins (14–12) leads the staff in wins, as six pitchers post double-digit win totals.

AT LAST, FIRST DIVISION

Fourth-Place Finish Holds Distinction in Phils History

Back when the Phillies spent three straight years in the National League's top two, including their pennant-winning 1915 season, the future of the organization looked promising. Few might have guessed that the club would go on to finish out of the NL's first division (top four) every year from 1918 through '48, with the exception of one season. That season was 1932.

This beacon of light in an otherwise long, dark stretch of baseball was largely fueled by offense—a familiar trend in franchise history. The '32 Phillies led the NL with a .292 batting average and 844 runs. The seven batters who played in more than 103 games batted .298 or better, with six players eclipsing the .300 mark.

Of course, Chuck Klein was the offensive catalyst. His .646 slugging percentage was tops in the NL during his MVP performance, as were his 38 home runs and 20 steals. Catcher Spud Davis and first baseman Don Hurst joined Klein in topping .330 from the plate.

Manager Burt Shotton knew that the key to his club's success would be improving the troubled pitching staff, which had been beaten up in previous seasons. Pitchers tended to look bad when delivering their throws in the pint-sized Baker Bowl, but the ones wearing Philadelphia jerseys had been particularly inept.

They finished last in the NL in ERA once again in 1932, but they reduced their mark from 6.71 in 1930 to 4.58 in '31 to 4.47 in '32. Perhaps the improvement from the previous year was a "baby step," but the difference helped the Phillies outscore their opponents in '32—the first time they had done that since 1917.

Philadelphia's pitching success—what success there was—came very much as a result of balance. Phil Collins' 14 wins led a team that had six hurlers claim 10 or more victories. One of those six was a colorful newcomer, South Carolina right-hander Flint Rhem, who was a former 20-game winner with the Cardinals.

Rhem's arrival, and unpredictable antics, certainly caused a stir in and around the Baker Bowl. Renowned for his "big thirst" when it came to alcoholic beverages, Flint once refused to pitch on what he called a substandard mound until the groundskeeper built him a new one. "If he'd ever stayed sober," teammate Dick Bartell offered, "what a pitcher he could have been. He was the nicest guy in the world, never mean or nasty, never bothered nobody."

The Phillies held each of the eight places in the NL standings at some point during the 1932 season. They were first after back-to-back wins to open the season, then dropped to eighth before an 18–11 June pulled them out of the cellar. They played 39–35 baseball during the season's second half, and they secured their upper-division finish by a single game over the Braves thanks to a 6–3 road win against the Giants in the regular-season finale.

> **PHILLIES PHACT**
>
> The Phillies finish with a winning record for the first time since 1917.

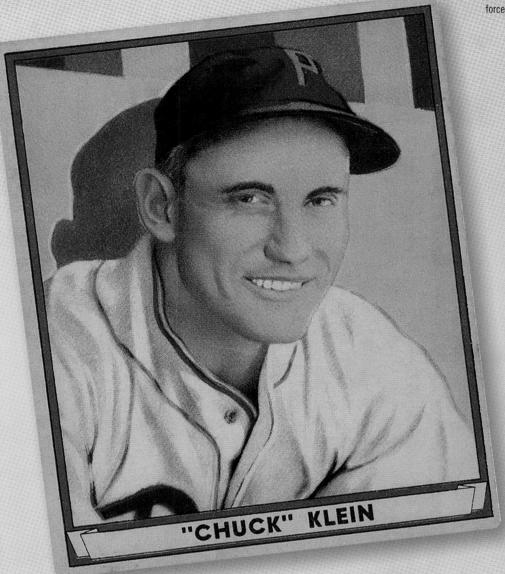

Chuck Klein, shown here on a Play Ball card, was a force at the plate in the late 1920s and early 1930s.

"CHUCK" KLEIN

Muscle Boy

After graduating high school, Chuck Klein worked for three years at an Indianapolis steel mill, heaving 200-pound hunks of metal into a blast furnace. With his bulging muscles and refined baseball talent—honed on semipro diamonds—Klein caught the attention of the Phillies, who signed him in the middle of 1928. Immediately, he set the league on fire.

Klein batted .360 in 1928, then blasted .356–43–145 a year later. His 1930 numbers were otherworldly: .386, 158 runs, and 170 RBI. His 250 hits, 59 doubles, 8 triples, and 40 home runs that year resulted in 445 total bases, which would remain a National League twentieth-century record for a left-handed hitter. Klein won home run titles the next three seasons and took home the NL MVP Award in 1932.

With its short right-field fence and Klein's powerful left-handed stroke, Baker Bowl was no match for the Phillies slugger. In his career at that ballpark, Klein bashed .395–164–594 in 581 games. He also shined in right field, as evidenced by his 44 assists in 1930—a twentieth-century record for a big-league outfielder. He finished his Hall of Fame career with a .320 average and 300 home runs, including 4 in a game in 1936.

Highlights

May 26: Chuck Klein hits for the cycle against St. Louis.

July 6: Klein and shortstop Dick Bartell start for the National League in the very first MLB All-Star Game.

July 7: Neal Finn, the team's starting second baseman, dies of complications from a stomach ulcer.

November 15: The Phils trade star catcher Spud Davis to St. Louis for catcher Jimmie Wilson, who will serve as player/manager, replacing fired skipper Burt Shotton.

November 21: The Phillies trade Klein to the Cubs for three players and $125,000.

NOTES

Chuck Klein wins the Triple Crown with marks of .368–28–120. He also leads the league in hits (223), doubles (44), total bases (365), OBP (.422), and slugging (.602).

Klein finishes second in MVP voting to Giants ace Carl Hubbell.

Spud Davis is second in the NL with a .349 average; **outfielder Wes Schulmerich** hits .334.

Don Hurst, a spring training holdout, sees his numbers drop to .267–8–76.

Ed Holley (13–15, 3.53) is the only pitcher to win in double digits.

In the heart of the Depression, **attendance falls** to 156,421.

DOWNRIGHT DEPRESSING

Fans, Victories Scarce for Disappointing Phillies

Commissioner Kenesaw Mountain Landis (center), with Phillies manager Burt Shotton at right, was in attendance at Shibe Park for the 1933 Opening Day.

Manager Burt Shotton, entering his sixth season at the helm, predicted a National League pennant for the 1933 Phillies during spring training. The club was coming off a winning season and its first upper-division finish since 1917. It boasted one of the game's most prolific sluggers in Chuck Klein along with potent hitters surrounding him, and it fielded a pitching staff that had improved its performance in each of the previous two seasons.

As the Great Depression continued to cripple the nation, however, there were few smiling faces in the stands at the Baker Bowl. The tragedy of second baseman Neal "Mickey" Finn epitomized the hard luck that seemed to have befallen the Phillies franchise.

Finn had been brought in from Brooklyn in a trade for pitcher Ray Benge, and Shotton figured the fiery infielder would be good for 10–12 extra wins for his club. Early in the season, though, Finn was diagnosed with stomach ulcers. He went in for surgery in late June, but post-surgical complications cost the 29-year-old his life on July 7. The Phillies were stunned.

The season went on, of course. Klein and his outfield mates all batted over .300, but the Phillies got precious little production from the second- and third-base positions. And although the pitching staff improved its ERA for the third consecutive season, its 4.34 mark was still considerably higher than any other in the NL.

The results were all too familiar. The Phillies lost a bushel of high-scoring games and never mounted a challenge in the NL standings. They went 32–40 at Baker Bowl and a dismal 28–52 on the road. While Ed Holley went 13–15, no other Philadelphia pitcher won more than eight games.

Poor play and the worst economic times in United States history took their toll at the box office. The Phillies attracted only 156,421 patrons to their games, their lowest mark since the war-shortened 1918 season.

ENTER MR. WILSON

Phillies Catcher Follows Shotton to the Helm

Considering he won barely 40 percent of his games and finished in the upper division just once, it was somewhat remarkable that Burt Shotton had been the longest-tenured Phillies manager of the twentieth century at the time he was replaced—after six seasons—by Jimmie Wilson in 1934. Wilson had begun his career as a catcher with the Phillies and was serving behind the plate for St. Louis when he got the call to manage his first team.

Consider it a classic case of "be careful what you wish for." The 33-year-old inherited a club with unproven pitching, shaky defense, and, like most Phillies clubs of this era, some pop at the plate. Charged with turning a seventh-place team into something better, Wilson began the year with high hopes, which took a beating when he lost his first seven games. He completed his debut, lo and behold, in seventh place.

There were some bright spots along the way. Outfielder Johnny Moore, brought in from Cincinnati in the season's first month, hit a team-leading .343 in a Phillies uniform and .330 overall. The club's .284 team average ranked third in the National League. And Al Todd did a fine job splitting catching duties with Wilson. Todd hit .318; Wilson, .292. Each appeared in 91 games.

Neither one of them could coax better performances out of their pitchers—a far-too-familiar problem for the Phillies. Curt Davis, a 30-year-old, side-arming rookie brought in from the Pacific Coast League, enjoyed a smashing debut with 19 wins against 17 defeats. His 2.95 ERA should have merited an even better win-loss fate, but hurting his cause was the fact that Philadelphia led the NL in errors.

The rest of the pitching staff was awful, resulting in an NL-worst 4.76 ERA. Not surprisingly, the Phillies also trailed each of their NL rivals at the gate, attracting fewer than 170,000 fans.

A skinny sidearmer, Curt "Coonskin" Davis ranked eighth in NL MVP voting after his sensational rookie year in 1934—at age 30.

Highlights

April 24: The Phillies start the year at 0–7.

April 29: The Phillies play their first-ever Sunday home game. A referendum passed by the Philadelphia electorate in November 1933 allowed for Sunday games between 2 p.m. and 6 p.m.

July 14: The Phils blow out the Red 18–0.

August 4: The Giants rout the Phillies 21–4, as reliever Reggie Grabowski coughs up 11 runs in the top of the ninth.

September 24: Phillies third baseman Bucky Walters gives pitching a try and throws two no-hit innings. He will wind up recording 198 career wins.

November 1: After another bad year at the gate, the Phillies trade standout shortstop Dick Bartell to the Giants for four players and cash.

NOTES

Early-season pickup **Johnny Moore** hits .343 with the Phils and leads the team in RBI (93).

Outfielder **Ethan Allen** raps .330 with a league-high 42 doubles, while **Dick Bartell** cracks .310 with a team-high 102 runs.

Thirty-year-old **rookie pitcher Curt Davis** ranks among the NL's top five in wins (19–17) and ERA (2.95).

Washed-up legend Hack Wilson goes 2-for-20 as a Phillie.

Highlights

April 19: The Phillies beat the Giants 18–7, as second baseman Lou Chiozza rips five hits and first sacker Dolph Camilli tallies two homers and seven RBI.

April 21: Philadelphia ties an NL record by turning six double plays.

May 8: The Phillies open the season at 2–10, a hole they'll never dig out of.

May 15: Pittsburgh routs the Phils 20–5.

May 24: The Phillies play the first night game in major league history, losing to the Reds 2–1 at Cincinnati's Crosley Field.

July 8: Catcher Jimmie Wilson represents the Phillies at the All-Star Game.

NOTES

Curt Davis is the ace of the staff, going 16–14 with a 3.66 ERA.

Dolph Camilli leads the team with 25 home runs.

Outfielder Johnny Moore tops the Phils with a .323 average and hits a career-best 19 homers.

Ethan Allen ranks second in the NL with 46 doubles.

Attendance improves to 205,470, but the Phils still rank last in the league.

PROGRESS ON THE HILL

Pitchers Halt an Embarrassing Run of Futility

As usual, there was not a great deal for Phillies fans to celebrate in 1935. Though Jimmie Wilson's club won eight more games than the previous year's contingent, another seventh-place finish plagued a club that consistently experienced pain both on the scoreboard and at the box office. Even with the economy beginning to take a turn for the better, only slightly more than 200,000 came out, the worst showing in the National League.

However, one notable feat was worth praise, perhaps with a subtle smile. For the first time since 1917—a run of nearly two full decades—Philadelphia pitchers did not register the highest ERA in the league. That dubious distinction belonged to the Boston Braves, whose 4.93 ERA was fatter than the Phillies' 4.76.

Jimmie Wilson (right) had many aggravating moments in his five seasons as Phillies skipper. The 1935 club won the most games during his tenure (64)—and finished 35 ½ games out of first place.

Side-arming Curt Davis followed his 19–17 rookie season with a 16–14 record as staff ace. He was joined by two teammates in double figures, Syl Johnson and Orville Jorgens. To be sure, having the second worst ERA in the NL was not exactly a catapult to rocket the Phils toward the top of the standings. But at least the slump was over.

What wasn't over was the team's financial struggles, and club president Gerry Nugent chose to ease the burden through a trade. He sent fine shortstop Dick Bartell to the Giants before the season for four players and cash to help balance the books.

Bartell's .300 bat was tough to replace. With Mickey Haslin hitting .265 in Bartell's position, the Phillies' team average—historically a bright spot in the hitter's palace that was the Baker Bowl—dropped to .269. Outfielders Johnny Moore and Ethan Allen were the only two regulars at .300 or better.

While the eight-game jump showed modest progress, the Phillies did make a big stride toward diversity. Middle infielder Chile Gomez made the club as a reserve to become the first Latin player in franchise history.

Opposite: Star outfielder Dolph Camilli scores a run for the Phillies, something he did more than 100 times in both 1936 and 1937 before being traded to Brooklyn for a nondescript player and cash in 1938.

WELCOME BACK, CHUCK

Slugger's Return Doesn't Stop the Bleeding

Leave it to Chuck Klein to find the silver lining—if one could call it that—in playing for a Phillies team that perennially finished at or near the bottom of the standings. "With the Phillies, nobody paid much attention whether I hit or not," offered Klein, who spent the 1934 and '35 seasons with the pennant-contending Cubs. "[In Chicago], they watch you on every pitch."

That's not to say that Klein stopped hitting when he returned to the Phillies in a trade for Curt Davis and Ethan Allen early in the 1936 season. Nothing could be further from the truth. His .309 average was third on the team—behind fellow outfielder Johnny Moore and first baseman Dolph Camilli—and his 20 homers (including four in one game) were second to Camilli's 28. Klein's point was that the Phillies, compared with the contending National League clubs, seemed to be playing in a vacuum.

The nation was clawing its way out of the Great Depression, but fewer than 250,000 fans came out to support Philadelphia's National Leaguers in 1936. That was an improvement over the previous season, but it still ranked dead last among the eight NL teams.

Those who did come out to the aging Baker Bowl witnessed a team that lost 100 games for the first time since 1930, including 14 in a row at one point. They went 4–24 in August and landed a whopping 13 games behind seventh-place Brooklyn in the final standings.

After a one-year reprieve, Philadelphia's pitching staff regained its familiar position of posting the highest ERA in the league (4.64). Starters Bucky Walters and Joe Bowman recorded 21 and 20 losses, respectively.

Klein wasn't the only former Phillies standout brought back to participate in the carnage. Pinky Whitney, who had been with the Braves since 1933, returned to play third base. He hit .294 and was the only Phillies representative at the All-Star Game.

Highlights

May 21: The Phillies trade Curt Davis and Ethan Allen to the Cubs for Chuck Klein.

July 10: At Pittsburgh, Klein becomes the fourth player in MLB history—and the first in the NL in the twentieth century—to belt four home runs in a game, including one in the tenth inning.

July 7: The only Philadelphia players in the All-Star Game are Pinky Higgins of the Athletics and third baseman Pinky Whitney of the Phillies.

July 22: Outfielder Johnny Moore socks three home runs in a 16–4 rout of the Pirates.

August 16: The Phillies lose their fourteenth game in a row.

NOTES

First baseman Dolph Camilli (.315) ranks second in the NL in slugging (.577) and leads the team in homers (28), RBI (102), and runs (106).

Chuck Klein hits .309–20–86 in just 117 games with the Phillies.

Johnny Moore leads the team with a .328 average and belts 16 home runs.

Bucky Walters (11–21) and **Claude Passeau** (11–15) lead the team in wins; **Joe Bowman** goes 9–20.

The Phillies finish last in the NL in ERA (4.64) and go a startling 12–34 in one-run games.

69

▶ 60-92   7th ◀

Highlights

April 30: Star hitter Dolph Camillli signs with the Phillies after a long holdout.

May 9: Cincinnati routs the Phils 21–10.

May 22: The Phillies return the favor, clubbing the Reds 19–9.

July 7: Bucky Walters, the sole Phillie in the All-Star Game, shuts down the AL in the eighth.

July 11: Boston's Lou Fette outduels Philly's Syl Johnson 1–0 in 13 innings.

September 23: With a win over the Reds, the Phillies climb out of the cellar.

NOTES

Despite his holdout, **Dolph Camilli** hits .339 and leads the team in homers (27) and RBI (80).

Pinky Whitney ranks fifth in the NL in batting at .341.

Chuck Klein hits .325 but falls to 15 home runs.

Wayne LaMaster (15–19), **Claude Passeau** (14–18), and **Walters** (14–15) are the staff's big three.

Hugh "Losing Pitcher" Mulcahy goes 8–18.

Baker Bowl continues to plague Phillies pitchers, who give up 6.5 runs per game at home.

Both Philadelphia teams rise from eighth place in 1936 to seventh place in 1937. The A's draw more than twice as many fans as the Phils.

POWER, BUT NO SURGE

Homers Abound, Even If Wins Don't Follow

The Phillies had spent much of the previous decade as one of the best home run–hitting teams and worst pitching clubs in all of baseball. So in their last full season playing in the homer-happy Baker Bowl, it was no surprise that the song remained the same.

Slugging first baseman Dolph Camilli, a contract holdout through the first week of the season, joined the club in time to swat 27 home runs. Chuck Klein added 15 and Morrie Arnovich 10, as Philadelphia was one of just two National League teams to top 100 round-trippers for the year. Yes, the Phillies could plate runs at a rapid pace in their sparsely populated home ballpark. Trouble was, opponents could score with even greater ease there.

The Phillies gave up 481 runs at the Baker Bowl—93 more than they yielded on the road. As a result, their home record was a dismal 29–45, contributing to a 61–92 overall record that was good only for seventh place despite their hitting prowess.

If the tiny dimensions of the Baker Bowl weren't making the Phillies feel at home, neither were the fans. Although the Athletics, across town, boosted their attendance from 285,000 to 430,000 despite a matching seventh-place finish (in the American League), the Phillies saw their gate turnout drop from 250,000 to 212,000. Who wanted to watch an out-of-contention team in a decrepit facility? Not many, it seemed.

What never seemed to change on the Phillies' side of town was ineffective pitching. Their 5.05 ERA was nearly a full run higher than that of any other NL team. Every pitcher on the team who started more than two games suffered a losing record.

Bucky Walters (14–15) didn't have the worst mark on the team, but he did suffer the indignity of losing twice on the same day—as the starter in a doubleheader opener against the Cardinals and a reliever in the nightcap.

The bad luck of Hugh "Losing Pitcher" Mulcahy (45–89) dragged into real life, as he was the first big-leaguer drafted into the military in 1941.

SHARING SHIBE
New Home Does Not Bring Predicted Success

A Philadelphia baseball legend made a matter-of-fact prediction regarding the Phillies, and his own Athletics, during the 1938 season. "I think the change will benefit both clubs and make for better baseball in Philadelphia," said Philadelphia A's leader Connie Mack as he completed a deal that allowed the Phillies to call "his" Shibe Park their new home facility. "I am sure the Phils will play better at Shibe Park."

Mack was many things. A smart catcher. A world champion manager. A successful team owner. A Baseball Hall of Famer. In this case, however, he was no prophet.

Jimmie Wilson's Phillies were happy to make the move. Baker Bowl was not only outdated, sparsely populated, and home to loss after loss for the locals; structurally, it was dangerous. Shibe Park, for many reasons, made a lot more sense.

Truth be told, it was not any park or location that contributed to the club's failures in 1938 and beyond. It was the team. Financially strapped, the Phillies were forced to unload top players, including Dolph Camilli and Bucky Walters, for less expensive talent and cash to stay viable. The result was some of the worst baseball in franchise history—and that's saying something.

The 1938 Phillies won just 45 games. The next worst team in the National League, Brooklyn, won two dozen more! The Phillies, as usual, were the worst pitching team in the league with a 4.93 ERA. While usually much better at the plate, they hit an anemic .254 in 1938 and scored the fewest runs in the league.

Only one regular, Phil Weintraub, hit .300, and no one on the team hit more than eight home runs. Just 166,111 fans could stomach this awful baseball. And with two games remaining in the season, Wilson could take no more himself. He stepped down, leaving Hans Lobert to manage, and lose, the final two contests.

Outfielder Hersh Martin led the Phillies in runs in 1937 (102) and again in 1938 (a mere 58). The team averaged just 3.6 runs per game in '38.

Highlights

March 6: The Phillies trade Dolph Camilli to Brooklyn for a fringe player and $45,000.

April 30: The team is 1–10 after losing its ninth straight game.

June 13: The Phils ship Bucky Walters to the Reds for two players and $50,000.

June 30: Phillies pitchers get blasted (14–1) one last time at Baker Bowl.

July 4: The Phils play their first game in their new home, Shibe Park, which they will share with the Athletics, who have played there since 1909.

July 6: Outfielder Hersh Martin is the team's sole All-Star.

September 19–21: Phillies home games are canceled due to a hurricane that hammers the Northeast.

October 2: The Phillies close the season on a 16–46 skid.

NOTES

Jewish players **Phil Weintraub** and **Morrie Arnovich** lead the Phillies in batting (.311) and RBI (72), respectively.

Chuck Klein leads the team in homers, but with only eight.

Claude Passeau paces the team in wins (11–18), while **Hugh Mulcahy** goes 10–20.

Tucked into its urban neighborhood, Shibe Park was an elegant ballpark designed in a French Renaissance style and featuring a tower topped by a dome-shaped cupola at the main entrance.

Home for 33 Years

Shibe Park, later renamed Connie Mack Stadium, saw the best and worst of Philadelphia baseball. Built in 1909 for an exorbitant $300,000 by Athletics owner Ben Shibe, who designed the park with manager Connie Mack, the ballpark hosted seven World Series in its first 22 seasons.

While the Phillies had set a precedent by rebuilding the burnt-down Baker Bowl using steel in 1894, Shibe Park was the first park built with concrete and steel. Reinforced with brick, Shibe Park also had a distinctive Beaux Arts cupola as well as decorative arches and columns. Plus, it was the first ballpark with standard seating for more than 20,000. By the time the Phillies made the five-block move from decrepit Baker Bowl to Shibe during the 1938 season, the A's had double-decked the place with seating for 33,000. Meanwhile, Phillies pitchers could appreciate a right-field power alley that was 90 feet deeper than that in the tiny Baker Bowl.

Philadelphians could show up at Shibe any day—or night, once lights were installed in 1939—and see a ball game. Unfortunately, the baseball was often an eye-averting spectacle. The A's and Phillies both finished last in four of their first five seasons of shared occupancy. Misery loves company, and the last-place Philadelphia Eagles moved

into Shibe in 1940. They played football there for 18 seasons until transferring to Franklin Field on the University of Pennsylvania campus.

In 1949, the Phillies and A's both went 81–73, finishing 16 games out in their respective leagues and drawing just over 800,000 fans apiece. When the Phillies claimed the pennant the following year, however, their attendance jumped by 400,000 while that of the last-place A's went down by 500,000. The shift in allegiance for fans in Philadelphia was irreversible.

The impoverished Athletics moved to Kansas City after the 1954 season. The ban on advertisements in the park was lifted the following year, and soon ads were plastered all over the place. A new scoreboard—actually the old one from Yankee Stadium—was erected in right field, and beer was finally sold at the park in 1961. Neighborhood decline and the need for a modern venue resulted in a move to Veterans Stadium in 1971. Progress received its due.

Richie Ashburn, who played at Connie Mack Stadium for 12 years, called games there for 8 years, and spent 26 years in the Phillies booth at the Vet, memorably said of his former home: "It looked like a ballpark. It smelled like a ballpark. It had a feeling and a heartbeat, a personality that was all baseball."

WHAT'S UP, DOC?

New Skipper Can't Cure Ailing Team

P hillies fans—or what was left of them—had to have mumbled to the empty seats next to them during a 45–105 nightmare in 1938, "Oh well. There's nowhere to go but up!" Yet a year later, they began to realize that their ragtag team had not yet hit bottom.

Yes, the Phillies were even worse in 1939. They matched their measly 1938 win total with 45, but they threw in one more loss for good measure. Their 106 setbacks were the most since the 1928 team lost 109 games, and they joined that '28 club as just the second Phillies ensemble since 1883 to prevail in less than 30 percent of its games.

Former big-league third baseman Doc Prothro was hired to manage the floundering Phillies—his first and only major league skipper job. A more important order of business for team president Gerry Nugent was paying the bills, a task that during this era frequently resulted in the sale of quality players for cheaper players and cash. This time, it was pitcher Claude Passeau to the Cubs.

Prothro, who practiced dentistry in the offseason, had few tools to work with. His first Phillies club won four in a row in late April, but that wound up being its best stretch of the season. An 11-game losing streak spanned June and July. In 45 games decided by five or more runs, the Phillies lost 37.

PHILLIES PHACT

Rookie catcher Dave Coble makes the play of the year, catching a ball dropped from the top of Philadelphia's City Hall, 520 feet above ground.

Poor pitching had become a team tradition by this point, and 1939 was no exception. The Phillies' 5.17 ERA was more than a run higher than any other in the National League. Names like Hugh "Losing Pitcher" Mulcahy (9–16), Boom-Boom Beck (7–14), and Max Butcher (2–13) didn't inspire confidence.

Philadelphia also fielded the worst hitting team in the NL, with league lows in average (.261) and runs. It was an embarrassing combination, really, and there was not much hope on the horizon.

Highlights

May 29: Pitcher Claude Passeau is traded to the Cubs for pitcher Kirby Higbe, two other players, and cash.

June 1: The Phillies play their first-ever night game at Shibe Park, losing to Pittsburgh 5–2.

June 7: Chuck Klein signs with Pittsburgh after being released from Philadelphia, for whom he batted .191 with one homer.

July 8: The Phils lose their eleventh straight game.

September 23: The Phillies, who go 6–27 in September, lose to Brooklyn 22–4.

NOTES

Morrie Arnovich leads the club in batting (.324) and RBI (67).

First baseman Gus Suhr (.318) and **catcher Spud Davis** (.307) hit over .300, but no Phillies player cracks more than nine home runs.

Kirby Higbe paces the staff in wins (10–14), while **Syl Johnson** (8–8, 3.81) is the team's most effective pitcher.

The Phillies finish 18 games out of seventh place. They are 25–25 in one-run games and 20–81 in all others.

Despite the move out of tiny Baker Bowl, the Phillies' team ERA (5.17) is still more than a run higher than any other NL staff's.

THE 1930s RECORD BOOK

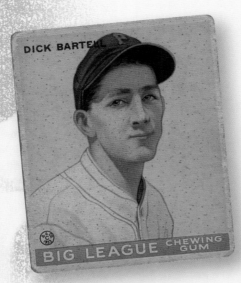

After batting .308 and scoring 118 runs in 1932, Dick Bartell was selected for the NL squad in the very first All-Star Game the following year.

Team Leaders

Batting
1930: Chuck Klein, .386
1931: Chuck Klein, .337
1932: Chuck Klein, .348
1933: Chuck Klein, .368
1934: Johnny Moore, .343
1935: Johnny Moore, .323
1936: Johnny Moore, .328
1937: Pinky Whitney, .341
1938: Phil Weintraub, .311
1939: Morrie Arnovich, .324

Home Runs
1930: Chuck Klein, 40
1931: Chuck Klein, 31
1932: Chuck Klein, 38
1933: Chuck Klein, 28
1934: Dolph Camilli, 12
1935: Dolph Camilli, 25
1936: Dolph Camilli, 28
1937: Dolph Camilli, 27
1938: Chuck Klein, 8
1939: Joe Marty, 9;
Heinie Mueller, 9

RBI
1930: Chuck Klein, 170
1931: Chuck Klein, 121
1932: Don Hurst, 143
1933: Chuck Klein, 120
1934: Johnny Moore, 93
1935: Johnny Moore, 93
1936: Dolph Camilli, 102
1937: Dolph Camilli, 80
1938: Morrie Arnovich, 72
1939: Morrie Arnovich, 67

Runs
1930: Chuck Klein, 158
1931: Chuck Klein, 121
1932: Chuck Klein, 152
1933: Chuck Klein, 101
1934: Dick Bartell, 102
1935: Ethan Allen, 90
1936: Dolph Camilli, 106
1937: Hersh Martin, 102
1938: Hersh Martin, 58
1939: Morrie Arnovich, 68

Doubles
1930: Chuck Klein, 59
1931: Dick Bartell, 43
1932: Chuck Klein, 50
1933: Chuck Klein, 44
1934: Ethan Allen, 42
1935: Ethan Allen, 46

This baseball was signed by Jimmie Wilson, who batted .292 in 91 games in 1934 in his first season as player/manager.

1936: Lou Chiozza, 32
1937: Hersh Martin, 35
1938: Hersh Martin, 36
1939: Hersh Martin, 28

Stolen Bases
1930: Fresco Thompson, 7
1931: Don Hurst, 8
1932: Chuck Klein, 20
1933: Chick Fullis, 18
1934: Dick Bartell, 13
1935: Dolph Camilli, 9
1936: Lou Chiozza, 17
1937: George Scharein, 13
1938: George Scharein, 11
1939: Morrie Arnovich, 7

Wins
1930: Phil Collins, 16–11
1931: Jumbo Elliott, 19–14
1932: Phil Collins, 14–12
1933: Ed Holley, 13–15
1934: Curt Davis, 19–17
1935: Curt Davis, 16–14
1936: Claude Passeau, 11–15;
Bucky Walters, 11–21

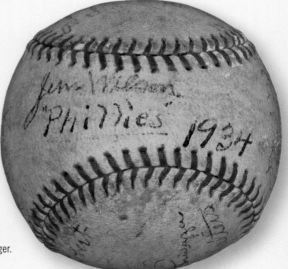

Spud Davis, shown on this Big League Collectibles card, opened the decade as the Phillies catcher from 1930 to 1934 and returned to Philadelphia in 1938–1939 after stints in St. Louis and Cincinnati.

VIRGIL L. DAVIS *Phi-N C*

1937: Wayne LaMaster, 15–19
1938: Claude Passeau, 11–18
1939: Kirby Higbe, 10–14

ERA

1930: Phil Collins, 4.78
1931: Ray Benge, 3.17
1932: Snipe Hansen, 3.72
1933: Ed Holley, 3.53
1934: Curt Davis, 2.95
1935: Syl Johnson, 3.56
1936: Claude Passeau, 3.48
1937: Claude Passeau, 4.34
1938: Max Butcher, 2.93
1939: Boom-Boom Beck, 4,73

Strikeouts

1930: Phil Collins, 87
1931: Ray Benge, 117
1932: Ray Benge, 89
1933: Ed Holley, 56
1934: Curt Davis, 99
1935: Syl Johnson, 89
1936: Claude Passeau, 85
1937: Wayne LaMaster, 135; Claude
          Passeau, 135
1938: Claude Passeau, 100
1939: Kirby Higbe, 79

NL Leaders

1930: Runs—Chuck Klein, 158;
          Doubles—Klein, 59
1931: Runs—Klein, 121;
          Home Runs—Klein, 31;
          RBI—Klein, 121

1932: Runs—Klein, 152;
          Hits—Klein, 226;
          Home Runs—Klein, 38;
          RBI—Don Hurst, 143;
          Stolen Bases—Klein, 20
1933: Batting Average—Klein, .368;
          Hits—Klein, 223;
          Doubles—Klein—44;
          Home Runs—Klein, 28;
          RBI—Klein, 120
1934: Doubles—Ethan Allen, 42
1936: Shutouts—Bucky Walters, 4

NL Awards

NL MVP Voting

1930: No voting this year
1931: Chuck Klein, 2nd
1932: Check Klein, 1st;
          Don Hurst, 7th
1933: Chuck Klein, 2nd
1934: Curt Davis, 8th

NL All-Stars

1933: Dick Bartell, SS;
          Chuck Klein, OF
1935: Jimmy Wilson, C
1936: Pinky Whitney, 3B
1937: Bucky Walters, P
1938: Herschel Martin, OF
1939: Morrie Arnovich, OF

PHILLIES 1930s All-Decade Team	
1B	DOLPH CAMILLI
2B	LOU CHIOZZA
SS	DICK BARTELL
3B	PINKY WHITNEY
C	AL TODD
OF	CHUCK KLEIN
OF	JOHNNY MOORE
OF	HERSH MARTIN
SP	CLAUDE PASSEAU
SP	CURT DAVIS
RP	SYL JOHNSON

The 6-foot-3, 235-pound Jumbo Elliott posted a winning record (36–34) for the 1931–1933 Phillies when the team had an overall mark of 204–256.

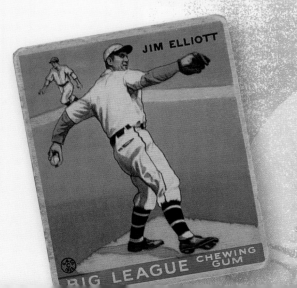

JIM ELLIOTT

BIG LEAGUE CHEWING GUM

RISING FROM THE ASHES

With new ownership and a fruitful farm system, the Phillies ascend from their lowest depths to become a promising pennant contender by decade's end.

As the 1940s dawned, the Phillies were in the midst of a streak of five seasons with more than 100 losses. In the first three years of the decade, they lost 323 games. The 1945 outfit would lose 108, marking the seventh time in eight years that the Phillies finished in last place.

This was the last full decade in which two major league teams played in Philadelphia. The 1946 Phillies outdrew the Athletics by almost a half-million fans. While the teams stayed relatively even in attendance through the rest of the decade, the ascendance of the Whiz Kids coincided with a downturn by the A's, who moved to Kansas City for the 1955 season.

The Phillies, however, were hardly a model of stability. William B. Cox bought the team in 1943, becoming baseball's youngest owner at 33 years old. For that season, Cox hired Bucky Harris as manager, an inspired move. Harris had won a World Series with Washington and would win another with the Yankees on his way to the Hall of Fame. What could go wrong?

Everything, as it turned out. Cox was a meddler who hired his high school track coach as the Phillies' trainer, and Harris fumed at his interference. When Cox fired Harris in July, Harris shot back by charging publicly that Cox was gambling on his own team. The resulting investigation found Cox guilty, and Commissioner Kenesaw Mountain Landis banned him for life.

The new owner, Bob Carpenter Jr., had the backing of the DuPont family fortune. He emphasized the minor league system and tried to liven the Phillies'

The Fightin' Phillies were fighting to stay out of the cellar for most of the 1940s.

With his spectacular debut season in 1948, speedy, hard-hitting Richie Ashburn helped turn around a franchise that had averaged 100 losses per season over the previous 10 years.

image by unofficially changing the team name to "Blue Jays" in the mid-1940s. The name never stuck and was dropped by the end of the decade.

The Phillies' talent level did improve. Pitcher Robin Roberts and center fielder Richie Ashburn made their debuts in 1948 and would spend their prime seasons as teammates. Both wound up in the Hall of Fame. Other homegrown future stars signed as amateurs by the Phillies included Del Ennis, Granny Hamner, and Curt Simmons.

The long-term problem for the Phillies was their refusal to participate in the trend that would soon reshape baseball. Jackie Robinson broke the color barrier for the Brooklyn Dodgers in 1947, but it would be 10 years before the Phillies welcomed their first African American player, infielder John Kennedy. They were the last National League team to integrate.

In the meantime, the Dodgers thrived with Robinson, Don Newcombe, and other black players. Monte Irvin and Hank Thompson debuted for the Giants in 1949. By the early '50s the Giants had added Willie Mays, and soon Hank Aaron would star for the Braves and Ernie Banks for the Cubs. The Phillies lagged behind, and they paid the price in the standings.

But that shameful reality wasn't immediately evident in the late 1940s. The Phillies, so often residents of last place throughout their history, were subtly making strides. They avoided the cellar in 1946, 1947, and 1948 under manager Ben Chapman, who was replaced in '48 by Eddie Sawyer.

In his first full season, Sawyer led the Phillies to a 15-game improvement, their record rising to 81–73 in 1949. The third-place finish was the team's highest since 1917. Ennis and Andy Seminick combined for 49 home runs and three pitchers won 15 games. It was by far the best season of the decade, an encouraging way to end a 10-year span that had begun with such gloom.

▸ 50-103   8th ◂

Highlights

May 20: The Phillies erupt for seven runs in the bottom of the ninth to stun Pittsburgh 8–7.

June 17: Now on a 2–13 skid, the Phillies fall into last place.

August 21: Pitcher Charlie Frye hits a pinch-hit home run in the top of the tenth to defeat the Cubs 7–5.

November 11: Pitcher Kirby Higbe is dealt to the Dodgers for three players and $100,000. Owner Gerald Nugent laments that the team lost more than twice that amount of money during the season.

NOTES

Outfielder **Johnny Rizzo** paces the club in HRs (20) and RBI (53).

Third baseman **Pinky May** tallies team bests in batting (.293) and runs (59).

In his third stint with the Phils, **Chuck Klein** hits .218 with seven homers as a regular outfielder.

Rookie **Danny Litwhiler** raps .345 in 36 games and authors a 21-game hitting streak.

Kirby Higbe (14–19, 3.72) and **Hugh Mulcahy** (13–22, 3.60) are the heart of the staff, although Mulcahy leads the league in losses for the second time.

The team posts a **losing record** in every month and against every National League team.

SOUND FAMILIAR?

Another Year, Another 100-Loss Season

Danny Litwhiler grew up in the quiet borough of Ringtown, Pennsylvania, and was quite familiar with the Phillies and their struggles. He was a smart kid, too, having graduated from Bloomsburg State Teacher's College—later to become Bloomsburg University. The vast majority of pro ball players during this era had not set foot on a college campus.

So when the 23-year-old Litwhiler was called up to the Phillies in 1940, he was well aware of the losing proposition facing him. What the rookie could not have known is that he'd be the lone bright spot that year.

Litwhiler played outfield and hit .345 in 36 games in the majors. His 21-game hitting streak was far and away the most consistent stretch of solid baseball played by anyone on the team.

Once again, the Phillies fielded the treacherous combination of anemic hitting (a .238 team average—by far the lowest in the National League) and generous pitching (a league-worst 4.40 ERA). Their resulting 50 wins, against 103 setbacks, were 15 fewer than the next worst team in the standings.

A rookie sensation in 36 games with the Phillies in 1940, left fielder Danny Litwhiler became, two years later, the first known player to stitch together the fingers of his glove.

Whatever Philadelphia tried—beyond bringing Litwhiler into the mix—was doomed to fail. The club brought back former power-hitting hero Chuck Klein for a third stint in Philadelphia, but the 35-year-old outfielder hit .218 with seven homers. No other position player in the regular lineup had celebrated his 30th birthday. No starter hit .300.

Opponents, on the other hand, simply teed off against Philadelphia pitchers. Kirby Higbe, obtained the previous year from the Cubs in the Claude Passeau deal, and Hugh Mulcahy were the steadiest starters. They led the team in wins with 14 and 13, respectively, and kept their ERAs under 4.00. However, they also combined for 41 losses.

It was a year that must have had manager Doc Prothro, a dentist, in need of anesthesia. And the worst, unbeknownst to the good doctor and his players, was yet to come.

STRANGE MAGIC

Joltin' Joe, Teddy Ballgame, and the Futile Phillies

The 1941 baseball season forever stands as one of the most magical summers in history. It was the year that Yankees legend Joe DiMaggio hit safely in an unfathomable 56 consecutive games, still considered one of the most unbreakable records in sports. It was also the year that Boston's Ted Williams refused to sit out of a doubleheader on the season's final day to preserve his .400 average. He wound up hitting .406, and no one has batted .400 since.

Then there were the Philadelphia Phillies. If they could perform magic, their first trick might be making the 1941 season disappear from the record.

Like 56 and .406, the numbers speak for themselves. The Phillies scored 91 fewer runs than anyone else in the National League. They gave up 73 more runs than any of their NL rivals. They were the worst team in baseball by far, and one of the worst in major league history.

The Phillies' 43 wins against 111 losses put them in a dubious class among twentieth-century losers. It was one of just eight times in the entire century that a big-league club dropped that many games.

Their two best pitchers from the 1940 season—another last-place, 100-loss showing—were gone. One, Hugh Mulcahy, became the first major-leaguer drafted for service in World War II. The other, Kirby Higbe, was traded to the Dodgers following the '40 season for three players and cash to help eliminate some of the red ink in the team's books.

Higbe, much to the chagrin of Phillies fans, went on to lead the NL with 22 wins for the Dodgers in 1941. Meanwhile, not even the top two Philadelphia pitchers *combined* produced that many victories. In fact, no Phillies pitcher even reached double digits.

The 1941 season marked the end of the Doc Prothro managerial era. The dentist, probably to the delight of his patients, never managed in the majors again.

A hard-hitting first basemen, Nick Etten spent two years with the Phils in 1941 and 1942 before being traded to the Yankees, with whom he would lead the AL in RBI in 1945.

Highlights

March 8: Hugh "Losing Pitcher" Mulcahy becomes the first major leaguer to be drafted during World War II.

August 17: The Phillies rout the Giants 18–2, as Lee Grissom improves his record to 1–11.

August 18: The Phils tie a team record with eight errors in a loss to the Reds.

NOTES

First baseman Nick Etten (.311–14–79) paces the team in batting and RBI.

Outfielder Danny Litwhiler rips .305 with a club-high 18 homers.

Rookie second baseman Danny Murtaugh tops the NL in steals (18).

Johnny Podgajny (9–12) and **Tommy Hughes** (9–14), both 21 years old, lead the staff in victories.

The Phillies set a team record with 111 defeats. They are one of only eight MLB teams to lose that many games in the twentieth century.

The team finishes last in the NL in runs and runs allowed—both by large margins.

The last-place A's outdraw their ballpark mates 528,894 to 231,401.

1942

▸ 42-109   8th ◂

Highlights

February: Management announces that the team will now be known as the Phils. (They'll revert to Phillies the next season.)

August: The Phils are shut out for the third game in a row.

September 7: The club loses its thirteenth consecutive game.

September 11: Only 393 fans attend a Phils game at Shibe Park.

December: National League officials meet to determine what to do with the debt-ridden Phils. They tell owner Gerald Nugent to sell the team.

NOTES

All-Star outfielder Danny Litwhiler hits .271–9–56, leading the team in each category.

Litwhiler, who made three errors in one game in 1941, goes errorless in 151 games this year.

Tommy Hughes (12–18, 3.06) tops the staff in wins and ERA.

The Phils set a **franchise low** for team batting average (.232) while scoring just 2.6 runs per game.

The team is 19–80 in games decided by two runs or more.

In debt to the National League, the Athletics, and others, owner Gerald Nugent trades more players (first baseman Nick Etten, pitcher Rube Melton) for cash after the season.

CALL THEM "PHILS"
Changing Names, Managers Offers Little Impact

No "lie." The Phillies became the "Phils" for 1942, losing three letters from their nickname because a cigar company was using "Phillies" and the club did not have the money to pursue a court case. But make no mistake. They were instantly recognizable by their futility, which in some ways was even worse than it was during their laughable 1941 slate.

Longtime coach Hans Lobert took over as manager. Lobert had managed the final two games of the 1938 season, losing both, so he was quite familiar with the results he'd get in his first full season at the helm. Devoid of talent, it was another long year in Philadelphia.

The 1942 Phils lost 109 games—two fewer than their franchise record-setting total from a year earlier. However, because the '42 club played three fewer games, its winning percentage of .278 was actually worse than the previous season's.

But enough hairsplitting. The problems were all the same. The Phils were the only team in the National League to score fewer than 400 runs. Every other club, in fact, totaled 515 or more.

Danny Litwhiler, at a mere .271, was the toughest out in the lineup. He also played all 151 games without an error in the outfield. There was little talent around him. Four of eight regulars in the regular batting order failed to hit even .240.

If the bats were cold, the pitching was even worse. Philadelphia's 4.12 ERA was easily the highest in the league, with the Braves' 3.76 rate next in line. The Phils finished a mind-boggling 62½ games behind the powerhouse St. Louis Cardinals.

While war was dominating the headlines, Major League Baseball was urging club president Gerry Nugent to sell the team. Its debt was growing, its fan base was shrinking, and its ability to play competitive baseball was at the lowest point in team history.

Opposite page: The Phillies' catching crew was so anemic in 1942 that starting shortstop Bobby Bragan donned the tools of ignorance for 22 games that season.

Wartime Characters

When Phillies players arrived for spring training in 1943, they had to feel good about their playing time. After all, there were only 14 of them. During the war years, a large number of able-bodied ballplayers had joined the fight against Hirohito and Hitler. MLB rosters were filled with the very young and very old, as well as 4-Fs, men deemed unfit for military service.

The 1941 to '45 Phillies were unfit for baseball, averaging 102 losses per season. For the last three years of the war, the manager was Fat Freddie Fitzsimmons, and one of his "aces" was the short, plump Dick Barrett. "Kewpie Dick" posted a 2.39 ERA in 1943 but lost an NL-high 20 games in 1945. Tall, bespectacled Charley Schanz went 4–15 that year, hitting four batters in one game.

The Phillies suited up several teenagers during the war years, including a pair of 16-year-olds: pitcher Rogers McKee, who got torched in four outings, and infielder Ralph "Putsy" Caballero, who went 0-for-4 in '44. The Phils also found a place for has-beens, most notably Jimmie Foxx. Number 2 on the career homer list when he joined the Phillies in 1945, Double X still had a bit of gas left in the tank at age 37. He hit .268 with seven homers before calling it quits.

Jimmie Foxx earned Hall of Fame credentials with the Athletics and Red Sox before joining a war-depleted Phillies roster in 1945.

1943

Highlights

February–March: Prior to the season, the National League purchases the Phillies (and assumes the team's large debts) from Gerald Nugent and then sells the franchise to a syndicate headed by wealthy New Yorker William D. Cox, age 33.

February 26: Bucky Harris is hired to manage the Phillies.

July 8: Phillies pitcher Dick Barrett pitches a 14-inning shutout over Cincinnati.

July 27: Cox fires Harris as manager. The players are so outraged that they threaten to strike.

November: Major League Baseball Commissioner Kenesaw Mountain Landis bars Cox from baseball for betting on the Phillies to win games.

NOTES

Outfielder Ron Northey leads the team in homers (16) and RBI (68).

Infielder Babe Dahlgren paces the club with a .287 average.

Pitcher Schoolboy Rowe (14–8, 2.94) leads the team in wins.

After the season, the Carpenter family of Delaware buys the team. Bob Carpenter, 28, is named team president.

While attendance is down throughout baseball, the **Phillies' attendance** more than doubles from 1942 to 1943 (466,975).

ONE AND DONE

Though Banned for Betting, Cox Lays Groundwork

It was some sight when new Phillies owner William Cox donned a team uniform while taking part in spring training in Hershey, Pennsylvania. (Commissioner Kenesaw Mountain Landis had ordered all but two teams to train in the North during wartime.) However, a 33-year-old businessman in full uniform was hardly the strangest occurrence between a wretched 1942 season and the end of the '43 slate.

Most of the big news occurred off the field. The National League took control of the failing franchise from Gerry Nugent at a time when the club was more than $300,000 in the hole. Legendary trickster Bill Veeck tried to purchase the Phillies, with the goal of loading the roster with top African American players. Eventually, former Senators and Tigers infielder Bucky Harris was installed by Cox as manager—at least for a while.

The way the Phillies had played under Nugent's presidency—six last-place finishes over the previous seven years—it was a wonder that Cox didn't contend for a starting position as he fielded grounders and made throws that spring. After all, Cox had played ball at Yale. He also had some great ideas for how to improve the club. Among them: invest money in the farm system, bring in a strength and conditioning coach (Cox did, hiring his former track coach for the position), and add a veteran pitcher to lead the younger arms on the staff.

The latter man was Schoolboy Rowe, who went 14–8 with a 2.94 ERA as the Phillies' new ace. As a result, the club boosted its record considerably to 64–90, avoiding the NL cellar for the first time since '37 despite playing 43 doubleheaders.

However, it wasn't improvement enough for Cox, a hands-on owner who not only worked out with the team from time to time but who passionately craved a winner and wore his emotions on his sleeve. In addition to his success in the business world, he owned two pro football teams and created a professional soccer league. He fired Harris after 92 games and a 39–53 record, a move that proved to be more costly than Cox ever could have imagined.

After being stripped of his duties, Harris publicly called Cox "a fine guy to fire me, when he gambles on games his club plays." It was a revelation to the baseball world.

So while Freddie Fitzsimmons was assuming the managerial job, Landis was springing into investigative action over Harris' parting shot. It turned out that Cox's bets were all low-stakes wagers that he called "sentimental" bets, and they were always on his own team to win—never to lose. Still, it was a violation of baseball's cardinal sin. There was no tolerance for gambling of any kind in the game, and Landis banned Cox for life. He became the last man banned for life before Pete Rose was handed the same punishment 56 years later.

Cox's run lasted less than a year, ending shamefully. But he left a lasting impression on the Phillies.

> "I had tried to buy the Philadelphia Phillies and stock it with Negro players."
>
> —Bill Veeck, who said his plan was sabotaged by the commissioner

CARPENTERS TO THE RESCUE

This Time, New Ownership Offers Hope

Money talks. And for decades, it had been telling Philadelphia Phillies fans there was not much hope for their baseball team. The franchise's history of cash-strapped ownership led directly to its annual second-division finishes. Finally, before the 1944 season, the team's bank account took a turn for the better.

Robert R. M. Carpenter, who married into the wealthy DuPont family and was vice president of their giant chemical company, purchased the Phillies after previous owner Bill Cox was banned from baseball for placing small bets on his team to win. The elder Carpenter bought the team for his 28-year-old son, Bob Carpenter Jr.

The younger Carpenter would have to preside from overseas, as shortly after assuming the post he was drafted into the U.S. Army. Former pitching great Herb Pennock, a friend of the family, was hired as general manager and given the task of constructing a solid farm system to serve as the club's foundation. It would take time, but it would give the Phillies something they never enjoyed before.

PHILLIES PHACT

Through fan balloting during the 1944 season, the Phillies decide to change their name to Blue Jays. However, fans and writers will still call them the Phillies.

The loss of many regulars to World War II made the '44 season a strange one all around. For the Phillies—who actually tried calling themselves the Blue Jays, though reporters never really acknowledged the new name—it was strange in that they pitched far better than they hit.

Ken Raffensberger, the winning pitcher in the 1944 All-Star Game, headed the staff with a 3.06 ERA. He was one of four starters to post ERAs under 4.00 and double-digit victory totals. Just two clubs, Cincinnati and St. Louis, yielded fewer runs than the Phillies.

It was weak hitting that kept the club from winning more than 61 games against 92 defeats, a ledger that produced another last-place National League finish. Philadelphia scored a league-low 539 runs, and not a single regular in the lineup hit as high as .290.

Highlights

April 18: The Phillies open the season with more new faces, as many ballplayers are contributing to the war effort.

May 2: Phillies pitcher Charlie Schanz one-hits the Giants and wins the game with a three-run triple in the ninth.

May 18: The Phils beat the Reds 2–0 to improve to 14–10.

July 11: Ken Raffensberger, the sole Phillie in the All-Star Game, pitches two innings and gets the win.

June 22: The Phils nip the Braves 1–0 on a home run by Ron Northey in the top of the fifteenth.

August 6: The team loses its twelfth consecutive game.

NOTES

The Phillies have the weakest offense in the league, averaging just 3.5 runs per game.

Ron Northey rips .288–22–104, leading the team in each category.

Outfielder Buster Adams hits .283 with 17 homers and 64 RBI, placing second on the club in each category.

First baseman Tony Lupien is second in the NL in steals (18).

Ken Raffensberger (13–20) earns the win in the All-Star Game but ends up leading the NL in losses for the season. He ranks fourth in the league in strikeouts with 136.

Charlie Schanz (13–16) ties Raffensberger for the team high in wins.

1945

▶ 46-108   8th ◀

Highlights

April 17: The Phillies open the season without star outfielder Ron Northey, who's off to war.

April 29: The Phils fall to 3–7 and enter last place for good.

June 29: With the team at 18–51, Ben Chapman takes over managerial duties from Freddie Fitzsimmons.

July 15: Pitcher Charley Schanz walks none but hits four batters in a 6–1 loss to the Reds. The final 2 2/3 innings are pitched by hitting legend Jimmie Foxx, who allows no hits but walks four in a rare appearance on the mound.

September 1: Outfielder Vince DiMaggio smacks his fourth grand slam of the year, tying an MLB record.

NOTES

Vince DiMaggio, the least-accomplished of the three big-league brothers, arrives from the Pirates and leads the Phils in homers (19) and RBI (84).

Outfielder Jimmy Wasdell paces the club in batting (.300) and runs (65).

Legendary slugger Jimmie Foxx belts seven homers in his only season as a Phillie and his last in the majors.

Foxx gives pitching a whirl and posts a 1.59 ERA in 22 2/3 innings.

Dick Barrett (8–20, 5.38) and reliever **Andy Karl** (8–8, 2.99) tie for the team lead in wins.

The Phillies finish in last place for the seventh times in eight years.

THAT'S LIFE

Magazine Correctly Predicts Long Year for Phils

The fourth straight year of "wartime baseball" and the death of MLB Commissioner Kenesaw Mountain Landis the previous November were among the reasons *Life* magazine, in the spring of 1945, chronicled the troubles facing the national pastime. The Phillies were pointed to as the prime example of a franchise facing an uphill climb. The publication pointed out that Philadelphia's players were either too young or too old to make the team competitive.

"The prize 1945 example of a team in trouble," the magazine wrote, "is the National League Phillies, managed by Freddie Fitzsimmons." Of the Phillies players pictured in the issue, five had not celebrated their twenty-first birthdays, and nine were over 35.

So into the season the Phillies raced, with that national disclaimer following them. And they lived down to their billing. Two weeks into the season, they tumbled into last place for good. They finished last in the National League in fielding, batting average, slugging percentage, and home runs. On the mound, they amassed the most wild pitches and balks and recorded the highest ERA in the league.

With 46 wins and 108 losses, it was only the fifth time since the turn of the century that the Phillies failed to win even 30 percent of their games. However, it was the fourth time it had happened in a seven-year span. And the 1945 season marked the eighth time in a 10-year stretch that the Phils finished in last place in the NL.

With attendance declining and wins elusive, the club's new management group decided to make its first managerial change. In late June, former Yankees standout and recent Phillies player Ben Chapman was chosen to replace Fitzsimmons at the helm. General manager Herb Pennock was the first to admit it was not entirely Fitzsimmons' fault. "We have been unable to provide Fitz with adequate material because of the scarcity of good players," Pennock said.

PHILLIES PHACT

With many big-league players serving in the military, the young Hamner brothers make the Phillies—18-year-old Granny at shortstop and 21-year-old Garvin at second base.

SIMPLY DEL-LIGHTFUL

Philadelphia Native Ennis Fulfills Childhood Dream

Delmer Ennis was an accomplished war hero before he became an accomplished major-leaguer. As baseball fans were welcoming their favorites back from the war before a highly anticipated 1946 season, few outside of Philadelphia had ever heard of this Ennis kid.

Raised swinging a bat in the Olney area of town, Del grew up a Phillies fan. A hot-hitting outfielder, he had enjoyed a promising minor league season in Trenton in 1943, ripping .346 with power. In fact, he was offered a late-season call-up to the majors that year, but he turned it down so he could spend time with his family before going overseas.

Ennis was not discharged from the Navy until after spring training in '46. Still, Phillies owner Bob Carpenter, general manager Herb Pennock, and skipper Ben Chapman decided to take a chance on the hometown kid.

Their faith paid early dividends. Ennis, just 21, enjoyed a smashing debut in 1946. The *Philadelphia Inquirer* captured the enthusiasm for this new ray of hope following a difficult road trip in May: "The journey was successful if for no other reason than the discovery of a new left fielder who promises to develop into one of baseball's brightest lights."

Ennis would go on to become the club's career home run king—a distinction he held until Mike Schmidt came around a quarter-century later. In '46, the youngest player in the lineup showed no nerves swinging the bat in front of his hometown fans, powering the team with a .313 average (no one else hit .300), 17 homers, and 73 RBI. He also earned his first of three All-Star Game selections. Though just a rookie, a day was held in his honor at Shibe Park.

In fact, Del's arrival on April 28 was the greatest factor in the Phillies winning 23 more games than the previous season. They climbed to fifth place in the NL standings and drew more than a million fans for the first time in history.

In the first postwar season, big crowds cheered on a new hitting hero: local-boy Del Ennis.

Highlights

April 16: The Phillies open the season with colorful new uniforms and many new faces. With dozens of MLB players returning from the war, the Phillies have opened their pocketbooks to acquire teams' "excess" players.

June 30: After an 8–24 start, the Phils go 17–9 in June.

July 9: First baseman Frank McCormick, second baseman Emil Verban, and rookie outfielder Del Ennis play in the All-Star Game.

August 11: After Brooklyn wins 18 straight games at Shibe Park, the Phillies sweep the Dodgers in a doubleheader.

September 15: The Phils edge Pittsburgh 6–5 in 11 innings to move into fifth place for good. It will be their highest finish since 1932.

September 25: The Phillies score five in the top of the ninth to surpass Brooklyn 11–9.

NOTES

Del Ennis ranks fourth in the NL in batting (.313) and homers (17) and second in slugging (.485).

Frank McCormick is second on the team in average (.284) and RBI (66).

Schoolboy Rowe goes 11–4 with a 2.12 ERA.

The 1946 Phillies become the first Philadelphia team to draw a million fans (1,045,247).

Highlights

April 22–24: Phillies manager Ben Chapman assault Dodgers rookie Jackie Robinson with a barrage of racial insults.

May 3: GM Herb Pennock ships Ron Northey to the Cardinals for outfielder Harry Walker.

May 11: A Shibe Park-record 41,660 fans (many African American) show up to see the Phillies host Robinson and the Dodgers.

May 18: Ken Raffensberger throws a 12-inning shutout against St. Louis to improve the team record to 15–13.

May 20: Walker goes 4-for-4 at Chicago to raise his average to .400.

July 8: Walker, Schoolboy Rowe, and Emil Verban represent Philadelphia in the All-Star Game.

September 28: Walker concludes the season having ripped .434 in September.

NOTES

Harry Walker bats .371 with the Phillies, .363 overall, and wins the batting title by 46 points.

Del Ennis leads the team with 81 RBI.

In a **rare achievement,** the Phils post a team ERA (3.96) that's below the league average. The team's three top workhorses are in their late 30s.

Dutch Leonard (17–12, 2.68) ranks among league leaders in wins and ERA.

OLD GUYS RULE

Veteran Pitchers Keep the Phillies Afloat

It was a tumultuous time in baseball, as teams began integrating and a largely white fan base, in many cases, took exception. Phillies manager Ben Chapman added fuel to the fire early in the 1947 season when he let loose a barrage of insults directed toward Dodgers rookie Jackie Robinson, who that year broke the major league color barrier.

The two later made amends, but the buildup led to the largest crowd in Shibe Park history when an overflow crowd of 41,000 fans descended on the park for a May 11 doubleheader the next time the Dodgers were in town. It was not Robinson or Chapman, though, who stole the show. It was 38-year-old Dutch Leonard and 37-year-old Schoolboy Rowe who pitched the Phillies to one of the greatest doubleheader sweeps in franchise history.

The Dodgers, on their way to the pennant that year, could not handle Leonard's knuckleball in the first game. The veteran right-hander, who had been acquired from the Washington Senators before the season, twirled a 7–3 victory before handing the ball to Rowe for the nightcap.

Schoolboy, coming off an 11–4 record the previous season, matched his elder pitch for pitch. He held off the Dodgers 5–4, sending the crowd into a spirited celebration. Each game lasted just one hour, 58 minutes.

Throw in 39-year-old Oscar Judd, and three members of the Phillies' starting rotation could have been the easy targets of nursing-home jokes from opposing fans. That is, except for the fact that Leonard went 17–12 and Rowe 14–10 to lead the club.

Still, the Phillies clearly had their eye on the future. While aging arms were doing the bulk of the pitching and newly acquired Harry Walker was carrying the offense with a sizzling .371 average toward a tie for seventh place in the National League, several up-and-coming players were honing their talents in the farm system.

SIMMONS CRACKS ROTATION
Alongside Veteran Hurlers, Teenager Takes His Place

You never get a second chance to make a first impression, so Curt Simmons made his one and only such opportunity count. The year was 1947, and Simmons was a Pennsylvania high school pitcher. Given a chance to face the Phillies in an exhibition game, the left-hander struck out 11 and pitched the Lehigh Valley High School All-Stars to a 4–4 draw against the major-leaguers.

The Phillies were so impressed, they gave Simmons a $65,000 signing bonus and promoted him to the majors for his debut—a complete-game victory—that year. He was 18 at the time. And when the '48 season opened, there was Simmons in the starting rotation along with 39-year-old Dutch Leonard and 38-year-old Schoolboy Rowe.

No one knew at the time, of course, that Simmons would go on to become one of the most successful pitchers in Philadelphia history, with 115 victories and more than 1,000 strikeouts during 13 seasons in a Phillies jersey. He later pitched for the Cardinals, Cubs, and Angels as well.

As a rookie, Simmons took his lumps. He went 7–13 in '48 with a 4.87 ERA on a team that finished sixth in the National League (66–88). Leonard and Rowe continued to prove there was something to be said for experience, leading the team with 12 and 10 wins, respectively. But a youth movement was in full swing, and better days were just around the corner.

That didn't help manager Ben Chapman keep his job in 1948. During the All-Star break, owner Bob Carpenter showed Chapman the door. Coach Dusty Cooke managed the club for two weeks until a replacement was found. That man was Eddie Sawyer, an Ithaca College professor who was familiar to many of the players from his days as a manager in the Phillies' farm system.

Sawyer went 23–40 down the stretch, managing a lineup in which seven of eight position players were in their 20s.

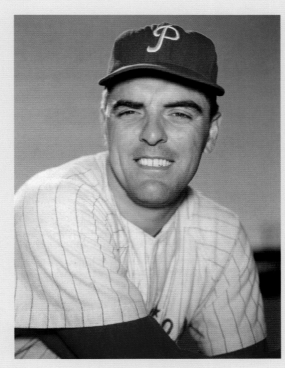

The Phillies opened their pocketbooks to prep phenom Curt Simmons after the hurler averaged 17 strikeouts per game in high school.

Highlights

January 30: General manager Herb Pennock dies at age 53.

April 20: Speedy outfielder Richie Ashburn makes his major league debut with the Phillies.

June 5: Ashburn caps off his 23-game hitting streak, which is a twentieth-century NL rookie record. His average is now .380.

July: Phillies owner Bob Carpenter replaces Ben Chapman with interim manager Dusty Cooke and then permanent skipper Eddie Sawyer, a biology professor in the offseason.

July 17: Granny Hamner drives in seven runs to help defeat the Cardinals 11–10.

August 13: Hosting the Giants, the Phillies set an MLB record by scoring nine runs before making their first out of the game. They win 12–7.

NOTES

Del Ennis ranks fifth in the NL with 30 homers and leads the team with 95 RBI.

Richie Ashburn (.333) finishes runner-up for the batting crown and leads the league in steals (32). He earns Rookie of the Year honors by *The Sporting News.*

Dutch Leonard (12–17, 2.51) tops the staff in wins and ERA.

Rookie pitcher Robin Roberts goes 7–9 with a 3.19 ERA after debuting on June 18.

Opposite page: Phillies manager Ben Chapman was particularly harsh in his heckling of Jackie Robinson during the latter's debut season. Here the two are shown together in a more peaceful pose.

Highlights

June 2: Catcher Andy Seminick belts three home runs—and the team hits five four-baggers in the eighth inning—in a 12–3 rout of Cincinnati.

June 9: Pittsburgh beats the Phils 4–3 in 18 innings.

June 17: After downing St. Louis 2–0 on a Robin Roberts shutout, the Phillies conclude a 13–3 run that puts them at 33–25, two games out of first.

August 19: Shibe Park hosts "Eddie Waitkus Night" on behalf of the Phillies player who was shot in June by a deranged fan.

August 21: Phillies fans throw soda bottles onto the field in protest of an umpire's decision of a disputed catch by Richie Ashburn. The Phillies are forced to forfeit the game to the Giants.

NOTES

Del Ennis ranks among the league leaders in batting (.302), homers (25), RBI (110), doubles (39), and other categories.

Andy Seminick socks 24 home runs.

Ken Heintzelman (17–10, 3.02) and **Russ "Mad Monk" Meyer** (17–8, 3.08) pace the staff in wins and ERA.

With a 16–10 finish, the Phillies place third in the NL, their highest spot in the standings since 1917.

PHILLIES CLIMB TO THIRD

"Mild-Mannered" Sawyer Coaxes Big NL Jump

Compared with his predecessor, new Phillies manager Eddie Sawyer was as stoic as a statue. A biology professor at Ithaca College in the offseason with no major league experience as a player or manager, Sawyer preferred quiet, well-thought-out solutions to loud, emotional ones. Previous manager Ben Chapman, conversely, had gained infamy in 1947 for his racially charged tirade toward Jackie Robinson and rarely held anything back.

With the young, up-and-coming Phillies in 1949, Sawyer's intellectual style seemed a better fit. So as the 38-year-old prepared for his first full season as a major league manager, spring training hopes were high—if rarely verbalized.

"Sawyer was a very different type of manager than Ben Chapman," outfielder Del Ennis explained. "He was mild-mannered, a professor. He grew on us. We learned a lot of baseball under Eddie Sawyer."

"Although I did not realize it at the time, the hiring of Eddie Sawyer was a real turning point for the Phillies, and for me personally," pitcher Robin Roberts said. "Eddie had a hands-off leadership style that I did not grow to appreciate until much later in my baseball career."

Their manager might have been quiet, but the young Phillies began making noise in the National League standings for the first time in decades. They had not finished in the league's upper division since a fourth-place showing in 1932, but a stretch of 13 wins over 16 games had the club sitting a mere two games out of first place in mid-June.

It was also in mid-June when the cerebral Sawyer became a rock for his players after first baseman Eddie Waitkus was shot by a deranged young woman in Chicago. The day after the incident hit the press, the Phillies trailed the Cubs 3–0 after seven innings but rallied with four runs in the eighth and ninth to prevail 4–3.

The Dodgers and Cardinals soon began pulling away in a two-team NL pennant race, but Sawyer and his young troops were earning a reputation for battling. They were rarely out

Schoolboy Rowe was far from school age when he wrapped up his 15-year major league career in 1949. The 39-year-old won only three games that year after a four-year run of double-digit victories with the Phillies.

Fightin' Phillies

THERE'S FUN AT THE PARK WHEN THE PHILS ARE IN TOWN!

OFFICIAL
SCORE
CARD

1949
1ST. No.

FEATURES:
STAN BAUMGARTNER
FRANK YEUTTER
LANSE McCURLEY

10 CENTS

TRY THIS PHILCO...
for 10 days FREE!

Let Vic Hendler put this great new "wide screen" Philco 1150 in your living room for a 10 day free trial!

Vic Hendler's sensational offer scores with every sports fan . . . a sporting offer that lets you test Philco television in your own home . . . at no cost to you. No foolin', no money.

FIRST WITH THE FINEST!

Vic Hendler
ST 2-5454   6th & DIAMOND STREETS
Open Wednesday and Friday Evenings

Fans could watch their beloved Fightin' Phillies either at the ballpark or on their Philco television in 1949.

of games due to their improved pitching and refusal to throw in the towel.

The Phillies won 19 of their final 30 games despite being out well out of the race. They wound up a considerable 16 games behind flag-winning Brooklyn in the standings, but the third-place finish was their best in 32 years.

Roberts and the pitching staff led the charge, dropping the team ERA to 3.89, among the best in the NL. Russ Meyer and Ken Heintzelman each won 17 games, and Roberts won 15 for a club that bucked Phillies tradition by posting a winning record in one-run games.

Offensively, the young Phillies would need better than they mustered in '49. Just one regular, Ennis, hit .300. And the Phils were outscored by their opponents despite finishing eight games over .500. Still, it was progress. And it was just getting started.

The Waitkus Affair

Eddie Waitkus survived fierce fighting in the Philippines in World War II only to be shot by an obsessed woman in a Chicago hotel room. After hitting .297 over three seasons with the Cubs after the war, the first baseman was sent to the Phillies in December 1948. Waitkus was batting .306 as the team visited Chicago in June 1949.

In an incident eerily similar to the shooting of the Cubs' Billy Jurges in 1932, Ruth Ann Steinhagen had secured a room at the Edgewater Beach Hotel, where the Phillies stayed. Steinhagen lured Waitkus to her room with an urgent note. When he arrived after 11 p.m., she told him, according to *Time* magazine: "For two years, you've been bothering me and now you're going to die." She shot him with a rifle, and Waitkus nearly died on the operating table. He missed the rest of the 1949 season.

The next year, Waitkus earned Associated Press Comeback Player of the Year honors for the pennant-winning Phillies. While Waitkus was still playing, writer Bernard Malamud penned a novel based on the incident entitled *The Natural*, which was made into a memorable film in 1984, a dozen years after Waitkus died of cancer.

Eddie Waitkus, on a Topps card.

THE 1940s RECORD BOOK

Team Leaders

Batting

1940: Pinky May, .293
1941: Nick Etten, .311
1942: Danny Litwhiler, .271
1943: Babe Dahlgren, .287
1944: Ron Northey, .288
1945: Jimmy Wasdell, .300
1946: Del Ennis, .313
1947: Harry Walker, .371
1948: Richie Ashburn, .333
1949: Del Ennis, .302

Home Runs

1940: Johnny Rizzo, 20
1941: Danny Litwhiler, 18
1942: Danny Litwhiler, 9
1943: Ron Northey, 16
1944: Ron Northey, 22
1945: Vince DiMaggio, 19
1946: Del Ennis, 17
1947: Andy Seminick, 13
1948: Del Ennis, 30
1949: Del Ennis, 25

RBI

1940: Johnny Rizzo, 53
1941: Nick Etten, 79
1942: Danny Litwhiler, 56
1943: Ron Northey, 68
1944: Ron Northey, 104
1945: Vince DiMaggio, 84
1946: Del Ennis, 73
1947: Del Ennis, 81
1948: Del Ennis, 95
1949: Del Ennis, 110

Runs

1940: Pinky May, 59
1941: Nick Etten, 78
1942: Danny Litwhiler, 59
1943: Ron Northey, 72
1944: Buster Adams, 86
1945: Jimmy Wasdell, 65
1946: Johnny Wyrostek, 73
1947: Harry Walker, 79
1948: Del Ennis, 86
1949: Del Ennis, 92

Doubles

1940: Art Mahan, 24;
 Pinky May, 24
1941: Danny Litwhiler, 29
1942: Danny Litwhiler, 25
1943: Ron Northey, 31
1944: Buster Adams, 35;
 Ron Northey, 35
1945: John Antonelli, 27
1946: Del Ennis, 30;
 Johnny Wyrostek, 30
1947: Harry Walker, 28
1948: Del Ennis, 40
1949: Del Ennis, 39

Stolen Bases

1940: Art Mahan, 4
1941: Danny Murta
1942: Danny Murta
1943: Jimmy Wasde
1944: Tony Lupien,
1945: Vince DiMag
1946: Roy Hughes,
 Johnny Wyro
1947: Harry Walker, 13
1948: Richie Ashburn, 32
1949: Richie Ashburn, 9

Wins

1940: Kirby Higbe, 14–19
1941: Tommy Hughes, 9–14;
 Johnny Podgajny, 9–12
1942: Tommy Hughes, 12–18
1943: Schoolboy Rowe, 14–8
1944: Ken Raffensberger, 13–20;
 Charley Schanz, 13–16
1945: Dick Barrett, 8–20;
 Andy Karl, 8–8
1946: Oscar Judd, 11–12;
 Schoolboy Rowe, 11–4
1947: Dutch Leonard, 17–12
1948: Dutch Leonard, 12–17
1949: Ken Heintzelman, 17–10;
 Russ Meyer, 17–8

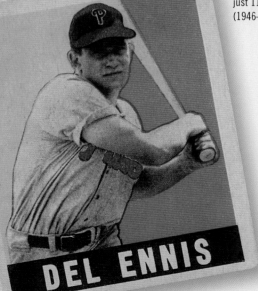

A team leader and fan favorite, Del Ennis amassed 1,124 RBI in just 11 seasons with the Phillies (1946–1956).

DEL ENNIS

This 1947 scorecard insisted that the Phillies would skyrocket up the standings in 1947. Instead, they fell from fifth (in 1946) to seventh.

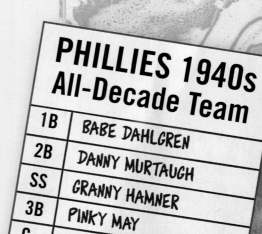

ERA

1940: Hugh Mulcahy, 3.60
1941: Cy Blanton, 4.51
1942: Tommy Hughes, 3.06
1943: Dick Barrett, 2.39
1944: Ken Raffensberger, 3.06
1945: Andy Karl, 2.99
1946: Schoolboy Rowe, 2.12
1947: Dutch Leonard, 2.68
1948: Dutch Leonard, 2.51
1949: Ken Heintzelman, 3.02

Strikeouts

1940: Kirby Higbe, 137
1941: Si Johnson, 80
1942: Rube Melton, 107
1943: Al Gerheauser, 92
1944: Ken Raffensberger, 136
1945: Dick Barrett, 72
1946: Ken Raffensberger, 73
1947: Dutch Leonard, 103
1948: Dutch Leonard, 92
1949: Robin Roberts, 95

Andy Seminick, portrayed here on a Bowman card, was the National League's starting catcher in the 1949 All-Star Game.

NL Leaders

1940: Strikeouts—Kirby Higbe, 137
1941: Stolen Bases—
    Danny Murtaugh, 18
1947: Batting Average—
    Harry Walker, .363;
    Triples—Walker, 16
1948: Stolen Bases—
    Richie Ashburn, 32
1949: Shutouts—Ken Heintzelman, 5

NL Awards

NL MVP Voting
1946: Del Ennis, 8th
1949: Ken Heintzelman, 9th

NL All-Stars
1940: Kirby Higbe, P;
    Pinky May, 3B;
    Hugh Mulcahy, P
1941: Cy Blanton, P
1942: Danny Litwhiler, OF
1943: Babe Dahlgren, 1B
1944: Ken Raffensberger, P
1945: No game
1946: Del Ennis, OF;
    Frank McCormick, 1B;
    Emil Verban, 2B
1947: Emil Verban, 2B;
    Harry Walker, OF;
    Schoolboy Rowe, P
1948: Richie Ashburn, OF
1949: Andy Seminick, C;
    Eddie Waitkus, 1B

PHILLIES 1940s All-Decade Team

1B	BABE DAHLGREN
2B	DANNY MURTAUGH
SS	GRANNY HAMNER
3B	PINKY MAY
C	ANDY SEMINICK
OF	DANNY LITWHILER
OF	RON NORTHEY
OF	DEL ENNIS
SP	DUTCH LEONARD
SP	SCHOOLBOY ROWE
RP	ANDY KARL

SIZZLE AND FIZZLE

After soaring to the World Series in 1950, the young Phillies fall back to earth. Star players Robin Roberts and Richie Ashburn thrive but lack a strong supporting cast.

The Phillies entered the 1950s with something preciously rare in the franchise's sorry history: optimism. The third-place finish and winning record in 1949 signaled a new direction, a change from a wretched stretch of 31 years in which the team managed only one winning season.

What better way to test that optimism than by opening the decade against the defending National League champions, the Brooklyn Dodgers? The Phillies were up to the task, driving Don Newcombe from the Shibe Park mound after one inning as Robin Roberts cruised to a 9–1 victory.

The rest of the 1950 season was a joyride, the most memorable in Phillies history to that point. With a one-game lead over Brooklyn on the final day of the season, Roberts faced Newcombe again, this time at Ebbets Field. Both pitchers went 10 innings until Philly triumphed on a three-run homer by Dick Sisler.

Robin Roberts, who won 20 games six consecutive seasons in the 1950s, celebrates after winning his 200th game in 1958.

The Phillies' second World Series went much like their first—a one-sided loss, this time to the Yankees, who swept the Phillies in four. But with October experience and youth on their side, Philadelphia's "Whiz Kids" figured to have a bright decade ahead.

Owner Bob Carpenter had fortified the farm system, which boasted 11 affiliates in 1950, up from one in 1943. But the pipeline of young talent suddenly ran dry after the Whiz Kids' magical run, and future stars stopped flowing to Philadelphia. Moreover, the stars of 1950 quickly faded.

Pitcher Jim Konstanty, the MVP of the National League in 1950, was mortal again. Curt Simmons, a 17-game winner in '50, missed the next season with army duty. Roberts and Ashburn excelled, as usual, but the 1951 team lurched to a 73–81 record, and by mid-1952 manager Eddie Sawyer had lost the players.

Sawyer's attempts to discipline his cocky young team had failed, and under his cool-headed replacement, Steve O'Neill, the 1952 Phillies went 59–32 the rest of the way. It was good for only fourth place, and the 1953 edition finished third.

Yet the rest of the decade brought six .500-or-below seasons and more managerial changes, from O'Neill to Mayo Smith back to Sawyer. Through it all, Roberts and Ashburn were dominant. For years, their retired uniform numbers—36 for Roberts, 1 for Ashburn—were the only ones hanging above the outfield wall at Veterans Stadium.

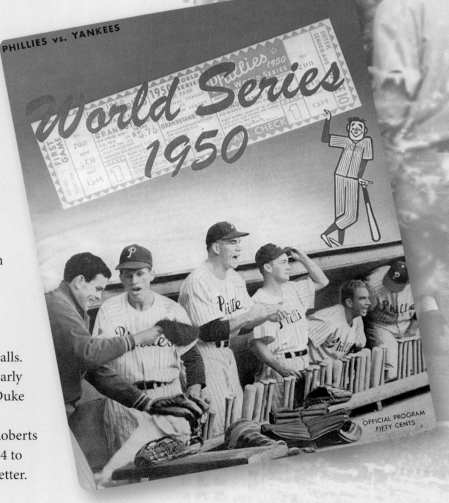

They earned that honor—and eventual Hall of Fame enshrinement—for their extraordinary work in the '50s. Roberts led the league in innings and complete games five times, in victories four times (and twice in losses). He won at least 20 games six seasons in a row (1950–1955), logging more than 300 innings every year.

Among everyday players, Ashburn was the face of the franchise. No player in the majors had as many hits as Ashburn in the '50s. He captured two batting crowns (.338 in 1955 and .350 in 1958) and led the league in on-base percentage three times in the decade.

Ashburn also used his speed to score at least 90 runs eight times in the '50s, and nobody was better at tracking down fly balls. In an era romanticized for outstanding center fielders (particularly the fabled New York trio of Willie Mays, Mickey Mantle, and Duke Snider), Ashburn led NL outfielders in putouts nine times.

But 1959 would be Ashburn's last season as a Phillie, and Roberts was also declining. The Phils dropped to 69 wins in 1958 and 64 to close out the decade. Things would get worse before they got better.

1950

▶ **90-63   1st** ◀

Highlights

April 18: The Phillies open with new uniforms—red and white pinstripes. Their road games, in addition to home games, will now be broadcast live on the radio (WPEN).

September 15: The Phils edge the Reds 8–7 in 19 innings to maintain a 7 1/2-game lead.

October 1: With their lead down to one game over the Dodgers, the Phillies win the season finale at Brooklyn 4–1 in 10 innings, as Dick Sisler smashes a three-run homer. Tens of thousands of fans will greet the team as it arrives in Philadelphia that night.

October 4: The Yankees edge the Phillies 1–0 in Game One of the World Series.

October 5: New York takes Game Two 2–1 on a Joe DiMaggio homer in the top of the tenth.

October 7: After winning Game Three 3–2 with a ninth-inning run, the Yankees sweep the series with a 5–2 triumph in Game Four.

NOTES

Del Ennis swings the big bat, belting a .311 average with 31 home runs and an NL-high 126 RBI.

Pitcher Jim Konstanty (16–7, 2.66 as a reliever) wins the NL MVP Award.

Robin Roberts goes 20–11, and Curt Simmons, 17–8.

Dick Sisler (8) is greeted by elated teammates after belting his historic tenth-inning home run at Brooklyn in the 1950 season finale.

94

THE "KIDS" ARE ALL RIGHT

Phillies Whiz to Top of National League

Brooklyn's Jackie Robinson strode to the plate in the 1950 season opener, having just watched the Phillies rough up Dodgers ace Don Newcombe before a delighted Shibe Park crowd in Philadelphia. "What do you guys think you're going to do?" Robinson asked catcher Andy Seminick with a joking grin. "Win the pennant?"

History said such an idea was outlandish. The Phillies had been outscored by their opponents for 17 consecutive seasons. They had not finished as high as second place in the National League since 1917. And they had spent 24 of the 31 years since then in last or next-to-last place.

What's more, the Phillies were far too young. The oldest man in the 1950 batting order was 30-year-old Eddie Waitkus, and he was returning after being shot in the chest the previous June. None of the top five starters had celebrated a twenty-seventh birthday.

Still, Robinson and the Dodgers learned something during that 9–1 Opening Day loss that the rest of the league would discover soon enough. These kids could play.

"You bet," Seminick told Robinson.

The 1950 Phillies debuted white jerseys with red pinstripes, but it wasn't their fashion that made the most lasting statement. It was their energy and hustle. It was their unwillingness to listen to those who told them they weren't ready to win it all. It was their defiance of logic.

Robin Roberts' mastery of mighty Brooklyn in that Opening Day gem was his first of 20 victories that season, nearly matching his age of 23. Curt Simmons finished four wins off his age, with 17 triumphs as a 21-year-old. Bob Miller, 24, added 11 wins.

The Whiz Kids

The 1950 Phillies had the youngest team in baseball with an average age just a tick over 26. Center fielder Richie Ashburn and shortstop Granny Hamner were both 23. All-Star third baseman Willie "Puddin' Head" Jones was just 24. Slugger Del Ennis, 25, was in the top 10 in batting—as was Ashburn.

But pitching paced the Whiz Kids and ultimately kept midnight from striking on Cinderella. With the Korean War just begun, stellar southpaw Curt Simmons, 21, was called to National Guard duty in September. The lead dwindled to a single game on the final day of the year, but Robin Roberts, just 23, won his 20th game with a 10-inning effort in Brooklyn to clinch the pennant.

Other youngsters on the roster included backup catcher Stan Lopata (24) and starting pitchers Bob Miller (24), Bubba Church (25), and Russ Meyer (26). Ironically, the National League MVP Award went to the oldest regular on the Phillies team. Reliever Jim Konstanty was 33 years old.

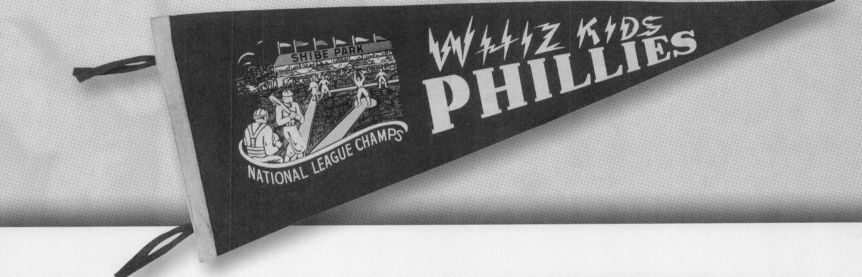

All three posted ERAs between 3.02 and 3.57, giving Philadelphia the stingiest staff in the league. With NL MVP Jim Konstanty emerging as the team's first legitimate relief ace with 22 saves, 16 wins, and a 2.66 ERA, the Phillies easily unleashed the NL's best arms.

Eddie Sawyer's team had pitched well the previous summer, too, but it did not have the offensive firepower to stay in contention. That changed in '50, as the club's young nucleus began to jell in a hurry.

Del Ennis hit .311 with 31 homers and 126 RBI. Fellow outfielder Richie Ashburn added a .303 average and led the league with 14 triples. Their energy fueled the Phillies to a sensational year in which they spent more than half the season in first place. They led by five games with six to play, but they needed a repeat victory by Roberts over Newcombe in the finale at Brooklyn to edge the Dodgers for their first pennant in 35 years. Dick Sisler's three-run homer off Newcombe in the top of the 10th secured the 4–1 victory.

Jim Konstanty earned the 1950 NL MVP award by winning 16 games, all out of the pen. He sometimes pitched long stretches as a reliever, including 10 innings of a 19-inning game.

The World Series was a quick one, swept by the Yankees, but the first three games were one-run contests. The Phillies were playing without Simmons, who had been called to Korean War duty. But it was their bats that failed them. They hit .203 despite Granny Hamner's .429 average.

1951

Highlights

May 20: Richie Ashburn collects eight hits as the Phillies sweep Pittsburgh in a doubleheader 17–0 and 12–4.

July 25–28: The Phillies post four straight shutouts—two at St. Louis and two at Chicago. They will extend the scoreless streak to 41 innings.

August 11: A Robin Roberts shutout puts the Phils at 58–52, but they will lose their next eight games.

August 27: The Phillies shut out the Reds three times in the span of approximately 26 hours.

September 30: In the season finale, Brooklyn edges the Phils 9–8 in 14 innings to enter its fabled playoff with the Giants. Jackie Robinson saves this game in extra innings with a sensational bases-loaded catch and then wins it with a homer in the fourteenth.

NOTES

Richie Ashburn leads the NL in hits (221) and is runner-up for the batting crown (.344).

Willie Jones leads all Phils in homers (22) and RBI (81).

Robin Roberts finishes 21–15 with a 3.03 ERA and six shutouts.

Jim Konstanty (4–11, 4.05) is among the many players who disappoint after the pennant-winning season of 1950.

EASY GO

Success Slips Away After 1950 Pennant

Finally at the top, Phillies fans wondered what their talented young club would do for an encore in 1951. They found out quickly, and the answer was far from pretty.

It was a rapid fall from grace. The defending National League champions went 73–81, making a beeline for the second division with a fifth-place showing. Several factors contributed to their demise.

For starters (literally), the Phillies lost one of their best. Curt Simmons had been called into active military duty during the Korean War the previous fall and missed the entire 1951 season. It was a colossal blow to Philadelphia's young pitching staff.

> **PHILLIES PHACT**
>
> On August 27, light-hitting backup catcher Del Wilber belts three home runs in his three trips to the plate, as the Phillies defeat the Reds 3–0.

Some felt the 1950 World Series sweep at the hands of the Yankees might have taken some of the pep out of the Phillies' stride. There was probably some truth to that. It should also be noted that the Phillies were among the last major league teams to integrate. While other teams were bringing top Negro League stars into the mix, Eddie Sawyer's club did not. In the blink of an eye, Philadelphia's talent was no longer the envy of the league.

Richie Ashburn was tearing the cover off the ball with a .344 average and burning up the base paths with 29 steals. However, the rest of the offense struggled. No other regular hit .290. As a team, the Phillies hit a modest .260 and were better than only two other NL teams in the run-scoring department.

Without Simmons, too much of a burden fell on Robin Roberts' shoulders. The ace did what he could, winning 21 games with a 3.03 ERA, and Bubba Church added a career-high 15 wins. But there was a significant drop-off after that starting pair. In addition, reliever Jim Konstanty did not get nearly as many opportunities to close the door on tight victories as he did during the pennant-winning season, nor was he as effective—a recurring theme among the '51 Phils.

No. 1

Richie Ashburn was a catalyst on the field, in the booth, and in the hearts of three generations of Phillies fans. The Hall of Fame center fielder was called "Whitey" for his light blond hair, but he was renowned for his great speed, superb glove, keen batting eye, quick bat, and even quicker wit.

A Nebraska native, Ashburn signed with the Phillies in 1945, batted .342 in the minors, and arrived in Philadelphia in 1948 to replace Harry "The Hat" Walker, the previous year's batting champion. Ashburn broke into the majors by hitting .333, second in the National League, and leading the league with 32 steals. A catalyst on the 1950 "Whiz Kids," he hit .303 and led the league with 14 triples. He saved the pennant on the season's final day, gunning down Cal Abrams at the plate in the ninth inning of a tie game at Ebbets Field. Dick Sisler's home run the next inning secured the Phillies' first pennant since 1915.

Number 1 has been retired since 1979, but the wearer of that uniform still ranks high in the team's record book. Three times in his dozen seasons with the Phillies he led the NL in hits, and he won the batting crown in 1955 and 1958. Ashburn rarely missed a game, playing in 150 or more games 10 times in 12 seasons. His 1,794 games, 7,122 at-bats, 2,217 hits, and 946 walks were Phillies records until surpassed by Mike Schmidt. He finished with 2,574 hits and a .308 career average in the majors, plus nine seasons leading NL outfielders in putouts.

Traded to the Cubs after the 1959 season, Ashburn joined the expansion Mets for their inaugural 1962 campaign. Ashburn was the team's first batter, first All-Star, first .300 hitter, and first to retire after a record-shattering 40–120 disaster of a season.

Armed with enough anecdotes and jokes for a lifetime, Ashburn returned to Philadelphia and joined By Saam and Bill Campbell in the broadcast booth. In 1971, Harry Kalas replaced Campbell, creating the most memorable on-air team the city has ever enjoyed. Whitey and Harry worked together until September 9, 1997, when Ashburn died of a heart attack after calling a game at Shea Stadium. Though he never saw Citizens Bank Park, the fleet center fielder is a part of the place in the popular outfield walkway known as Ashburn Alley.

At various times in his career, Richie Ashburn led the NL in batting, hits, walks, and steals—all marks of a dangerous leadoff man.

1952

▶ 87-67   4th ◀

Highlights

May 13: Curt Simmons tosses a two-hit shutout against the Cubs in his first start since returning from the army.

June 27: With the team at 28–35, manager Eddie Sawyer is replaced by Steve O'Neill.

July 8: Shibe Park hosts the All-Star Game. Pitchers Robin Roberts and Curt Simmons and shortstop Granny Hamner represent the Phillies.

August 31: Boston beats Philly 1–0 in the bottom of the ninth. With the bases loaded, an inside pitch accidentally hits the bat of ducking pitcher Virgil Jester, who beats it out for a single.

September 6: Roberts goes the distance in a 17-inning, 7–6 win over the Braves.

September 28: The Phils close the season with a record of 59–32 under O'Neill.

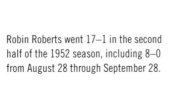

NOTES

Del Ennis bounces back to tally team highs in HRs (20) and RBI (107).

The Phillies lead the NL in ERA (3.07).

Roberts (28–7, 2.59) tops the league in wins and complete games (30). He finishes second in NL MVP voting.

Curt Simmons (14–8, 2.82), **Karl Drews** (14–15, 2.72), and **Russ Meyer** (13–14, 3.14) round out the rotation.

ROBIN SOARS

Roberts' 28 Wins Are 10 Better than NL Runner-Up

There were several reasons the Phillies shook off their post-pennant doldrums of 1951 and returned to winning baseball in '52. Curt Simmons, after missing the previous year, returned from the Korean War and went 14–8. Four players socked 12 or more home runs, led by Del Ennis' 20 round-trippers. The firing of Eddie Sawyer and promotion of easygoing Steve O'Neill as manager in midseason sparked a sizzling 59–32 finish after a 28–35 start.

But one reason stood out among all others for the Phillies' 1952 resurgence. He was a 25-year-old right-hander named Robin Roberts.

Roberts had been terrific for the Phillies in both the championship '50 season and '51, winning 20 or more games each year with an ERA just above 3.00. In '52, however, the Illinois native put together his greatest season. It was one of the best in baseball history.

Looking back, it's hard to believe that Cubs outfielder Hank Sauer edged Roberts for the 1952 National League MVP Award. While Sauer hit .270 with 37 home runs for a fifth-place club, Roberts won 28 games, the highest total in the majors since Dizzy Dean had won the same number in 1935. Since '52, only one major league pitcher—Denny McClain with a 31-win campaign for the Tigers—has won more games in a season.

Roberts amassed 10 more victories than any other pitcher in the NL in '52. He also racked up 40 more innings and nine more complete games than any of his fellow NL aces while compiling a 2.59 ERA.

"When he won, he was gracious," wrote James A. Michener in *The New York Times*. "When he lost, so often in extra innings with his teammates giving him no runs, he did not pout. Day after day he went out there and threw that high, hard one down the middle, a marvelously coordinated man doing his job. If he had pitched for the Yankees he might have won 350 games."

Robin Roberts went 17–1 in the second half of the 1952 season, including 8–0 from August 28 through September 28.

Proven Winner

O'Neill Guides Phils to Third-Place Finish

Steve O'Neill was confident entering his first spring training as manager of the Philadelphia Phillies. O'Neill knew a thing or two about winning as he put the club through its drills. As a 17-year major league catcher, he had won a World Series with Cleveland in 1920. As a veteran manager, he had steered the 1945 Detroit Tigers to the world title.

Just two seasons removed from their 1950 pennant, the Phillies still purported to be a National League contender, and they had won 59 of 91 games after O'Neill was brought in to replace Eddie Sawyer as manager in 1952. With a full season of O'Neill guiding their heroes, Philadelphians anticipated great success, particularly after the Phillies opened the season by capturing 9 of their first 11 games.

They had to settle for something close to it—a summer that did not live up to April hopes but that produced a tie for third place in the NL standings.

Robin Roberts and Curt Simmons provided one of the best one-two pitching punches in baseball, combining for 39 victories. Jim Konstanty added a 14–10 record, but the talent level on the mound dropped off significantly after that.

Offensively, Del Ennis drove in 125 runs and steady Richie Ashburn hit .330, but no other Phillies regular batted .300. The left side of the infield—shortstop Ted Kazanski and third baseman Willie Jones—struggled to .217 and .225, respectively.

With those weak spots in the lineup, there was no way for O'Neill's Phillies to keep up with the runaway train that was Brooklyn in the NL standings. The 1953 Dodgers won 105 games on their way to another World Series with the Yankees.

The Phillies tied with St. Louis for third place at 83–71, a full 22 games behind the NL pennant-winners.

Shortstop Granny Hamner, whose first name was short for Granville, drove in a career-high 92 runs in 1953.

Highlights

April 16: Second baseman Connie Ryan goes 6-for-6 in a 14–12 loss to Pittsburgh.

April 26: Ryan goes 5-for-5 against the Pirates.

May 16: After giving up a single to open the game, Phillies pitcher Curt Simmons is perfect the rest of the way, retiring 27 straight for a 3–0 shutout.

May 19: The Phillies are 17–8 and hold a one-game lead in the NL standings. They will drop out of first for good later in the week.

July 5: Robin Roberts goes 10 innings in a 2–0 shutout against Pittsburgh—his 28th consecutive complete game.

July 14: Roberts, Curt Simmons, Richie Ashburn, and Granny Hamner all play in the All-Star Game, with Roberts and Simmons pitching five shutout innings.

August 12: Roberts wins his twentieth game and his fifteenth straight versus the Pirates.

NOTES

Del Ennis (.285–29–125) ranks fourth in the league in RBI.

Richie Ashburn rips .330 and tops the NL in hits (205).

Granny Hamner amasses 21 homers, 92 RBI, and 90 runs.

Robin Roberts (23–16, 2.75) leads the league in wins, complete games (33), and strikeouts (198).

Highlights

April 14–18: After an Opening Day loss, Phillies pitchers throw three consecutive shutouts.

May 16: The Phils are 16–11 and all alone in first place.

June 12: Jim Wilson of the Braves no-hits the Phillies.

June 17: Robin Roberts goes the distance and scores the winning run in the bottom of the fifteenth in a 3–2 win over St. Louis.

July 13: Roberts, Granny Hamner, and catcher Smoky Burgess represent the Phils at the All-Star Game. During the All-Star break, Terry Moore replaces Steve O'Neill as the team's manager.

October 14: The Phillies announce that Mayo Smith will manage the team in 1955.

NOTES

Smoky Burgess places sixth in the NL in batting with a team-best .368 mark.

Richie Ashburn raps .313 and leads the league in walks (125) and OBP (.441).

Robin Roberts (23–15, 2.97) again paces the circuit in wins, complete games (29), and strikeouts (185).

Murry Dickson (10–20) leads the NL in losses.

KEYSTONE FOLLIES

Poor Choices, Inept Spy Characterize '54 Phils

The Phillies of the mid-1950s, as it turned out, could not even do espionage right. And that's to say nothing about their managerial decisions. It was a sad series of events all around that took the club to its second losing season since capturing the National League pennant in 1950.

The 1954 season started out swimmingly. After an Opening Day loss, Philly pitchers tossed three consecutive shutouts. The Phillies sat atop the National League standings in mid-May. They sent three standouts to the All-Star Game. And they were a quite respectable 40–37 and in third place when new general manager Roy Hamey decided to fire manager Steve O'Neill. He put former Cardinals outfielder Terry Moore, a man with no major league experience as a skipper, in charge. "The appointment of Moore is a shot in the dark," admitted Hamey himself.

It was hardly a ringing endorsement, but it was also not the most ridiculous thing the front office did during the '54 season. That "honor" went to the club's decision to hire a private investigator to follow rule-breaking third baseman Willie Jones. The P.I., however, wound up trailing the wrong man! He followed All-Star shortstop Granny Hamner, which incensed Hamner and created a rift between the player and management.

Short, hefty catcher Smoky Burgess batted .368 for the Phillies in 108 games in 1954. He would retire with the major league record for career pinch hits.

Meanwhile, Moore turned out to be a short-lived and unsuccessful skipper. He dropped his first four games and guided the team from third place to fourth. His 35–42 record was far worse than the winning ledger of his predecessor, and it was announced that Mayo Smith would take the reins the following year.

Pitchers Robin Roberts and Curt Simmons, holdovers from the "Whiz Kids" days, remained brilliant. Both posted ERAs under 3.00, and Roberts followed up his record 28-win season with a 23–15 mark. Offensively, however, only one team in the NL—the 101-loss Pittsburgh Pirates—scored fewer runs than the Phillies in 1954.

Control Freak

The numbers are impressive; his durability, legendary; his knack for allowing solo homers but getting the big outs with men on base, a survival trait. The key to Robin Roberts, however, was summed up best in a *Time* magazine cover story on the pitcher in 1956:

"Better than any of them now on the mound, Robin Roberts can put the ball where he wants. There is one precious-diamond word for him—control."

Roberts didn't walk batters. He rarely hit anyone, and he famously refused to even knock down hitters during a time when that was a way of life on a big-league mound. He never hit more than five batters in a season, and he led the league in innings and complete games five straight years. Of his 505 home runs allowed, 304 were with none on base. Only four were grand slams. He still holds the mark for homers allowed by a right-hander—or a Phillie—but his all-time gopher ball record was surpassed by southpaw Jamie Moyer.

Roberts' control came to him on the farm in Springfield, Illinois. While his brothers toiled in the fields—Robin once broke a hoe, so he didn't have to work—he took out an old mattress and threw against it repeatedly. An all-around athlete, he earned a basketball scholarship to Michigan State. Signed by the Phillies, he spent just 11 games in the minors (compiling a 9–1 mark) before being summoned to Philadelphia in 1948.

The first Phillies pitcher since Pete Alexander to win 20 games in a year, Roberts reeled off six straight 20-win seasons. His first time reaching that number, on the last day of the 1950 season in Brooklyn, also clinched the first Phillies pennant since 1915. Roberts won 234 times as a Phillie to break Alexander's club mark. And in 1976 Roberts, a 286-game winner

overall, became the first primarily Phillies player elected to the Hall of Fame since Alexander in 1938.

A five-time All-Star starter, Roberts helped get the players movement off the ground in the 1950s. He served as National League player representative when the owners still held the cards. Later he suggested that the players hire a chief executive, who turned out to be Marvin Miller. Sore feelings from management perhaps kept Roberts from joining the Phillies after his career, though the club retired his No. 36. An investment broker, Roberts filled his baseball itch as head coach at South Florida. He died in 2010 at age 83.

Before beginning his windup, Robin Roberts always tugged at his belt, pant leg, and cap.

Highlights

April 13: Richie Ashburn's team-record streak of 731 consecutive games comes to an end.

April 30: The team trades the potent-hitting Smoky Burgess to Cincinnati in a six-player deal. All three acquired players will turn out to be disappointments.

May 15: After a promising 9–6 start to the season, the Phillies lose their thirteenth game in a row to fall 14 ½ games out of first place.

July 12: Robin Roberts starts the All-Star Game, but he gives up four runs in the first inning. Outfielder Del Ennis and catcher Stan Lopata join Roberts on the NL roster.

July 22: The Phils win their eleventh consecutive game to pull their record to 48–48.

July 23: Ennis belts three home runs and knocks in seven in a 7–2 win over St. Louis.

NOTES

Richie Ashburn wins the batting crown at .338, 19 points better than runners-up Willie Mays and Stan Musial.

Del Ennis finishes third in the NL with 120 RBI and ninth with 29 home runs.

Robin Roberts goes 23–14 and leads the league in wins, complete games (26), and—for the fifth straight year—innings pitched (305).

ONLY TEAM IN TOWN

Phils Add Mayo while A's Move to Kansas City

For most of their existence, Connie Mack's Athletics had overshadowed the Phillies in Philadelphia. Their following was better. Their success was superior. And if a town the size of Philly could support only one major league team, most in the wagering business would have bet that the Phillies would be the team to go.

But along came 1955, and the A's headed for greener pastures in Kansas City. Meanwhile, the Phillies—unhappy with their late-season slide under manager Terry Moore in '54—decided to make another change before the '55 season that put a former A's player at the helm.

Mayo Smith, a onetime International League batting champion, played just one season in the majors. That was as an outfielder with Mack's Athletics in 1945. Smith achieved success as a minor league manager in the Yankees system, earning praise from the likes of Casey Stengel.

Outfielder Del Ennis drove in 120 runs in 1955, the fourth straight season and the sixth in seven years in which he topped the 100-RBI plateau.

"There's one minor [league] manager who comes to our preliminary camps loaded with curiosity and questions," Stengel said. "He watches everything and asks about everything. He never forgets. He is headed, for sure, for a big [-league] job."

Eventually, Smith would win a World Series championship as a manager. Unfortunately for the Phillies, that time would not arrive until 1968, when Smith was skippering the Detroit Tigers.

In Philadelphia, he was not so well received. Phillies star Del Ennis said Smith lacked confidence and did not stick up for his players. Some of his teammates simply felt that Smith was out of his league. They were looking to reclaim the glory they had experienced in winning a 1950 pennant, and such glory proved elusive.

Without the A's across town, Phillies attendance jumped nearly 200,000 to 922,886. But after Ennis (.296) and batting champ Richie Ashburn (.338), no one in the lineup hit better than .272, and there was only one Robin Roberts on the pitching staff. The Phillies won 77 and lost 77, splitting their decisions evenly for the first time in their history.

CROUCHING BACKSTOP

Catcher Lopata Alters Batting Stance, Breaks Out

Stan Lopata was a catcher, after all, and a pretty talented one at that. Crouching would seem to come quite naturally for someone playing his position.

A backstop who had been in and out of the Phillies lineup since 1948, he had reached the MLB All-Star Game for the first time in 1955 when he launched a career-high 22 home runs. Lopata longed to get better, though, so he tinkered with his stance in 1956. The suggestion was first made to him by one of the greatest hitters in history, Rogers Hornsby. The change: an exaggerated crouch.

The results were undeniable. From his squatting position in the batter's box, Lopata strode through the ball and unleashed 32 home runs in 1956, shattering his career high by 10. His 143 hits, 33 doubles, seven triples, and 95 RBI were also the loftiest totals of his career.

"After I changed my stance," he explained, "I just started hitting line drives and pulling the ball, and it was just one of those fabulous years. . . . I just kept hitting everything hard."

If a few other members of the 1956 Phillies would have enjoyed career years like their gritty catcher from Michigan, the club might have avoided its fate of a 71–83 ledger and fifth-place National League finish. It was their third losing season since claiming the 1950 pennant.

Philadelphia was by far the worst pitching team in the NL, with a 4.20 ERA. Robin Roberts again led the staff in wins (19), but his ERA jumped to 4.45 as he approached his 30th birthday. The Phillies gave up more home runs than any other team in the league.

Offensively, manager Mayo Smith's second Phillies club didn't have the firepower to keep up with the sluggers who were hammering his pitchers. Philadelphia hit .252 as a team and ended the year a distant 22 games behind Brooklyn in the standings.

In addition to changing his batting stance, Stan Lopata credited his improved production in 1956 to tinting his eyeglasses, which cut down on glare.

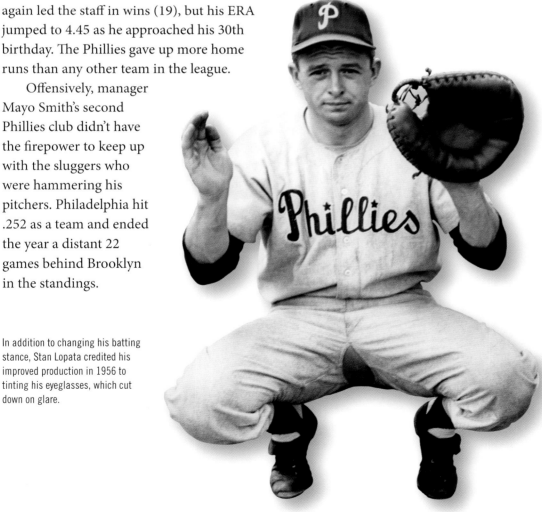

1956

▶ 71-83   5th ◀

Highlights

April 22: Police are called to Connie Mack Stadium after fans start throwing bottles and cans on the field in a game against the Giants.

May 13: After a 5–5 start, the Phillies lose their tenth straight game (all on the road). They will remain under .500 the rest of the year.

July 10: Robin Roberts and catcher Stan Lopata represent Philly at the All-Star Game, but neither plays.

July 17: The Cubs score two in the bottom of the ninth and one in the sixteenth to defeat the Phillies 3–2.

August 8: Roberts wins his fourth game in 10 days, defeating the Giants 9–3. In the same game, Phillies shortstop Ted Kazanski silences the New York crowd with an inside-the-park grand slam.

September 25: Sal "The Barber" Maglie of Brooklyn no-hits the Phils, walking two and striking out three.

NOTES

Richie Ashburn finishes fifth in the NL in hitting (.303) and second in hits (190).

Stan Lopata ranks among NL leaders in homers (32) and RBI (95).

Robin Roberts (19–18) leads the NL in losses and in runs, hits, and home runs allowed.

▶ 77-77   5th ◀

Highlights

April 16: Promising shortstop Chico Fernandez of Cuba, recently acquired from Brooklyn for five players and $75,000, becomes the first dark-skinned player to play for the Phillies.

April 22: Ten years and one week after Jackie Robinson broke the MLB color barrier, John Kennedy becomes the first African American player for the Phillies, entering the game as a pinch runner.

May 1: The Reds defeat the Phils 8–6 in 16 innings.

July 30: The Phillies improve to 56–44 and are only three games behind in the NL standings, but they will go 21–33 the rest of the way.

NOTES

Rookie **Jack Sanford** (19–8) leads the NL with 188 strikeouts and finishes second in wins and winning percentage.

First baseman **Ed Bouchee** hits .293 with 17 homers and 35 doubles. *The Sporting News* dubs him NL Rookie Player of the Year.

Relief pitcher **Turk Farrell** is another rookie star, going 10–2 with a 2.38 ERA.

Outfielder **Rip Repulski** leads the club with 20 homers.

Robin Roberts suffers through a 10–22 season.

LIGHTNING STRIKES TWICE

Bizarre At-Bat Stands Out During .500 Season

It was an at-bat that does not show up anywhere in the baseball record books. Certainly, however, what Richie Ashburn managed to do with his bat on August 17, 1957, is a feat that only he has accomplished in major league lore. Baseball fans everywhere hope no one else ever does.

In the second game of a four-game series against the Giants at Shibe Park, Ashburn hit a foul ball into the stands that struck and broke the nose of Alice Roth, the wife of *Philadelphia Bulletin* sports editor Earl Roth. Then, as medical personnel were carrying Roth out of the stands on a stretcher, Ashburn hit her again with a second foul ball in the same at-bat!

Alice, fortunately, made a full recovery and remained Ashburn's longtime friend. Whenever the conversation turned to the '57 campaign, that bizarre at-bat dominated the conversation.

The Phillies won that game 3–1 to go five games over .500 at 60–55. Their roster was loaded with rookies and young players, causing some to speculate that perhaps a "Whiz Kids II" was in the works. Two of the rookies were standout pitchers. Jack Sanford, 28, went 19–8 with a 3.08 ERA to pace the staff as one of the most surprising young arms in the game. Meanwhile, 23-year-old Turk Farrell was used out of the bullpen and posted a 10–2 record with 10 saves.

However, with longtime ace Robin Roberts struggling to a 10–22 record and the Phillies finishing next to last in the National League in runs (623) and batting average (.250), the club was never able to make a serious run in '57, the year the team suited up its first African American player, John Kennedy.

Another of the rookies, 24-year-old first baseman Ed Bouchee, was the offensive star with a .293 average and 17 homers. The fifth-place Phillies finished an even 77–77 for the second time in three years.

John Kennedy was the first African American to play for the Phillies, but his big-league career amounted to just two at-bats.

Milwaukee's Hank Aaron sends one soaring into the air against Robin Roberts. The two men hold twentieth-century MLB records for home runs hit (755) and homers allowed (505), respectively.

Highlights

May 11: Richie Ashburn's streak of 473 consecutive games comes to an end.

July 8: Phillies pitcher Turk Farrell fans four in two no-hit innings in the All-Star Game.

July 22: The Phillies replace manager Mayo Smith with former skipper Eddie Sawyer.

August 1: Robin Roberts defeats the Cubs 3–1 for his 200th victory.

August 20: Willie Jones belts two homers and drives in eight in a 12–2 win over St. Louis.

September 22: Seth Morehead, Farrell, and Jack Meyer strike out 21 Pirates in a 3–2, 14-inning win.

September 28: Ashburn smacks three hits in the season finale to win the batting title (.350) by three points over Willie Mays.

NOTES

Richie Ashburn leads the NL in hits (215), triples (13), walks (97), and OBP (.440).

Outfielder Harry Anderson paces the team in homers (23) and RBI (97) while batting .301.

Robin Roberts (17–14, 3.24) leads the staff in wins and ERA.

Following his sensational rookie season, **Ed Bouchee** is arrested for exposing himself to young girls. After undergoing psychiatric treatment, he returns to the team.

DOWN AND OUT

Phillies Youngsters Prove to Be No "Whiz Kids"

Philadelphia's 1957 youth movement had fans hopeful that a second coming of the "Whiz Kids" might be in the offing. In fact, more than a million fans spun the turnstiles in '57 to watch the Phillies, marking just the third time in history that the club hit the seven-figure attendance mark.

Before the '58 season started, however, fans had ample evidence that these young Phillies were not cut out for the achievements that their '50 predecessors had attained.

Bad news came all the way from Spokane, Washington. That's where Ed Bouchee was arrested and charged with exposing himself to young girls during the offseason. The man who earned the *Sporting News* 1957 NL Rookie of the Year Award spent some time in a psychiatric institution, pleaded guilty to indecent exposure, and returned to the Phillies in midseason, only to hit .257 with nine home runs in 89 games.

The top two young pitchers faltered as sophomores, too. Starter Jack Sanford, 19–8 as a rookie, saw his record slip to 10–13, and reliever Turk Farrell followed his 10–2 first-year ledger with a losing 8–9 mark. The results were predictable. Even though veteran Robin Roberts bounced back from a dismal year with 17 victories and a 3.24 ERA, the Phillies were once again pitching poor. Their 4.32 ERA was second worst in the league, and no National League team yielded more than their 762 runs.

Offensively, there was brighter news. Richie Ashburn captured the batting title after going 3-for-4 on the final day of the season. Still, it was not enough to avoid a last-place, 69–85 finish. Nor could Ashburn bring a million fans to the park or save Mayo Smith's job.

The Phillies turned to a familiar face after relieving Smith of his managing chores in midseason. They rehired Eddie Sawyer, who had skippered the original Whiz Kids to the 1950 pennant. A repeat would not be in the works.

From 1949 to 1958, Willie Jones manned the hot corner in Philly and was the best defensive third baseman in the National League.

Sparky, but No Spark

Once-Promising Decade Ends on Sour Note

The 1950s started with a rare Phillies pennant. The decade ended with a finish more typical of a franchise that could never seem to sustain its success: a 64–90 showing that landed the club dead last in the standings, last in paid attendance, and last in a host of other key categories. It was a dreary way to wrap up a decade that began with so much promise.

The admission of Alaska and Hawaii gave the United States 50 states in 1959, and there were probably some men in those outposts who could have hit better than those in the Phillies lineup. With a .242 team average, the Phillies were a full seven points worse than their nearest National League rival. They were the only team in the league to score fewer than 600 runs.

Unbeknown to the Phillies, there was a future Hall of Famer who made his debut in their lineup in '59. George Lee Anderson, a colorful minor league infielder who earned the nickname "Sparky" for his constant berating of umpires on the farm, was called up to try to fill the team's second-base void. "I only had a high school education," Anderson noted. "And believe me, I had to cheat to get that."

The 25-year-old Anderson struggled, hitting .218 with no homers in 152 games. He was sent back to the minors the following year, turned his efforts toward managing, and eventually became the first major league skipper to win World Series titles in both leagues.

If Anderson could have thrown a curveball, he might have been of more help. Robin Roberts' best days were behind him, leaving the Phillies without a reliable ace. It was a bad way for new general manager John Quinn to get started with the Phillies—a season that had him spending hour after hour on the telephone trying to deal his new club back into the NL conversation.

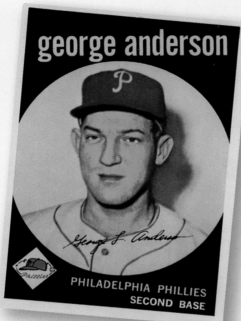

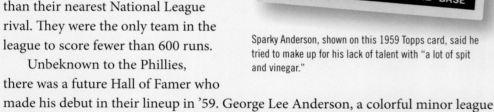

Sparky Anderson, shown on this 1959 Topps card, said he tried to make up for his lack of talent with "a lot of spit and vinegar."

Highlights

January: Owner Bob Carpenter replaces general manager Roy Hamey with John Quinn, who had been successful as the Braves' GM.

May 31: Gene Freese belts his fifth home run of the year—all as a pinch hitter.

June 9: The Phils lose to the Los Angeles Dodgers and fall into last place for good.

December 9: The Phillies trade Freese to the White Sox for outfielder Johnny Callison.

NOTES

Outfielder Wally Post leads the team with 94 RBI.

Gene Freese becomes the team's regular third baseman and leads the club in home runs (23).

Robin Roberts tops the team in wins (15–17).

Jim Owens (12–12, 3.21) and **Gene Conley** (12–7, 3.00) excel even though the Phillies have the weakest offense in the league.

Bob Carpenter talks about moving the Phillies unless he gets a new ballpark.

The Phillies drop to last in the NL in attendance (802,815).

THE 1950s RECORD BOOK

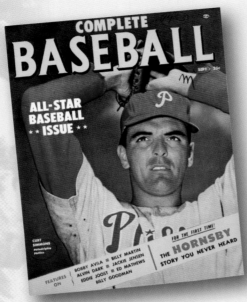

This baseball magazine displays one of the faces of the franchise in the 1950s, three-time All-Star pitcher Curt Simmons.

Team Leaders

Batting

1950: Del Ennis, .311
1951: Richie Ashburn, .344
1952: Smoky Burgess, .296
1953: Richie Ashburn, .330
1954: Smoky Burgess, .368
1955: Richie Ashburn, .338
1956: Richie Ashburn, .303
1957: Richie Ashburn, .297
1958: Richie Ashburn, .350
1959: Ed Bouchee, .285

Home Runs

1950: Del Ennis, 31
1951: Willie Jones, 22
1952: Del Ennis, 20
1953: Del Ennis, 29
1954: Del Ennis, 25
1955: Del Ennis, 29
1956: Stan Lopata, 32

1957: Rip Repulski, 20
1958: Harry Anderson, 23
1959: Gene Freese, 23

RBI

1950: Del Ennis, 126
1951: Willie Jones, 81
1952: Del Ennis, 107
1953: Del Ennis, 125
1954: Del Ennis, 119
1955: Del Ennis, 120
1956: Stan Lopata, 95;
Del Ennis, 95
1957: Ed Bouchee, 76
1958: Harry Anderson, 97
1959: Wally Post, 94

Wins

1950: Robin Roberts, 20–11
1951: Robin Roberts, 21–15
1952: Robin Roberts, 28–7
1953: Robin Roberts, 23–16
1954: Robin Roberts, 23–15
1955: Robin Roberts, 23–14
1956: Robin Roberts, 19–18
1957: Jack Sanford, 19–8
1958: Robin Roberts, 17–14
1959: Robin Roberts, 15–17

ERA

1950: Jim Konstanty, 2.66
1951: Robin Roberts, 3.03
1952: Robin Roberts, 2.59
1953: Robin Roberts, 2.75
1954: Curt Simmons, 2.81
1955: Robin Roberts, 3.28
1956: Curt Simmons, 3.36
1957: Jack Sanford, 3.08
1958: Robin Roberts, 3.24
1959: Gene Conley, 3.00

Strikeouts

1950: Robin Roberts, 146;
Curt Simmons, 146
1951: Robin Roberts, 127
1952: Robin Roberts, 148
1953: Robin Roberts, 198
1954: Robin Roberts, 185
1955: Robin Roberts, 160
1956: Robin Roberts 157
1957: Jack Sanford, 188
1958: Robin Roberts, 130
1959: Robin Roberts, 137

Saves

1950: Jim Konstanty, 22
1951: Jim Konstanty, 9
1952: Jim Konstanty, 6
1953: Jim Konstanty, 5
1954: Robin Roberts, 4
1955: Jack Meyer, 16
1956: Bob Miller, 5
1957: Turk Farrell, 10
1958: Turk Farrell, 11
1959: Turk Farrell, 6

NL Leaders

1950: Triples—
Richie Ashburn, 14;
RBI—Del Ennis, 126;
Saves—Jim Konstanty, 22;
Shutouts—Robin Roberts, 5
1951: Hits—Ashburn, 221
1952: Wins—Roberts, 28;
Complete Games—
Roberts, 30;
Shutouts—Curt Simmons, 6
1953: Hits—Ashburn, 205;
Wins—Roberts, 23;
Strikeouts—Roberts, 198;
Complete Games—
Roberts, 33

1954: Wins—Roberts, 23;
Strikeouts—Roberts, 185;
Complete Games—Roberts, 29
1955: Batting Average—Ashburn, .338;
Saves—Jack Meyer, 16;
Complete Games—Roberts, 26
1956: Compete Games—Roberts, 22
1957: Strikeouts—Jack Sanford, 188
1958: Batting—Ashburn, .350;
Hits—Ashburn, 215;
Triples—Ashburn, 13

NL Awards

NL MVP Voting

1950: Jim Konstanty, 1st;
Del Ennis, 4th;
Granny Hamner, 6th;
Robin Roberts, 7th
1951: Richie Ashburn, 7th
1952: Robin Roberts, 2nd
1953: Robin Roberts, 6th
1954: Robin Roberts, 7th
1955: Robin Roberts, 5th
1957: Jack Sanford, 10th
1958: Richie Ashburn, 7th

NL Rookie of the Year Winners

1957: Jack Sanford

NL All-Stars

1950: Robin Roberts, P;
Willie Jones, 3B;
Jim Konstanty, P;
Dick Sisler, OF
1951: Robin Roberts, P;
Richie Ashburn, OF;
Del Ennis, OF;
Willie Jones, 3B
1952: Curt Simmons, P;
Granny Hamner, SS;
Robin Roberts, P
1953: Robin Roberts, P;
Richie Ashburn, OF;
Granny Hamner, 2B;
Curt Simmons, P
1954: Robin Roberts, P;
Granny Hamner, 2B;
Smoky Burgess, C
1955: Robin Roberts, P;
Del Ennis, OF;
Stan Lopata, C
1956: Stan Lopata, C;
Robin Roberts, P
1957: Curt Simmons, P;
Jack Sanford, P
1958: Richie Ashburn, OF;
Turk Farrell, P
1959: Gene Conley, P

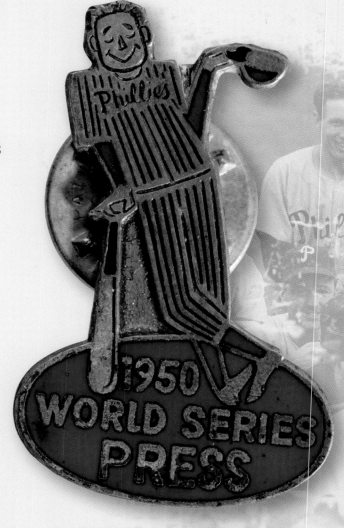

Though this character suggests that the Phillies breezed to the 1950 World Series, getting there was anything but easy.

Richie Ashburn burned up these spikes en route to 234 career stolen bases and 1,322 runs scored.

PHILLIES 1950s All-Decade Team

1B	EDDIE WAITKUS
2B	GRANNY HAMNER
SS	JOE KOPPE
3B	WILLIE JONES
C	STAN LOPATA
OF	RICHIE ASHBURN
OF	DEL ENNIS
OF	DICK SISLER
SP	ROBIN ROBERTS
SP	JACK SANFORD
RP	JIM KONSTANTY

BLOWING THEIR CHANCE

Manager Gene Mauch pulls the Phillies out of the doldrums and to the threshold of a pennant in 1964. But after a historic September collapse, it's all downhill from there.

One game into the 1960s, the Phillies' manager resigned. Eddie Sawyer, the skipper of the 1950 Whiz Kids, abruptly ended his second stint as manager with an infamous line: "I'm 49 years old, and I want to live to be 50." Maybe Sawyer knew something: This would be another cruel decade for the franchise.

For Sawyer's replacement, the Phillies hired the 34-year-old manager of the minor league Minneapolis Millers. He was Gene Mauch, and he piloted the Phillies until June 1968. He led the Phillies to six winning seasons, a fine accomplishment on its face. But he is forever remembered for 1964, when the Phillies held a 6½ game lead with 12 to play and lost 10 in a row to blow the pennant.

The psychic damage of that season would linger for many years, with the totality of the collapse obscuring most of the good work Mauch did. He took a team that had lost 107 games in 1961—including a twentieth-century record 23 in a row—and guided it to a winning record in 1962. The Phillies refused to be the league's doormat anymore, taking 31 of 36 games against the expansion Mets and Colt .45s.

JOHNNY CALLISON • RICHIE ALLEN

HURLERS BEWARE

Philadelphia's tandem of Johnny Callison and Richie Allen wreaked havoc on opposing pitchers throughout the late 1960s. Allen was emerging as a star just as Callison was beginning his decline.

They kept improving in 1963, when an old friend returned to the team. Whiz Kids legend Richie Ashburn joined Byrum Saam and Bill Campbell on the broadcast team, beginning a second career for Ashburn that endeared him to another generation of Phillies fans.

In '63, the Phillies finished fourth in the 10-team National League and played .603 ball in the second half. That foreshadowed the success of 1964, when Jim Bunning threw a perfect game, Johnny Callison won the All-Star Game with a home run, Dick Allen claimed the NL Rookie of the Year Award, and the Phillies started 90–60.

Their fold in late September, as traumatic as it was, did not cost Mauch his job or keep the Phillies from playing competitive baseball the next few seasons. They won 85 games in 1965 and 87 in 1966, a marginal upgrade aided by 40 homers from Allen and a combined 39 victories from Bunning and Chris Short.

Buried in the statistics of the 1966 Phillies is one game—2⅓ innings—pitched by Ferguson Jenkins. The young right-hander had also pitched 12⅓ innings for Philadelphia the previous season.

But the Phillies did not think much of Jenkins, and they included him in a five-player deal with the Cubs in April 1966 that brought pitchers Larry Jackson and Bob Buhl. By the end of the decade, Jackson and Buhl had retired. Jenkins, meanwhile, was into a stretch of six consecutive 20-win seasons on his way to the Hall of Fame.

With deals like that, it was no wonder where the Phillies were headed. Mauch's famed small-ball tactics, combined with the stardom of Allen, Bunning, and Short, propped up the team for a while. But Mauch feuded with Allen, and Bob Skinner replaced him in June 1968. The Phillies, at .500 under Mauch, limped to a 76–86 finish under Skinner.

They plunged to 99 losses in 1969 and became so irrelevant in Philadelphia that they drew only 519,414 fans, the second lowest total in the league, ahead of only the expansion San Diego Padres. The other NL expansion team, the Montreal Expos, saved the Phillies from finishing last in the first year of the newly formed NL East.

The manager of that first Expos team? None other than Gene Mauch.

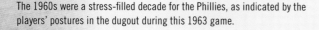

The 1960s were a stress-filled decade for the Phillies, as indicated by the players' postures in the dugout during this 1963 game.

1960

Highlights

January 11: The Phillies trade Richie Ashburn to the Cubs for John Buzhardt, Alvin Dark, and Jim Woods.

April 12: After losing 9–4 to Cincinnati on Opening Day, Phils manager Eddie Sawyer resigns. Minor league manager Gene Mauch, 34, will be hired to replace him.

May 14: For the third day in a row, the Phillies lose a 1–0 game, this time to Cincinnati.

July 21: Robin Roberts throws a one-hitter (an infield hit) at San Francisco.

August 18: The Phillies are no-hit by Milwaukee's Lew Burdette. Their sole baserunner is a hit batter.

September 16: Milwaukee's Warren Spahn no-hits the Phils.

NOTES

First baseman Pancho Herrera leads the team in homers (17) and RBI (71) but sets a league record for strikeouts (136).

Outfielder Ken Walters finishes second on the club in RBI with a mere 37, as the Phils rank last in the majors in runs scored (546) by a large margin.

Second baseman Tony Taylor hits a team-high .287 and ranks third in the NL in stolen bases (24).

Robin Roberts (12–16) is the only starter with more than eight wins.

MAUCH ERA BEGINS

Struggling Phillies Turn to Minor League Skipper

Ten years earlier, Eddie Sawyer managed the Phillies to the National League pennant. In 1960, he barely made it past Opening Day. After his team opened with a 9–4 loss to Cincinnati, he quit. "I'm 49 years old," Sawyer said, "and I want to live to be 50."

Managing the Phillies was no way to increase one's longevity. Andy Cohen led the club to a win over the Reds the following day, filling in until the club's permanent choice arrived the next day from the minors. His name was Gene Mauch, and he had earned a reputation as a combative skipper who would not settle for mediocrity.

Given the talent level of the 1960 Phillies, he would have to settle for something a little less than that—at least for the first year or two. With the fading Richie Ashburn dealt to the Cubs prior to the season, the Phillies hit a miserable .239, worst in the NL.

Philadelphia's pitching wasn't much better, but at least it was interesting. Turk Farrell, Jim Owens, and Jack Meyer became known as the "Dalton Gang." The moniker, coined by pitching coach Tom Ferrick, was in reference to the group's busy nightlife.

Sports Illustrated picked up on their shenanigans and published "The Dalton Gang Rides Again." The article contended, "Unlike some of the storied hell-raisers of old, the members of the Dalton Gang aren't really good enough to be so bad."

The highlight of the 59–95 slate was a one-hitter thrown by Robin Roberts on July 21 in San Francisco. Newly acquired third baseman Joe Morgan cleanly fielded a hot shot by Felipe Alou in the fifth inning, but the force knocked Morgan on his backside, and by the time he reached his feet he did not have a play. It was ruled an infield hit.

After the season, fans watched the cross-state rival Pirates defeat the Yankees in the World Series on Bill Mazeroski's fabled home run.

First baseman Pancho Herrera was Philly's top run producer in 1960 and finished runner-up for the NL Rookie of the Year Award.

TAYLOR MADE

Tony's a Bright Spot on Dismal Team

Tony Taylor spent his first spring training with the Phillies in 1961. The Cuban-born infielder had been acquired from the Cubs in May 1960 and endeared himself to his Phillies teammates with his willingness to apply his slick defensive skills at second base or third base. He would even play first base and the outfield later in his career, which culminated with more than 2,000 hits.

Taylor made the All-Star Game during his first season in Philadelphia. And as he fielded grounders and practiced throws during that '61 spring training, he looked around and said little about the relative lack of talent surrounding him. That was Taylor's way. He was a team player through and through. It made him a fan favorite for more than 15 years with the Phillies.

Tony Taylor was an infield fixture in Philadelphia for 15 seasons. Though lacking range, he was fast on the base paths, stealing home six times for the Phils.

It was also the first full season for manager Gene Mauch, who had taken over the club two days into the 1960 season. Mauch knew it was the beginning of a rebuilding project, and his first task was getting his players to think of themselves as Phillies, rather than ex-Cubs or ex-Giants.

To that end, the manager said the '61 team made progress. In the standings (47–107, last place) and on the stat sheets, that progress was not evident.

From the end of July until late August, the '61 Phillies lost 23 consecutive games, a losing streak that would stand as MLB's longest of the twentieth century. They hit .243, a staggering 12 points worse than anyone else in the National League. Their 4.61 ERA was also worst in the league. The '61 season was the last in a Phillies uniform for longtime ace Robin Roberts, who won just 1 of 11 decisions. He was sold to the Yankees after the season.

Taylor hit .250, worked hard, and welcomed new teammates into the fold. There was nowhere to go, he thought, but up.

Highlights

April 11: Robin Roberts ties the NL pitching record with his twelfth straight Opening Day start.

April 23: Art Mahaffey strikes out 17 Cubs hitters in a nine-inning shutout.

May 12: The Phillies lose their tenth game in a row.

July 13: The team suffers its 15th loss in 16 games.

August 20: With a 5–2 defeat at Milwaukee, the Phillies lose their twenty-third consecutive game, which sets and will remain a twentieth-century MLB record. Their record is 30–87.

August 25: The Phillies win their fourth straight game after their record losing streak.

September 12: Philly defeats the Dodgers 19–10 in L.A. as Don Demeter goes 4-for-5 with three homers and seven RBI.

NOTES

In just 106 games, outfielder/first baseman **Don Demeter** leads the club in homers (20) and RBI (68).

Art Mahaffey, the Phillies' sole All-Star, is the ace of the staff at 11–19, 4.10.

Robin Roberts goes 1–10 with a 5.85 ERA in his final season with the Phils.

Attendance plummets to 590,039, the lowest since the end of World War II.

1962

Highlights

March 10: The Phillies leave a hotel in Florida because it does not allow black players.

March 21: The team retires Robin Roberts' No. 36.

April 10: The season begins with two new NL teams, the New York Mets and Houston Colt .45s, and an expanded schedule (162 games).

September 3: The Phils defeat Houston for the seventeenth consecutive time.

September 27: The Phillies rout the Cubs 7–0 to complete an 18–5 run and clinch the team's first winning record in nine years.

NOTES

Third baseman Don Demeter leads the team in batting (.307), home runs (29), and RBI (107).

Outfielder Johnny Callison bats .300, cracks 23 homers, and belts a league-high 10 triples in an All-Star season.

All-Star Art Mahaffey (19–14) finishes fifth in the NL in wins.

Screwballer Jack Baldschun goes 12–7 with a 2.95 ERA in relief.

Gene Mauch is named NL Manager of the Year after winning 34 games more than the year before.

A year after going 19–35 in one-run games, **the Phils** go 26–14 in such contests.

EXPANSION, PROGRESS

Phillies Top .500 for First Time Since '53

Few teams were happier about the arrival of the New York Mets and Houston Colt .45s in 1962 than the Phillies. After all, the National League's expansion teams were expected to struggle, and they did. With the Mets winning only 25 percent of their games (40–120), the Phillies were no longer the team everyone kicked around.

In fact, it was time the Phillies did some kicking of their own. Thanks to 19 wins in a 24-game span down the stretch, they finished at 81–80 in the lengthened schedule, topping .500 for the first time in nine seasons.

General manager John Quinn and skipper Gene Mauch had begun rebuilding two years earlier by bringing in a group of young, untested players. The players took their lumps in '60 and '61, but they began to reach their potential during the summer of '62.

With the exception of 35-year-old first baseman Roy Sievers, every member of the Phillies' regular lineup was 27 or younger. Don Demeter, acquired from the Dodgers in a trade during the previous season, hit .307 with 29 homers and 107 RBI—the best offensive season by a Phil in a long while. Tony Gonzalez, 25, and 23-year-old Johnny Callison also swung hot bats.

The pitching staff was remarkably young. In fact, all but 24 of the team's 161 games were started by a pitcher 28 or younger. Three of the top four in the rotation were

Like Garry Maddox a decade later, Tony Gonzalez had great range in center field and occasionally batted over .300. In 1962, he ripped .302.

22-year-old Dennis Bennett, 23-year-old Jack Hamilton, and 24-year-old phenom Art Mahaffey, who went 19–14 with a 3.94 ERA and 177 strikeouts. They turned in mound performances that were a far cry from the ones that had plagued the Phillies over the previous few seasons.

For his efforts, Mauch was honored as NL Manager of the Year. "I don't know of a better strategist," said Bobby Wine, a rookie shortstop for the 1962 Phillies. "He knew the rules better than the umpires."

FANTASTIC FINISH

Late-Season Success Bodes Well for '64

History shows that the Los Angeles Dodgers swept the two-time defending champion New York Yankees in the 1963 World Series. Dodgers general manager Buzzy Bavasi had no doubt that the Philadelphia Phillies could have accomplished the same feat had they been representing the National League.

"Aw, we just ought to let the Phillies go [to the Series]," Bavasi told reporters before the Fall Classic. "They played the best ball in the league the last two months."

Bavasi and his powerful team witnessed the Phillies' dramatic improvement first-hand. In addition to being one of the hottest clubs in baseball down the stretch, Philadelphia took 11 of 18 decisions against the Dodgers in 1963. They outscored the World Series champs by a 78–54 margin in those contests.

It was a true team effort by Gene Mauch's club. In fact, only one member of the team—rookie pitcher Ray Culp—was selected for the All-Star Game. At the time, it did not seem like a slap in the face. The Phillies spent most of the first half of the season below the .500 mark. They played losing baseball in April, May, and June. Midway through the year, they were 40–44.

Then, sitting three games under .500 in mid-July, the Phillies caught fire. They won 43 of their final 71 outings, including eight wins in a row in August, to climb to fourth place in the standings with an 87–75 record. It was their best winning percentage in a decade.

The outfield of Tony Gonzalez, Wes Covington, and Johnny Callison was one of the best in baseball, and Mauch's team was much improved on the mound. Cal McLish, the veteran in the rotation, went 13–11 in his last full season in the majors, while the rookie Culp added a team-high 14 wins and Jack Baldschun was a savior in the bullpen.

The pieces were finally in place for the Phillies to return to pennant contention.

In the first half of his very first big-league season (1963), Ray Culp went 10–6 with a 2.40 ERA. He was selected as an NL All-Star.

Highlights

April 9: The Phillies open the season with Richie Ashburn as part of the broadcast team.

May 17: Don Nottebart of Houston no-hits the Phillies.

June 23: After homering off Phillies pitcher Dallas Green in New York, the Mets' Jimmy Piersall runs around the bases backwards.

July 9: Ray Culp, a 21-year-old rookie pitcher, is the team's sole representative at the All-Star Game.

August 19: The Phils beat the Mets 1–0 for their eighth consecutive win.

September 29: The Phillies close the season with five wins in six games after manager Gene Mauch overturned a food table in a clubhouse tirade.

NOTES

Johnny Callison leads the team in HRs (26), while **Don Demeter** is tops in RBI (83).

Outfielders Tony Gonzalez and **Wes Covington** hit .306 and .303, respectively.

Tony Taylor ranks sixth in the league in runs (102) and seventh in stolen bases (23).

Ray Culp (14–11, 2.97) and 37-year-old **Cal McLish** (13–11, 3.26) anchor the pitching staff.

Shortstop Bobby Wine wins a Gold Glove Award.

Highlights

June 4: Sandy Koufax of the Dodgers no-hits the Phillies, allowing just one walk.

June 21: Jim Bunning throws the first perfect game in the National League in 84 years, overpowering the Mets at Shea Stadium.

September 21: Two thousand fans greet the Phillies as they return from the West Coast road trip up 6½ games. They lose later this day—the first loss in a 10-game losing streak.

September 27: Johnny Callison cracks three homers in a 14–8 loss to Milwaukee.

September 29: The Cardinals defeat the Phils 4–2 for their seventh straight win and move into first place.

October 4: On Closing Day, the Phillies beat the Reds but the Cardinals defeat the Mets, giving St. Louis a one-game margin over Philadelphia and Cincinnati.

NOTES

Third baseman Dick Allen is named NL Rookie of the Year. He hits .318–29–91 with 38 doubles and league highs in triples (13), total bases (352), and runs (125).

Johnny Callison leads the team in home runs (31) and RBI (104).

Jim Bunning (19–8, 2.63) and **Chris Short** (17–9, 2.20) star on the hill.

IMPERFECT 10

September Swoon Amounts to Epic Collapse

The 1964 Philadelphia Phillies could have lost *nine* games in a row down the stretch and wound up in a playoff with a chance to win the National League pennant. They could have lost *eight* games in a row and earned the pennant outright, as they showed every indication of doing all season long.

Instead, the 1964 Philadelphia Phillies did the unthinkable. They solidified their place on history's dubious list of all-time collapses by losing the last 10 games of September to hand the pennant to St. Louis by a single game.

"The one thing we never got in '64," recalled the team's best pitcher, Jim Bunning, "was the one performance, the one big hit, the one huge pitching performance that could have stopped the bleeding."

And, oh, what bleeding there was. When the Phillies sprung out of their beds on

Manager Gene Mauch watches his team defeat the Reds in the last game of 1964. By then, the season was already lost.

Monday morning, September 21, they were in first place by 6½ games with just 12 games to play. The teams chasing them—the Cardinals and Reds—appeared on the brink of surrender. St. Louis was in the process of negotiating with new managers to take over for Johnny Keane the following spring, and Cincinnati was under the leadership of interim skipper Dick Sisler, the former Phillies hero.

With second-place Cincinnati in Philadelphia for a three-game series, just one Phillies' win might have slammed the door. The lead could have been 7½ with 11 games to play if not for a brazen, sixth-inning straight steal of home by the Reds' Chico Ruiz. It led to a 1–0 Cincinnati victory, and the Phillies' celebration would have to wait.

The Reds followed with 9–2 and 6–4 wins to sweep the set, and Philadelphia's collective collar grew tighter. Still, with Bunning opening a four-game home series against Milwaukee, there was no reason to panic—that is, until the Braves beat Bunning 5–3 and won a 12-inning game the next day. The Braves took the last two games of the series, too, sending the Phillies to St. Louis riding a seven-game losing streak and sitting in second place for the first time since July.

Bunning had pitched a Father's Day perfect game at Shea Stadium—the first NL perfect game since 1880—and was finishing up a 19–8 slate in his Phillies debut

Jim Bunning was 19–5 with a 2.25 ERA—and was perfect against the Mets on June 21 (seen here)—but the ace went 0–3 with a 10.95 ERA during the Phillies' crippling 10-game losing streak.

The Phillies seemed such a lock for the NL pennant that World Series tickets were printed. They were useless, except as collectors' items.

season. Teammate Chris Short went 17–9. Phillies manager Gene Mauch worked the duo hard with the pennant slipping away, pitching them on limited rest in hopes of ending the slump. Nothing seemed to work.

The Cardinals swept the three-game series in St. Louis by scores of 5–1, 4–2, and 8–5, stretching Philadelphia's misery to 10 straight games as the calendar turned to October. The Phillies finally snapped out of it with a pair of season-ending wins in Cincinnati, but the damage had been done. St. Louis won the pennant and added a World Series title in the coming days.

"It was like swimming in a long, long lake," Phillies utility man Cookie Rojas told *Sports Illustrated*, when asked about the slump. "And then you drown."

In the Wake of the Collapse

At the beginning of the Phillies' 1964 meltdown, fans were still buying "Go! Phillies Go!" bumper stickers and pins. By the end of the 10-game losing streak, they were left dazed and confused.

"We were shell-shocked," wrote fan Mike Walsh. "The 1964 season ingrained something insidious in my brain, something defeatist."

Needing a scapegoat, many pundits blamed manager Gene Mauch for the disaster. His pitching of Jim Bunning and Chris Short on short rest hadn't work, and the normally fiery skipper had become withdrawn as the streak wore on. "Everybody blamed Gene for what happened," Bunning said, "but to this day and until the day I die I will never blame him."

Much like the Kennedy assassination in 1963, many Philadelphia fans consider the collapse a "loss of innocence" moment. The year 1965 saw an escalation in the Vietnam War and the beginning of troubled times throughout the nation. The Phillies were so desperate to make amends in 1965 that they traded away prospects for veterans, but the result that year was a sixth-place finish. True healing was more than a decade away.

April 12: The Phillies shut out Houston 2–0 in the first game ever played at the Astrodome, MLB's first indoor stadium.

May 5: Jim Bunning cracks a homer and beats Warren Spahn of the Braves 1–0.

June 6: Johnny Callison belts three homers against the Cubs.

July 3: A fight between teammates Frank Thomas and Dick Allen results in Thomas being released and Allen being booed.

July 9: The Phillies improve to 45–38 and are just three games out of first place, but they won't get any closer.

September 10: Future Hall of Fame pitcher Fergie Jenkins debuts with the Phillies, throwing 4 1/3 innings of shutout ball.

October 2: Phillies pitcher Chris Short strikes out 18 Mets in 15 innings, but the game ends in a 0–0 tie after 18 innings.

NOTES

Johnny Callison tops 30 homers and 100 RBI for the second straight year while leading the team in both categories (32, 101).

First baseman **Dick "Dr. Strangeglove" Stuart** tallies 28 homers and 95 RBI, but his glovework leaves a lot to be desired.

Jim Bunning (19–9, 2.60) and **Chris Short** (18–11, 2.82) are the stars of the pitching staff again.

HANGOVER EFFECT
After the '64 Debacle, Phillies Fall to Sixth

Those fans who expected the Phillies to bounce back from their 1964 collapse might have been guilty of wishful thinking. The 1965 Phillies, except for a brief time, failed to contend for the National League pennant and finished a disappointing sixth.

Shoddy glovework plagued the Phillies, who committed 51 errors in their first 40 games. The poor fielding, along with a shaky bullpen, undermined the efforts of starters Jim Bunning and Chris Short. Bunning tallied 19 wins while racking up a workhorse 291 innings. Short won 18.

Ray Culp also pitched well, but the Phillies could not find an effective fourth starter. Art Mahaffey fell from 12 wins to two. Playboy left-hander Bo Belinsky, one of the team's major winter acquisitions, was also a bust. Belinsky, plagued by a broken rib that he kept secret until late May, won only four games.

The team's other heralded pickup also disappointed. Dick Stuart walloped 28 home runs but reached base only 28.7 percent of the time. "Dr. Strangeglove" contributed to the woeful defense, as he committed 17 errors at first base.

A five-tool outfielder, Johnny Callison topped 30 homers and 100 RBI in both 1964 (when he was runner-up for NL MVP) and 1965.

Team harmony was a concern. Frank Thomas allegedly uttered a racial slur at Richie Allen, prompting a fight. Thomas was sold to Houston, while Allen became a target of Phillies fans.

On a positive note, the Phillies had their share of contributors at the plate. Allen batted .302 with 20 home runs, while veteran Johnny Callison reached a career high with 32 home runs. The Phillies also received surprising support from Cookie Rojas, who batted a career-best .303 while playing seven different positions.

From June 9 through July 9, the Phillies went 22–10 to move within three games of the top spot, but they faded after that. They played their worst ball in late August, when they started a stretch that saw them lose 13 times in 17 games.

No Relief

New-Look Phils Done In by Poor Bullpen

High expectations ruled the day during the spring of 1966. General manager John Quinn had produced much of that optimism by acquiring two high-profile infielders, first baseman Bill White and shortstop Dick Groat, who were expected to improve the Phillies' inner defense. Even after Opening Day, Quinn continued to wheel and deal, picking up veteran Cubs pitchers Larry Jackson and Bob Buhl (in a deal that cost them future Hall of Fame pitcher Fergie Jenkins).

At the time, the moves looked good. Unfortunately, many of the plans were waylaid by continuing bullpen problems and a major injury to Dick Allen. On April 29, Allen dislocated his shoulder while sliding. The separation knocked him out of the lineup for four weeks.

Allen finished the season with 40 home runs, becoming the first Phillie to reach the milestone since Chuck Klein in 1930. White provided a fine left-handed complement to Allen; after a dreadful start, the ex-Cardinal hit at a .338 clip over nearly a three-month stretch.

The Phillies played some of their best ball in early August, when they put the finishing touches on a seven-game winning streak. But the team faded over the final six weeks, done in by an inexperienced bullpen. Promising rookie Darold Knowles, who pitched well over the first half, was among the relievers who struggled down the stretch.

Another concern was the decline of aging right fielder Johnny Callison, who belted only 11 home runs while slugging a mere .418.

The Phillies' late fade spoiled another terrific season from their top two starters. Chris Short became the first Phillies left-hander to win 20 games since Eppa Rixey in 1916. Jim Bunning was even better, finishing fourth in the league with a 2.41 ERA. Jackson also pitched well, but Buhl and Ray Culp were disappointments, as the Phillies settled for a fourth-place finish behind the pennant-winning Dodgers.

In 1966, a year when 29 homers was good enough for tenth best in the NL, Dick Allen blasted 40—despite a dislocated shoulder.

Highlights

April 3: The Mets sign college pitching phenom Tom Seaver after winning a lottery involving the Indians and Phillies.

April 21: In a five-player trade with the Cubs, the Phils acquire reliable starting pitcher Larry Jackson, 34, but give up budding Hall of Fame pitcher Fergie Jenkins.

June 8: With their ninth win in 10 games, the Phillies move to within 1½ games of first place. They will slowly drop further back.

July 12: Dick Allen and Jim Bunning represent the Phillies at the All-Star Game.

July 27: In the first-ever meeting of perfect-game pitchers, Sandy Koufax of L.A. and Bunning each leave after 11 innings of a 1–1 game, having struck out a combined 28.

NOTES

Dick Allen ranks fourth in the NL in batting (.317), third in RBI (110), second in homers (40), and first in slugging (.632).

First baseman Bill White, acquired along with funnyman catcher Bob Uecker in the offseason, knocks in 103 runs.

Jim Bunning goes 19–14 with a 2.41 ERA and ranks second in the league with 242 strikeouts.

Chris Short (20–10, 3.54) and **Larry Jackson** (15–13, 2.99) bolster the staff.

Highlights

May 10: Against Jim Bunning, Hank Aaron cracks the only inside-the-park home run of his career.

May 21: The Phillies outlast the Reds 2–1 in 18 innings, as Don Lock delivers a walk-off single.

August 24: Dick Allen severely cuts his hand while pushing a car and is lost for the season.

August 28: The Phillies win their eighth straight game to improve to 68–59, but they are still 11 games out of first.

September 15: The Dodgers need just two runs total to sweep a doubleheader from the Phillies.

September 27: Bunning suffers his fifth 1–0 loss on the season.

December 15: The Phillies trade Bunning to Pittsburgh for Woody Fryman, Don Money, Bill Laxton, and Harold Clem.

NOTES

Outfielder **Tony Gonzalez** finishes second in the NL in batting with a career-high mark of .339.

Dick Allen leads the team in homers (23) and RBI (77).

Starting **shortstop Bobby Wine** hits .190 and starting **catcher Clay Dalrymple** bats .172.

Jim Bunning goes 17–15, 2.29 and leads the league in strikeouts (253).

After three straight seasons surpassing one million, **attendance drops** to 828,888.

CAVALCADE OF AILMENTS

Team Tops .500 Despite Rash of Injuries

Injuries have often been used as a sorry excuse for the failures of disappointing teams. Yet, in the case of the 1967 Phillies, a rash of injuries turned out to be a genuine reason for a mediocre finish of 82–80, well short of the first-place Cardinals.

Four key players, in particular, fell prey to the injury bug: Bill White (torn Achilles tendon), Dick Groat (bad ankle), Dick Allen (cut hand), and Chris Short (knee and back problems).

PHILLIES PHACT

In May, voters in Philadelphia approve a $13 million bond issue to build a new stadium. The groundbreaking begins after the season.

The Phillies played sluggishly over the first half. After missing the first month of the season, White returned to hit only eight home runs. Short went down twice, first with the knee and later with a bad back. Without their second best power hitter and pitcher, the Phillies played sub-.500 ball for much of the summer. They did not hit their stride until August, when they put together a pair of eight-game winning streaks. In late August, the Phillies moved into second place, but they still trailed the Cardinals by 11 games.

Just as the Phillies made their run, they lost Allen on August 24, when he cut his hand while trying to push an old motor vehicle. Beginning August 29, the Phillies went only 14–21 the rest of the way.

There were bright spots, however. Outfielder Tony Gonzalez rapped .339 when the league average was only .249. Bobby Wine replaced Groat and formed a dazzling double play combination with Cookie Rojas. The Phillies pitchers also shined. Jim Bunning led the league in strikeouts and innings, and he would have won 20 games if not for five 1–0 defeats. Young Rick Wise moved up in the rotation and won 11 games.

The bullpen emerged as the most improved part of the team. Veterans Dick Hall and Turk Farrell arrived via trade and combined for 19 wins and 20 saves. After two seasons of bullpen failures, the Phillies finally found respectability in the late innings.

Phillies fans heckle the opposing Atlanta Braves—
or, based on their reputation, perhaps their own team—
at Connie Mack Stadium in the late 1960s.

1968

▸ 76-86   7th ◂

Highlights

May 2: In a loss to the Mets, Phillies reliever John Boozer is ejected for throwing a spitball.

June 1: With a 12–0 rout of the Reds, the Phillies improve to 22–20 and are one game out—the closest they will come to first place.

June 8: Dodgers pitcher Don Drysdale sets an MLB record for consecutive scoreless innings, but in the same game the Phillies score to end the record at 58 2/3.

June 14: While on leave to visit his sick daughter, manager Gene Mauch is fired. His 646 managerial wins are a Phillies record. Bob Skinner is named as his replacement.

July 29: Despite an upset stomach, Cincinnati's George Culver no-hits the Phillies.

NOTES

Dick Allen ranks second in the NL in homers (33) and fifth in RBI (90).

Second baseman Cookie Rojas is second on the team in RBI with a mere 48.

The Phillies score just 543 runs in "The Year of the Pitcher."

At 19–13, **Chris Short** is the ace of the staff.

Starters Larry Jackson and **Woody Fryman** win a combined 25 games with a 2.77 ERA.

Attendance plummets to 664,546.

CAN'T BUY A HIT

Phillies Bat .233 in "Year of the Pitcher"

Slim hopes greeted the Phillies in the spring of 1968, in part because of the offseason decision to trade staff ace Jim Bunning to the Pirates. Right from the outset, the Phillies played to expectations. They lost six of their first seven games before recovering to move into second place on two different occasions. And then, in mid-June, controversy struck.

Outfielder Dick Allen butted heads with manager Gene Mauch, a noted disciplinarian. Allen asked for a meeting with owner Bob Carpenter. Four days later, the Phillies fired Mauch, who had been at the helm for eight-plus seasons. They replaced him with Bob Skinner.

For the next month, the Phillies played well as Allen heated up. After the All-Star break, the Phillies strung together seven straight wins to move up to third place. But the team lacked staying power, with the offense being the biggest culprit. Allen cooled off, batting only .210 after the middle of July. Bill White finished at .239. Infielders Cookie Rojas, Roberto Pena, and Tony Taylor provided little punch at the plate.

Once Chris Short developed a curveball, he was devastating, going 83–54 for the Phillies from 1964 through 1968.

The outfielders also slumped. Johnny Callison batted .244 with 14 home runs. Tony Gonzalez, a .339 hitter in 1967, fell to .264. Completing the dreary picture, catchers Mike Ryan and Clay Dalrymple batted .179 and .207, respectively. During baseball's "Year of the Pitcher," the Phillies batted .233 as a team.

On the hill, Chris Short bounced back and delivered 19 wins. Larry Jackson pitched well, but in hard luck, posting a staff-best 2.77 ERA but with a losing record (13–17). After the top two, the rotation looked like a crapshoot. Woodie Fryman was 10–5, 1.61 on June 18 but finished 12–14, 2.78. Rick Wise had a disappointing season, amassing 15 losses and a 4.54 ERA. The bullpen regressed badly.

With so many disappointments, it was no surprise that the Phillies finished in a tie for seventh place, well behind the back-to-back champions from St. Louis.

Up in Smoke

Allen Controversy at Center of Troubling Season

For the second straight year, the Phillies changed managers in midseason. The revolving managerial door did not bode well for the 1969 Phillies, who suffered through their worst summer since losing 107 games in 1961. It was clearly a rebuilding year in Philadelphia as a number of young players took over for fading or injured veterans.

With the National League split into two divisions because of expansion, the realignment increased the Phillies' chances of winning the newly formed Eastern Division. But in reality, the Phillies were dealt a death blow early when Chris Short made only two starts before undergoing season-ending back surgery. Without Short, the Phillies lacked a No. 1 starter.

Rick Wise and young lefty Grant Jackson pitched credibly, winning 15 and 14 games, respectively, but they would have been better fits as second and third starters. Beyond Wise and Jackson, few on the staff pitched effectively.

Another problem occurred when Dick Allen clashed with manager Bob Skinner. In May, Allen showed up late to a game in St. Louis and was fined. On June 24, he failed to show up for a game at Shea Stadium and was suspended indefinitely. After returning, Allen told Skinner he would not play in an August exhibition game against minor league Reading. Skinner then resigned, upset with the front office for failing to back him. Owner Bob Carpenter denied the charge, while Skinner's departure forced the Phillies to promote coach George Myatt.

The Phillies lost their first five games under Myatt before responding with a remarkable string of four consecutive shutout wins. But the Phils soon reverted to losing form, suffering losing streaks of seven and five games.

Two young outfielders did emerge amid the failures. Center fielder Larry Hisle hit 20 home runs and stole 18 bases, while Johnny Briggs contributed 12 home runs and 64 walks in a part-time role. They were two of the few beacons in a long and difficult Philadelphia summer.

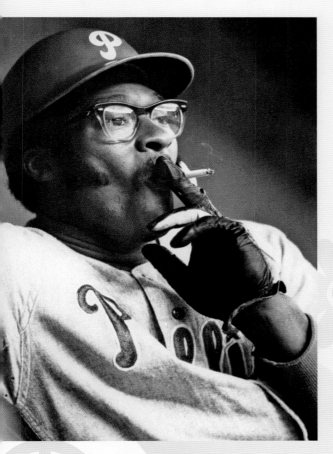

At times, Dick Allen took a lackadaisical attitude toward baseball. In 1969, he missed team flights, arrived late for games, and—after hearing he was suspended—went AWOL for two weeks.

Highlights

April 8: The season opens with four new MLB teams, including the Montreal Expos and San Diego Padres in the NL. The leagues are divided into East and West divisions, with the Phillies in the East.

April 17: Montreal's Bill Stoneman throws a no-hitter in Philadelphia.

June 10: The Phils lose their 12th game in 13 tries, dropping to 18–32.

June 24: The team suspends malcontent Dick Allen, who responds by disappearing for two weeks.

July 2: The Phillies blow out the Pirates 14–4 for their ninth win in a row.

August 3: With 10 runs in the fifth, the Reds outlast the Phillies 19–17.

August 7: Fed up with Allen's disruptions, manager Bob Skinner quits. Third-base coach George Myatt replaces him.

October 7: The Phillies trade Allen to St. Louis in a seven-player trade, getting Tim McCarver and Curt Flood in return. Flood, however, refuses to report.

NOTES

Playing just 118 games, **Dick Allen** leads the team in batting (.288), homers (32), and RBI (89).

Attendance falls to 519,414, the lowest mark since World War II.

THE 1960s RECORD BOOK

Team Leaders

Batting

1960: Tony Taylor, .287
1961: Tony Gonzalez, .277
1962: Don Demeter, .307
1963: Tony Gonzalez, .306
1964: Dick Allen, .318
1965: Cookie Rojas, .303
1966: Dick Allen, .317
1967: Tony Gonzalez, .339
1968: Tony Gonzalez, .264
1969: Dick Allen, .288

Home Runs

1960: Pancho Herrera, 17
1961: Don Demeter, 20
1962: Don Demeter, 29
1963: Johnny Callison, 26
1964: Johnny Callison, 31
1965: Johnny Callison, 32
1966: Dick Allen, 40
1967: Dick Allen, 23
1968: Dick Allen, 33
1969: Dick Allen, 32

RBI

1960: Pancho Herrera, 71
1961: Don Demeter, 68
1962: Don Demeter, 107
1963: Don Demeter, 83
1964: Johnny Callison, 104
1965: Johnny Callison, 101
1966: Dick Allen, 110
1967: Dick Allen, 77
1968: Dick Allen, 90
1969: Dick Allen, 89

Wins

1960: Robin Roberts, 12–16
1961: Art Mahaffey, 11–19
1962: Art Mahaffey, 19–14
1963: Ray Culp, 14–11
1964: Jim Bunning, 19–8
1965: Jim Bunning, 19–9
1966: Chris Short, 20–10
1967: Jim Bunning, 17–15
1968: Chris Short, 19–13
1969: Rick Wise, 15–13

ERA

1960: Gene Conley, 3.68
1961: Don Ferrarese, 3.76
1962: Dennis Bennett, 3.81
1963: Chris Short, 2.95
1964: Chris Short, 2.20
1965: Jim Bunning, 2.60
1966: Jim Bunning, 2.41
1967: Jim Bunning, 2.29
1968: Larry Jackson, 2.77
1969: Rick Wise, 3.23

Strikeouts

1960: Robin Roberts, 122
1961: Art Mahaffey, 158
1962: Art Mahaffey, 177
1963: Ray Culp, 176
1964: Jim Bunning, 219
1965: Jim Bunning, 268
1966: Jim Bunning, 252
1967: Jim Bunning, 253
1968: Chris Short, 202
1969: Grant Jackson, 180

Saves

1960: Turk Farrell, 11
1961: Frank Sullivan, 6
1962: Jack Baldschun, 13
1963: Jack Baldschun, 16
1964: Jack Baldschun, 21
1965: Gary Wagner, 7
1966: Darold Knowles, 13
1967: Turk Farrell, 12
1968: Turk Farrell, 12
1969: Bill Wilson, 6;
John Boozer, 6

NL Leaders

1962: Triples—
Johnny Callison, 10
1964: Runs—Dick Allen, 125;
Triples—Allen, 13
1965: Triples–Callison, 16
1966: Doubles—Callison, 40;
Shutouts—Jim Bunning, 5
1967: Strikeouts—Bunning, 253;
Shutouts—Bunning, 6

Bobbleheads, known as "nodders" at the time, were not nearly as common in the 1960s as they are today.

NL Awards

NL MVP Voting
1964: Johnny Callison, 2nd;
Dick Allen, 7th
1966: Dick Allen, 4th

NL Rookie of the Year Winners
1964: Dick Allen

Gold Glove Winners
1963: Bobby Wine, SS
1966: Bill White, 1B

NL All-Stars
1960: Tony Taylor, 2B
1961: Art Mahaffey, P
1962: Johnny Callison, OF;
Art Mahaffey, P

1962: Art Mahaffey, P
1963: Ray Culp, P
1964: Jim Bunning, P;
Johnny Callison, OF;
Chris Short, P
1965: Dick Allen, 3B;
Johnny Callison, OF;
Cookie Rojas, 2B
1966: Dick Allen, 3B;
Jim Bunning, P
1967: Dick Allen, 3B;
Chris Short, P
1968: Woodie Fryman, P
1969: Grant Jackson, P

The 32,000-plus fans who purchased a ticket to the Phillies–Mets game at New York's Shea Stadium on June 21, 1964, were treated to a perfect game by Jim Bunning.

This 1964 Phillies ball is signed by such notables as Pat Corrales, Rick Wise, Alex Johnson, and Tony Taylor.

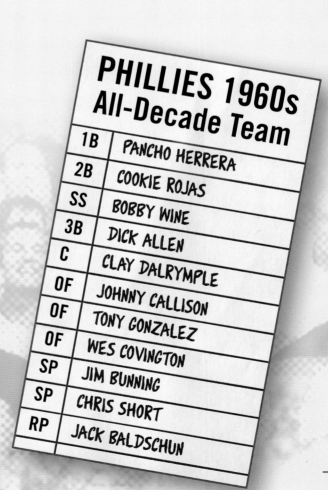

PHILLIES 1960s All-Decade Team

1B	PANCHO HERRERA
2B	COOKIE ROJAS
SS	BOBBY WINE
3B	DICK ALLEN
C	CLAY DALRYMPLE
OF	JOHNNY CALLISON
OF	TONY GONZALEZ
OF	WES COVINGTON
SP	JIM BUNNING
SP	CHRIS SHORT
RP	JACK BALDSCHUN

PLAYOFF BOUND

Steve Carlton, Mike Schmidt, and Greg "The Bull" Luzinski lead the Phillies to three division titles from 1976 to 1978.

The Phillies, who started the 1970s in a dilapidated ballpark in North Philadelphia, hadn't won a pennant in 20 years. They ended it in a modern, concrete bowl in South Philadelphia with three division titles to their credit and some of baseball's most prominent stars.

The final season at Connie Mack [...] 1938, ended with Oscar Gamble sin[...] October 1, 1970, with bedlam brea[...] looted the place, carrying off scrap[...] Few had seemed too interested in th[...] 700,000 fans showed up all season.

Yet somewhere in the rubble of t[...] finished 73–88, there was hope. New[...] with a scrawny rookie shortstop, Lar[...] position for 12 seasons. Bowa was th[...] added during the l[...]

In [...]

B[...]
Luzinsk[...]
who would become the greate[...]
The next season, the Phillie[...]
pitcher ever: Steve "Lefty" Carl[...]
Rick Wise, who had spun a no-[...]
in the game) in 1971. Carlton [...]
everything else in a Phillies ca[...]
Carlton won the 1972 [...]
for a team that won just 5[...]
ERA (1.97), and strikeo[...]
the staff throughout th[...]
After Danny Oza[...]
steadily nudged the [...]
rose to 71 in 1973, [...]

Steve Carlton fire[...]
helped lead the P[...]
but the club faile[...]

bookstores that are listed for sale in the Barnes & Noble Booksellers inventory management system.

Opened music CDs/DVDs/audio books may not b[...] returned, and can be exchanged only for the sam[...]

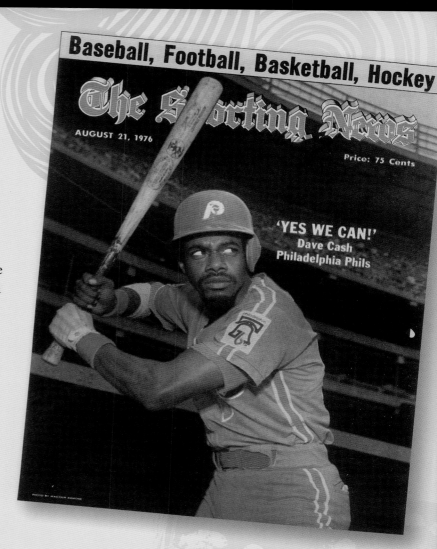

The Sporting News

AUGUST 21, 1976

Price: 75 Cents

'YES WE CAN!'
Dave Cash
Philadelphia Phils

season of 1976, when the Phillies celebrated the bicentennial with the first 100-win season in franchise history and an NL East title. Second baseman Dave Cash coined "Yes We Can" as the team's rallying cry, many years before it would pop up in politics. But the Phillies' run fizzled in the National League Championship Series when they were swept in three by the Cincinnati Reds.

More key components had joined the team by then, including outfielder Garry Maddox and pitchers Larry Christenson, Tug McGraw, and Ron Reed. The 1977 squad matched the previous year's total for victories (101), and Carlton captured another Cy Young Award while Schmidt and Luzinski teamed for 77 home runs. But the Los Angeles Dodgers defeated the Phillies in four games in a bitter playoff series. The Dodgers prevailed in four again in the 1978 NLCS, helped by Maddox's dropped fly ball in the finale in Los Angeles.

After three playoff defeats in three seasons, the Phillies signed the Reds' Pete Rose, who brought two World Series rings, more than 3,000 hits, and plenty of swagger to the Vet. They also traded for second baseman Manny Trillo, giving the Phillies a dynamic right side of the infield to go with Bowa and Schmidt on the left side.

The 1979 season featured a managerial change, from Danny Ozark to Dallas Green, and the Phillies slipped to fourth place. But all the pieces were in place for a glorious season to come.

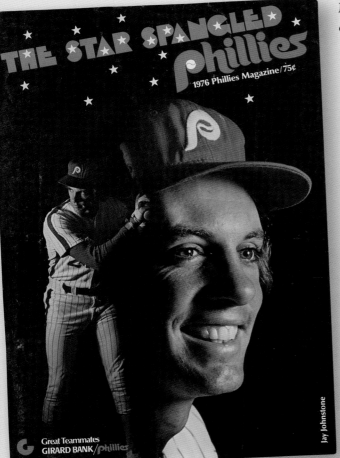

THE STAR SPANGLED Phillies
1976 Phillies Magazine/75¢

Jay Johnstone

Great Teammates
GIRARD BANK/phillies

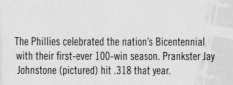

The Phillies celebrated the nation's Bicentennial with their first-ever 100-win season. Prankster Jay Johnstone (pictured) hit .318 that year.

exceptions:
A store credit for the purchase price will be issued (
for purchases made by check less than 7 days prior to
the date of return, (ii) when a gift receipt is presented
within 60 days of purchase, (iii) for textbooks, or (iv) for
products purchased at Barnes & Noble Colleg

1970

▶ 73-88   5th ◀

Highlights

April 7: The Phillies begin the season with a new manager, promoting minor league skipper Frank Lucchesi. They also have new uniforms. The Phillies had hoped to move into Veterans Stadium in 1970, but instead they play their final season in Connie Mack Stadium.

May 2: Phillies catchers Tim McCarver and Mike Ryan break their hands in the same inning.

May 18: The Phils lose their tenth game in a row to fall to 13–22. They will not again reach .500.

July 20: Bill Singer of the Dodgers no-hits the Phillies in L.A.

August 11: Jim Bunning, back with the Phils, becomes the first pitcher since Cy Young to win 100 games in both leagues.

October 1: A crowd of 31,822 attends the last game at Connie Mack Stadium. Many fans attempt to rip apart the seats to take home as souvenirs. The Phillies win the game against Montreal in the bottom of the tenth.

NOTES

First baseman **Deron Johnson** spearheads the NL's worst offense with 27 homers and 93 RBI.

Rick Wise (13–14) leads the staff in wins.

NOT BAD, CONSIDERING . . .

Phils Respectable Despite Injury Epidemic

A brand new skipper and some bright young talent gave the Phillies hope heading into the 1970 season. Unfortunately, an avalanche of injuries undermined any chance of the Phillies being competitive in the National League East.

The events of May 2 epitomized the extreme nature of the injury bug. In the very same inning, both of the Phillies' catchers—Tim McCarver and Mike Ryan—suffered broken bones in their hands. McCarver would miss four months while Ryan would not return until July. New manager Frank Lucchesi had to rely on minor league catchers Del Bates and Mike Compton, and when they suffered injuries, the team resorted to activating coach Doc Edwards.

Promising third baseman Don Money was also sidelined. With his average at .356, Money went down on May 21, taking a bad hop squarely in the eye. Other than first baseman Deron Johnson and shortstop Larry Bowa, no one played in more than 126 games.

Two of the Phillies' most highly touted players ended up as disappointments. Center fielder Larry Hisle and second baseman Denny Doyle barely hit above .200. With Richie Allen banished via trade, the Phillies finished dead last in the NL in runs scored.

The Phillies' improved pitching accounted for the team's increase in wins from 63 to 73. Rick Wise, Jim Bunning, and Woodie Fryman pitched decently. But Chris Short continued to show the effects of back trouble, while Grant Jackson's ERA ballooned to 5.29.

The staff's true strength could be found in the bullpen. Two trade acquisitions pitched brilliantly. Left-hander Joe Hoerner posted a 2.65 ERA and nine saves. Workhorse right-hander Dick Selma emerged as the top fireman, as he led the entire staff with 153 strikeouts while pitching exclusively in relief and logging 22 saves.

All in all, Lucchesi impressed observers with his patience and leadership, but injuries and inexperience doomed the Phillies to a fifth-place finish, well behind the division-winning Pirates.

Tony Taylor was traded to Detroit early in the 1971 season, but in 1970 the 34-year-old utilityman was the Phillies' only regular to hit over .300. He also scored a team-high 74 runs.

A New Beginning

Say Hello to Kalas, Schmidt, and the Vet

The 1971 season started with pomp and circumstance but ended in frustration, as the rebuilding Phillies actually regressed from their injury-filled 1970 performance.

The Phillies opened the home season by christening Veterans Stadium, the replacement for decrepit Connie Mack Stadium, while new Phillies broadcaster Harry Kalas served as the master of ceremonies. After the mirth of unveiling the artificial-turf stadium, the Phillies went into a freefall for most of the summer. They played especially poorly down the stretch, losing 29 of their last 43 games to finish last in a division won by the Pittsburgh Pirates.

The Phillies' hitting and pitching both failed badly. The offense finished 11th out of 12 teams in both runs scored and batting average. The pitching was only slightly better, ranking ninth in the National League. Jim Bunning struggled in his final season, Chris Short looked like a shell of his former self, and relief ace Dick Selma missed most of the season because of injury.

Only a few players qualified as bright spots, rewarding the franchise-record 1.5 million fans who ventured into Veterans Stadium. Deron Johnson hit a career-high 34 home runs. Willie Montanez clubbed 30 long balls, setting a record for a Phillies rookie. Larry Bowa set a major league record for the highest fielding percentage by a shortstop playing in at least 150 games (.987). And Rick Wise emerged as an ace by winning 17 games, including a no-hitter in which he belted two home runs.

Yet, the highlight of the season might have occurred well away from league play. In June, the Phillies selected a young shortstop named Mike Schmidt with their second-round choice in the annual draft. Schmidt made his professional debut in a June 17 exhibition game between the Phillies and minor league Reading. Playing for the Phils, Schmidt smacked a game-winning home run, a harbinger of many good things to come.

During his no-hit game in 1971, Rick Wise walked one Reds batter, fanned three, went 2-for-4 with two homers, and knocked in three runs in his 4–0 victory.

Highlights

April 10: The Phillies christen Veterans Stadium with a 4–1 victory over Montreal. A franchise-record 55,352 attend the game. Harry Kalas is the new voice in the broadcast booth.

May 15: With its eighth loss in nine games, the team drops to 9–22, 12 games out—a hole they won't be able to climb out of.

June 23: Phillies pitcher Rick Wise fires a no-hitter and belts two home runs—an achievement unprecedented in baseball history—in a 4–0 triumph over the Reds.

July 31: The Phillies defeat the Cardinals 5–4 in 16 innings on a walk-off walk.

August 28: Rick Wise, who threw a no-hitter and hit two home runs on June 23, cracks two homers against San Francisco, including a grand slam.

NOTES

Rookie Willie Montanez knocks 30 home runs and drives in a team-high 99 runs.

First baseman Deron Johnson slugs 34 homers, fourth most in the NL.

Rick Wise is the ace of the staff, going 17–14 with a 2.88 ERA. He also belts six homers from the plate, tied for fifth most on the team.

The Phillies set a team attendance record with 1,511,223 fans.

The Vet

In an era when striped bellbottom slacks were considered the height of fashion, Veterans Stadium—an oval, nondescript multipurpose facility—opened its doors. In the previous 84 years, the Phillies had played at Baker Bowl (1887–1938) and Connie Mack Stadium (1938–70). Those long-ago, state-of-the-art parks may have become rundown in their later years, but one thing you knew while sitting in either of them was that you were in Philadelphia.

By the time Veterans Stadium was completed at a cost of some $50 million, it was nearly indistinguishable from its concrete brethren built in the preceding few years in St. Louis, San Diego, Cincinnati, and Pittsburgh. The Vet wasn't in downtown; instead, it was part of a multi-stadium complex that included JFK Stadium and the Spectrum.

It was also late. When ground was broken in 1967, the Phillies expected to play at the new park in 1970, but cost overruns and weather delays meant that broadcaster Harry Kalas didn't call the inaugural Phillies game at the Vet until April 10, 1971. Carrying a radio—and binoculars—wasn't a bad idea if you had tickets in the uppermost 700 level, because those seats were miles from the action. The main reason for that was a block of luxury suites.

The acoustics of this large, enclosed stadium made it hard for players on the field to hear one another when the fans were raucous and the Vet was near capacity—a number that fluctuated between 56,000 when the place opened to nearly 66,000 in the 1980s. The noise mostly wreaked havoc on opponents during Eagles games, but a few visiting pitchers were rattled, notably Dodger Burt Hooton during a 1977 NLCS meltdown.

With notoriously bad AstroTurf, football yard markers that wouldn't fade in time for baseball games, and a rowdy enough reputation that a municipal court was set up in the stadium's basement during Eagles games in 1998, the Vet was far from perfect. However, it was where the Phillies saw their first real run of success. The Phillies won three straight division titles at the Vet from 1976 to 1978, and they won the franchise's first World Series in front of 65,838 on October 21, 1980. The Phillies also claimed pennants in 1983 and 1993 before playing their final game there in 2003. The stadium was imploded the following spring to become a parking lot for Citizens Bank Park.

PHILADELPHIA VETERANS STADIUM

PHILADELPHIA, PENNSYLVANIA

A One-Man Band

Carlton Wins 27 for Last-Place Team

The 1972 season represented rock-bottom for the Phillies. Only the performance of a newly acquired left-hander saved a 97-loss season from being an unmitigated catastrophe.

The Phillies actually catapulted to a good start, winning 13 of their first 20 games. From there, the team sputtered and then crashed. During their worst stretch, the Phillies lost 43 of 55 games, a string of ineptitude that cost popular manager Frank Lucchesi his job. He was replaced by Paul Owens, who had actually started the season as farm director before being promoted to general manager.

The reasons for the Phillies' collapse were numerous. Bothered by injury, Deron Johnson fell off his career-best performance of 1971. Willie Montanez suffered through a dreadful sophomore slump both at the plate and in center field. Heralded outfield prospect Roger Freed simply couldn't hit. Except for one pitcher, no full-time starter put up an ERA lower than 4.26. And onetime fireman extraordinaire Dick Selma struggled in his comeback from an injury-riddled 1971.

> **PHILLIES PHACT**
>
> In five starts from July 23 to August 9, Steve Carlton throws four shutouts and wins the other game 4–1—allowing only an unearned run.

All of these failures would have made the season unbearable—except for the presence of southpaw Steve Carlton.

Carlton actually began in spring training as a Cardinals holdout before being acquired in a straight-up swap for fellow holdout Rick Wise. With his crisp fastball and devastating slider, Carlton carved up National League batters. He led the league in ERA, innings pitched, complete games, strikeouts, and victories. With 27 of the team's 59 triumphs, Carlton accounted for 45.8 percent of the Phillies' wins. In so doing, he broke the MLB record of 44.6 percent set by Jack Chesbro of the 1904 New York Highlanders.

Though Carlton couldn't prevent the Phillies from remaining in the cellar, he made a major impact at the gate. In games in which he started, the Phillies drew an average of roughly 5,500 additional fans per game at Veterans Stadium. Every fourth game, Carlton made the Phillies worth watching.

The acquisition of Steve Carlton in 1972 was a watershed moment for the Phillies franchise, which would reach the playoffs in six seasons with Lefty on the hill.

STEVE CARLTON

TRADED

Highlights

February 25: The Phillies and Cardinals swap aces: Rick Wise for Steve Carlton.

April 16: Burt Hooton of the Cubs no-hits the Phils.

April 25: Carlton throws a one-hit shutout against the Giants, fanning 14 and walking one.

May 16: Rookie outfielder Greg Luzinski blasts a 500-foot home run off the Liberty Bell in center field at Veterans Stadium.

July 10: Former farm director Paul Owens, who replaced John Quinn as GM on June 3, adds managerial duties by replacing Frank Lucchesi.

August 17: Carlton wins his fifteenth straight decision to go 20–6.

September 12: Rookie third baseman Mike Schmidt debuts with the Phillies, striking out in his first at-bat.

NOTES

Greg Luzinski leads the team in batting, home runs, and RBI (.281–18–68).

Willie Montanez tops the league in doubles (39).

Shortstop Larry Bowa leads the NL in triples (13) and takes home a Gold Glove Award.

Steve Carlton leads the NL in wins (27–10), ERA (1.97), strikeouts (310), and complete games (30). He is the unanimous Cy Young Award winner.

Highlights

April 6: The Phillies open the season with new manager Danny Ozark.

April 17: Rookie pitcher Dick Ruthven, from Fresno St., debuts with the Phillies without ever having played in the minors.

May 4: The Phillies outlast the Braves 5–4 in 20 innings, winning on a game-ending sacrifice fly.

June 23: Phils pitcher Ken Brett sets an MLB record by homering in four consecutive starts.

July 21: Brett gives up Hank Aaron's 700th home run.

July 24: Pitcher Wayne Twitchell is the team's sole All-Star representative.

August 21: Despite a 58–66 record, the Phillies are only 4 ½ games out of first. They will not get any closer.

NOTES

Greg Luzinski leads the team in HRs (29) and RBI (97).

Outfielder Bill Robinson hits .288–25–65, placing second on the team in each category.

Mike Schmidt hits .196 and strikes out 136 times.

Steve Carlton slumps to 13–20 and 3.90. He leads the league in complete games (18) but also losses.

Wayne Twitchell (13–9, 2.50), **Ken Brett** (13–9), and **Jim Lonborg** (13–16) tie Carlton for the team high in wins.

SLIVERS OF HOPE

Several Newcomers Deliver the Goods

For the third straight season, the Phillies finished dead last, but they showed significant improvement over their dreadful record of 1972, thanks in part to improved depth in their rotation.

Left-hander Ken Brett and tall right-hander Wayne Twitchell spent the early weeks of 1973 in the bullpen before emerging as big-time starters. The youngsters each won 13 games, with Twitchell sporting a 2.50 ERA. Veteran Jim Lonborg, acquired with Brett in a winter blockbuster with Milwaukee, also tallied 13 wins.

Unfortunately, staff ace Steve Carlton did not live up to expectations. Bothered by a spring training illness, Carlton ended up losing 20 games against only 13 victories. The falloff of the reigning Cy Young winner hurt the Phillies badly in a year in which the Mets won the division with a record of only 82–79. "Turn Carlton's record around," player personnel director Paul Owens told *The Sporting News*, "and we have a shot at winning the pennant.

The season was marred by several conflicts between new manager Danny Ozark and his players. Rookie third baseman Mike Schmidt fell into Ozark's doghouse and struggled to a sub-.200 batting average. Valuable utility man Cesar Tovar also bristled under the manager and vowed that he would never play for him again.

Two unproven outfielders did thrive under Ozark. Left fielder Greg Luzinski, a 22-year-old rookie, led the club with 29 home runs and 97 RBI. Right fielder Bill Robinson suddenly discovered that he could hit at age 30; he wound up batting .288 with 25 home runs.

The Phillies also became a strong defensive team up the middle. Catcher Bob Boone handled the pitching staff deftly and earned consideration for Rookie of the Year. Larry Bowa and Denny Doyle formed a fine double play combination, while Del Unser played brilliantly in center field. Their play, along with that of the bookend outfielders, provided glimmers of hope amid another sixth-place finish.

Though considered a rising star after his All-Star 1973 season, the 6-foot-6 Wayne Twitchell never again won more than six games in a season.

Yes, We Can

New-Attitude Phils Become a Contender

As Mike Schmidt improved, so did the Phillies in 1974. No longer a last-place team, the Phils contended for much of the summer before settling for third place. At one point, the Phillies stood in first place for over a month, thanks in large part to Schmidt. Formerly a raw rookie who had batted below .200, Schmidt emerged as one of the National League's new stars. He led all major-leaguers with 36 home runs and flirted with the .300 mark before falling just short.

In pacing the offense, Schmidt received help from first baseman Willie Montanez, who batted .300 for the first time in his career, and spirited new second baseman Dave Cash, who gave the team the catch phrase "Yes, We Can." Acquired from Pittsburgh in a deal for Ken Brett, the free-swinging Cash collected 206 hits and batted .300 on the nose.

The Phillies' offense would have been even more explosive if not for a midseason injury to Greg Luzinski, their leading power man of 1973. "The Bull" hurt his knee in early June, underwent surgery, and finished with a .394 slugging percentage. "That hurt us more than anything," Schmidt told *The Sporting News*. "With 'The Bull' in there, we go all the way."

Still, the Phillies faced other problems, including a disappointing pitching staff. Wayne Twitchell missed the first six weeks of the season and never regained his 1973 touch. Steve Carlton, though much improved, went six weeks without a win. Young right-hander Dick Ruthven pitched erratically. Only Jim Lonborg, a 17-game winner, pitched up to expectation.

In the meantime, the bullpen flopped badly. Gene Garber and veteran left-hander Pete Richert were the only standout relievers, but Richert's season and career came to an end due to health issues.

Even without a reliable bullpen, the '74 Phillies managed to put on a good show, fielding their best team since 1967.

Booed often during his .196 rookie season of 1973, Mike Schmidt responded with a home run title in 1974. He also led the Phils with 108 runs and 116 RBI.

Highlights

May 20: The Phillies win to go 21–17 and move into first place, where they will remain until late June.

June 10: Mike Schmidt hits a fly ball off a speaker at the Astrodome, settling for a single instead of a home run.

July 12: Though just 44–42, the Phils again move into first place. They will stay in the top spot through August 2.

July 23: Four Phillies are on the NL All-Star team: Steve Carlton, Schmidt, Larry Bowa, and second baseman Dave Cash.

August 25: The Phillies are shut out in three straight games in Houston, dropping them to three games out of first place.

September 13: St. Louis beats the Phils 7–3 in 17 innings.

September 19: The Phillies lose their sixth straight game, a streak that takes them out of contention.

NOTES

Mike Schmidt leads the league in home runs (36) and ranks second in RBI (116).

Willie Montanez rips .304, and **Dave Cash** hits .300.

Steve Carlton rebounds with a 16–13 record and an NL-best 240 strikeouts.

Jim Lonborg finishes 17–13 with a 3.21 ERA.

The Phillies set a new team attendance record (1,808,648).

Highlights

May 4: The Phillies trade outfielder Willie Montanez to the Giants for outfielder Garry Maddox.

May 7: The Phils trade for prodigal son Richie Allen, now known as Dick Allen.

May 18: The Phillies defeat the Braves for the seventh straight victory.

August 18: With a win in Atlanta, the Phillies (67–55) move into first place for the first time all season. They will drop out of first for good the next day.

NOTES

Mike Schmidt repeats as NL home run champion (38), steals 29 bases, and strikes out 180 times.

Greg Luzinski hits .300, finishes third in the NL with 34 homers, and drives in a league-best 120 runs.

Slick-fielding keystone mates **Dave Cash** and **Larry Bowa** each hit .305.

Colorful outfielder **Jay Johnstone** bats .329.

Steve Carlton (15–14, 3.56 ERA) remains the staff ace.

Gene Garber saves 14 games, wins 10, and appears in an NL-high 71 games.

After the season, longtime Phillies broadcaster **Byrum Saam** retires.

LOADING UP

Well-Stocked Phillies Rise to Second Place

With young stars reaching lofty heights and an old hero returning to town, the 1975 Phillies made a strong run toward the top spot in the National League East. Unfortunately, they had to settle for a solid second-place finish behind the rival Pirates.

On August 18, the Phillies defeated the Braves to move into a first-place tie with the favored Bucs. With six weeks to go in the regular season, the Phillies seemed ready to claim their first postseason berth since 1950. But they lost their next game, the Pirates won theirs, and the Phils never again sniffed first place.

The Phillies did make it fun for a while, particularly when it came to hitting. Three of their star players led the league in key categories: Mike Schmidt with 38 home runs, Greg Luzinski with 120 RBI, and Dave Cash with 213 hits.

Even the lesser lights in the lineup contributed, including one returning veteran and a pair of newcomers who joined the team after Opening Day. Veteran shortstop Larry Bowa, better known for his fielding, batted a career-best .305. Johnny Oates, acquired in a large deal with Atlanta, overtook Bob Boone for the No. 1 catching job and hit .286. And Garry Maddox, obtained from San Francisco, hit surprisingly well while playing the best center field the Phillies had seen since the days of Richie Ashburn.

The Phillies' diverse offense, which featured three players with more than 20 stolen bases, would have been even more dynamic if not for the struggles of a returning star. Dick Allen, known as Richie when he last played in Philadelphia, rejoined the franchise in a May blockbuster trade with the Braves. Some observers felt that the acquisition of Allen would translate into a division title. Allen singled in his first at-bat, fueling the optimism of the prognosticators, but the excitement soon wore off as he finished with a .233 average and only 12 home runs. Nevertheless, Allen did provide some valuable veteran leadership, in contrast to his controversial manner of the 1960s.

The biggest obstacle for the Phillies could be found on the mound. Youngsters Tom Underwood and Larry Christenson showed legitimate promise, but two veterans struggled. Ace Steve Carlton, plagued by a sore elbow, tried to throw with reduced velocity

Larry Bowa holds the twentieth-century NL record for career fielding percentage by a shortstop (.980). His only .300 season at the plate came in 1975.

GREG LUZINSKI

The Bull

The middle of the Phillies' lineup in the 1970s made many an opponent mutter, "Bull Schmidt." The heart of the order featured Mike Schmidt followed by Greg "The Bull" Luzinski, and pitchers were in trouble either way.

A first-round pick in 1968, Luzinski became the Phillies' left fielder in 1972 at age 21, though the 255-pound Bull was often removed in late innings for defense. In 1975, he led the National League with 120 RBI and finished second to Joe Morgan in NL MVP voting. An All-Star four straight years (1975–78), Luzinski knocked in 130 and hit a career-best .309 in '77, again placing second in MVP balloting to a Red, George Foster.

Luzinski tumbled to .228 in 1980, but he came alive in the NLCS to help the Phillies win the pennant. He later thrived as a designated hitter in his native Chicago, hitting 32 homers in 1983 to help the White Sox claim their first American League West crown. He's again a rather conspicuous presence in Philly, operating Bull's BBQ at Citizens Bank Park.

and lacked his usual dominance. Top right-hander Jim Lonborg missed the final month of the season after attempting to pitch with an injured groin.

While the starting rotation was racked by injury, the bullpen thrived. After enduring the previous summer without a reliable fireman, the Phillies had a trio of effective relievers in side-arming Gene Garber and left-handers Tug McGraw and Tom Hilgendorf. Garber and McGraw combined to win 19 games and save 28 others.

The bullpen represented the greatest improvement over 1974, helping the Phillies play better than .500 for the first time since 1967. With just a little more starting pitching, they would have qualified for the first League Championship Series in franchise history.

With the infamous AMC Pacer as their official car, it's perhaps not surprising that the Phillies ran out of gas in late summer.

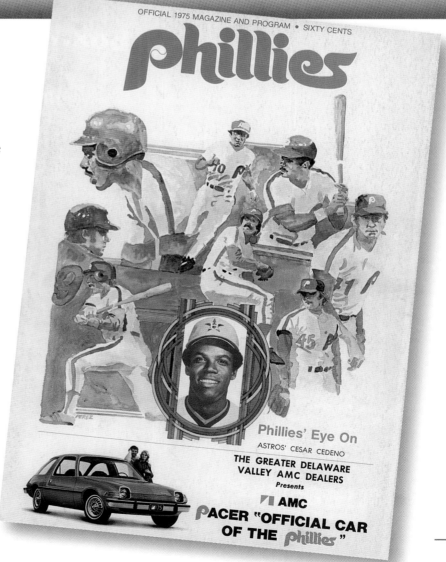

▶ 101-61   1st ◀

Highlights

April 17: Mike Schmidt socks four home runs as the Phillies win in Chicago 18–16 in 10 innings.

May 1: Schmidt strokes his twelfth homer in the season's fifteenth game.

July 4: The Phillies win on the nation's 200th birthday to go 52–21.

July 13: Philadelphia hosts the All-Star Game, with five Phils on the team.

August 24: The Phillies beat Atlanta 14–3 to go 82–41. They take a 15½ game lead in the NL East.

September 26: With a 4–1 win over Montreal, the Phils clinch the NL East.

October 12: After beating Philly 6–3 in Game One of the NLCS and 6–2 in Game Two, the Reds score three in the bottom of the ninth of Game Three to win 7–6 and clinch the series.

NOTES

Mike Schmidt leads the league in home runs (38).

Garry Maddox, Jay Johnstone, and **Greg Luzinski** all hit over .300.

Steve Carlton (20–7) and **Jim Lonborg** (18–10) star on a staff that posts a 3.08 team ERA.

The Phillies set franchise records for wins (101) and attendance (2,480,150).

Danny Ozark is named Manager of the Year by *The Sporting News.*

200 Years, 101 Wins

Bicentennial Culminates in Playoff Trip

It was fitting that in the year of the bicentennial, the citizens of Philadelphia—the onetime capital of the country—watched the Phillies claim their first postseason berth in 26 years.

On their way to winning at team-record 101 games, so many Phillies contributed that it was hard to keep track of all of them. Offensively, Mike Schmidt formed the cornerstone, smashing 38 home runs to lead the league for the third straight season. His season peaked on April 17, when he clubbed four home runs in a rollicking 18–16 win over the Cubs. Greg Luzinski played the role of solid second fiddle, crushing 21 home runs while batting .304.

While the power numbers of Schmidt and Luzinski were expected, the hitting of Garry Maddox might have been the season's biggest surprise. Known for his brilliant center-field play, Maddox not only blanketed the outfield but also hit a robust .330. He even contended for the batting title, finishing third, a mere nine points behind batting champion Bill Madlock.

The role players did their jobs, too. Bob Boone regained the starting catching job and made the National League All-Star team. Journeyman Jay Johnstone graduated from a platoon role to more regular duty in right field and hit a robust .318. Defensively, the Phillies might have had the strongest up-the-middle combination in the league. Not only did Maddox win his second Gold Glove, but Dave Cash and Larry Bowa sealed the middle of the infield, and Boone was a rock behind the plate.

The pitching staff also shined. Steve Carlton posted his best numbers since his Cy Young season of 1972, winning 20 games with a 3.13 ERA. Jim Lonborg bounced back from an injury-riddled season to win 18 games. Jim Kaat, who joined the Phillies in an offseason trade, emerged as a solid No. 3 starter.

In 1976, manager Danny Ozark led the Phillies to their first-ever NLCS, where they were swept in three games by Cincinnati's "Big Red Machine."

A beleaguered Jim Lonborg is removed from Game Two of the NLCS despite holding a 2–1 lead in the sixth inning. The Phillies would go on to lose 6–2.

The bullpen benefited from the acquisition of tall right-hander Ron Reed. Teamed with holdovers Tug McGraw and Gene Garber, Reed gave the Phillies a third effective fireman. Brilliantly mixing and matching his best relievers, Ozark coaxed successful seasons from his three bullpen aces, giving the opposition a variety of looks in the late innings.

Except for two faltering stretches, the Phillies dominated the competition. They lost eight consecutive games in late August and early September and then lost five in a row to the Pirates spread over two series, as they watched their 15-game lead fall to three. But with the season on the brink, the Phillies responded by winning 13 of their last 16 to conclude the year with a nine-game edge over the Bucs.

As well as the Phillies finished, the days leading up to the National League Championship Series provided a dose of controversy. A disgruntled Dick Allen became upset when he learned that the Phillies would not include veteran utility man Tony Taylor on the postseason roster. At one point, Allen left the team during a road trip, but he ultimately changed his mind about participating in the playoffs.

Even with Allen, the Phillies struggled in the NLCS. They were flattened by Cincinnati's "Big Red Machine," which swept the series in three straight. The Reds won the finale 7–6 when George Foster and Johnny Bench opened the bottom of the ninth with home runs off Reed to tie the score and Ken Griffey Sr. cracked a bases-loaded single off Tom Underwood to win it. Philly's few bright spots included the hitting of Johnstone, who collected seven hits in nine at-bats for a .778 average.

The playoff sweep notwithstanding, the Phillies had every reason to feel good about 1976. Not only did they erase the bad memories of the 1964 collapse, but they just might have put up the best season to date in the long history of the franchise.

The City of Brotherly Love hosted the All-Star Game in the Bicentennial year, and six Phillies saw action at the Midsummer Classic. President Gerald Ford threw out the first pitch before the game.

Highlights

April 9: Free agency is now part of baseball, and the Phillies open the season having lost one free agent (Dave Cash) and added one (infielder Richie Hebner).

August 5: In the midst of a 13-game winning streak, the Phillies moved into first place for the first time all season. They will not relinquish the top spot.

October 4: The Phils score two runs in the top of the ninth to defeat L.A. in Game One of the NLCS.

October 7: After cruising in Game Two 7–1, the Dodgers ride a wave of luck to score three in the top of the ninth of Game Three for a 6–5 victory.

October 4: With a complete game from Tommy John, L.A. clinches the series with a 4–1 victory in Game Four.

NOTES

Greg Luzinski, second in the NL MVP voting, hits .309–39–130.

Mike Schmidt wallops 38 homers.

Half-time players **Bake McBride, Tim McCarver,** and **Davey Johnson** all hit .320 or better.

Steve Carlton goes 23–10 with a 2.64 ERA and wins the Cy Young Award.

Larry Christenson finishes 19–6 for a .760 winning percentage.

Gene Garber, Ron Reed, and **Tug McGraw** anchor an outstanding bullpen.

OH, SO CLOSE

Phils Lose Frustrating NLCS to the Dodgers

The 1977 Phillies changed the right side of their infield, but they didn't miss a beat as they duplicated their 101 wins of the previous year and came within two games of a trip to the World Series.

Unlike the bicentennial season, the Phillies had to come from behind. By late June, the Phils found themselves 8½ games out of first place. But they rallied throughout the summer, compiling winning streaks of 8, 13, and 6 games along the way. They ended up winning the East by five games over Pittsburgh.

Greg Luzinski accounted for much of the resurgence. "The Bull" batted .309, led the Phillies with 39 home runs (exceeding Mike Schmidt by one), and reached a career high with 130 RBI.

Over the winter, the Phillies had let Dick Allen and Dave Cash depart via free agency. Faced with two holes in the infield, general manager Paul Owens responded by signing Richie Hebner (known for digging graves in the offseason) to play first and acquiring Ted Sizemore to fill the void at second. Both newcomers played well. Hebner swatted 18 home runs, while Sizemore hit .281 and played a steady second base.

Another important acquisition arrived at midseason when the Phillies snatched unhappy outfielder Bake McBride from the Cardinals. Splitting his time between right field and center field, McBride batted .339 and stole 27 bases. From the day that McBride made his debut, the Phillies went 69–33 to steal the division.

Mike Schmidt handles a hot shot in Game Three of the NLCS against the Dodgers. Los Angeles won the contest, 6–5, after scoring three runs in the top of the ninth.

> "I don't know why. I don't know why. I go to church, too."
>
> —Manager Danny Ozark, after errors and a bad call cost the Phillies Game Three of the NLCS

McBride's speed and range also strengthened a formidable defense. Schmidt, Garry Maddox, and Jim Kaat won Gold Gloves. In addition, Sizemore, Larry Bowa, and catcher Bob Boone, who played through a sore knee, fortified the middle of the diamond.

The flawless fielding supported a capable mound corps. Steve Carlton again pitched like an ace in winning the Cy Young Award. Young right-hander Larry Christenson moved up in stature, taking hold of the No. 2 slot and winning 19 games. The rest of the rotation provided mixed results. Kaat won only 6 of 17 decisions, rookie Randy Lerch struggled, and veteran Jim Lonborg pitched credibly. In the meantime, the bullpen repeated its success of the previous two summers.

Come October, the Phillies took aim at the Dodgers in the National League Championship Series. The teams split the first two games, setting up a critical Game Three in Philadelphia. The Phillies led 5–3 in the ninth with two outs, none on, and Gene Garber up 0–2 on Vic Davalillo, who then surprised everyone with a bunt single. After a double off Luzinski's glove by Manny Mota, the game seemingly ended on a ground out by Davey Lopes. But umpire Bruce Froemming mistakenly called Lopes safe, allowing the tying run to cross the plate. The Dodgers scored again that inning on a Bill Russell single to win 6–5, and they won the next day 3–1 to clinch the series.

The playoff defeat left the general manager disappointed. "I don't think there is any question we had the most talent," Owens told *The Sporting News*. "We had a better bench, a better bullpen, and better hitting. We just didn't play up to our capabilities."

Philly Phanatic

Historically speaking, the Philly Phanatic holds an esteemed place in baseball annals. He is one of the game's most venerable fuzzy mascots; the idea for him was hatched after the 1977 season as Philly's answer to the San Diego Chicken. The Phanatic, along with the Chicken and Youppi, are the only mascots on display at the National Baseball Hall of Fame.

But young Phillies fans don't care much about that. They just love his lime green fur, funny beak, jiggling butt, and hugs that are filled with brotherly love.

Once the Phanatic gets off his ATV, anything can happen. Certainly, he'll dance upon the Phillies dugout to sing his "Phanatic Dance." Other parts of his schtick include taunting the opposition, hexing their pitcher, and shooting hot dogs into the stands. At times, the Phanatic has gotten under the skin of opponents—most notably in 1988, when Dodgers manager Tommy Lasorda attacked him after he had stomped on a Lasorda dummy.

David Raymond wore the Phanatic costume from 1978 to '93, while Tom Burgoyne has had the honor ever since. The men within the suit will come and go, but the Philly Phanatic—fans hope— will live forever.

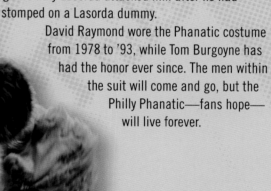

Highlights

April 16: Bob Forsch no-hits the Phillies in St. Louis.

June 5: Davey Johnson hits his second pinch-hit grand slam of the season, this one a walk-off, ninth-inning winner against L.A.

June 23: The Phillies move into first place for good.

September 30: The Phillies beat second-place Pittsburgh 10–8 in the season's penultimate game to clinch the NL East.

October 4: The Dodgers open the NLCS with a 9–5 win in Philadelphia.

October 5: Fans roundly boo the Phillies after they lose Game Two 4–0.

October 6: Steve Carlton homers, drives in four, and defeats L.A. 9–4 in Game Three.

October 7: Garry Maddox's dropped fly ball in the tenth inning of Game Four helps the Dodgers win 4–3 to clinch the series.

December 5: The Phillies sign longtime Reds star Pete Rose.

NOTES

Greg Luzinski hits only .265 but powers the offense with 35 homers and 101 RBI.

Steve Carlton (16–13), **Larry Christenson** (13–14), and **Dick Ruthven** (13–5) are the heart of the rotation.

Mike Schmidt, Larry Bowa, Garry Maddox, and catcher **Bob Boone** all win Gold Glove Awards.

THIRD STRAIGHT CROWN

But Phillies Fall Again in NLCS

In many ways, the 1978 season felt too much like the experiences of 1976 and '77. There was satisfaction in winning the National League East but an emptiness that came with a third consecutive failure in the postseason.

After a so-so start, the Phillies built a lead of five games on July 2. They held on to a slim lead for the rest of the season, and the Pirates breathed down their necks throughout September. The pennant race was indeed a struggle, as the Phillies fought through a rash of injuries. Two of the key ailments affected starting infielders: Mike Schmidt, who played through a serious hamstring pull, and Ted Sizemore, who missed nearly seven weeks with a broken hand.

Off the field, the Phillies had problems, too. Larry Bowa became embroiled in a nasty clubhouse argument with a New Jersey beat writer. In the front office, general manager Paul Owens took heat for breaking up the best bench in the National League when he traded away veterans Jay Johnstone and Davey Johnson. Owens felt he had to make the moves because of Johnson's unhappiness over playing time and the team's need for more bullpen depth. Owens sent Johnstone to the Yankees in June for Rawly Eastwick, the onetime relief ace for the "Big Red Machine."

While Owens sacrificed some of his positional depth, he made a terrific addition to the pitching staff when he acquired right-hander Dick Ruthven from the Braves in June. The addition of Ruthven, who pitched brilliantly over the second half, made a strong

A combined 2.43 ERA from relievers Warren Brusstar, Gene Garber, Tug McGraw, and Ron Reed (left to right) helped the Phillies repeat in the East in 1978.

Garry Maddox, a Gold Glove winner in 1978, makes a nice catch against the wall here in Game 3 of the NLCS in Los Angeles, although a costly error in Game 4 made him the goat of the series.

staff even more formidable. Steve Carlton battled shoulder pain to win 16 games. Larry Christenson would have easily won more than 13 games with better run support. Randy Lerch also chipped in, winning 11 games, including the pennant-clincher.

In the bullpen, 35-year-old right-hander Ron Reed emerged as the headliner. Pitching the best ball of his career, Reed posted a 2.24 ERA and a team-leading 17 saves. Veteran Tug McGraw and sinkerball pitcher Warren Brusstar provided ample support, giving manager Danny Ozark a multitude of capable options.

As it turned out, the Phillies needed all the pitching they could muster to counteract a disappointing offense. Most of the Phillies' regulars endured off seasons, with Bowa being one of the few exceptions. Not only did he hit .294, but he also led the team with 192 hits while stealing 27 bases.

The Phillies' other mainstays did not live up to expectation. Schmidt's production suffered because of his pulled hamstring. Greg Luzinski hit 35 home runs, but his batting average plummeted from .309 to .265. The hitting of Garry Maddox and Bake McBride fell off, as both speedsters struggled with a variety of minor injuries.

With so many of the hitters hobbled, the Phillies did not clinch the division until the final weekend of the season. The Phillies, protecting a lead of 3½ games and needing one more win to clinch, squared off against the Pirates for four games. The Phillies dropped the first two matchups before finally winning the third game—on the strength of two surprising home runs by Lerch—to officially end the race. "I feel like I've been through the playoffs and an entire World Series," Larry Bowa told *The Sporting News* after the decisive win.

The Phillies did not fare well in the actual playoffs. Repeating the outcome of the previous October, the Phillies fell to the Dodgers in four games. They lost the clinching game when a rare error by Maddox in center field set the scene for the deciding Dodger rally—and another postseason of disappointment in Philadelphia.

1979

▶ 84-78   4th ◀

Highlights

May 28: A 4–1 loss to the Cubs begins a six-game losing streak and drops the Phillies out of first place for good.

May 31: Two weeks after scoring 23 runs in one game, the Phils are shut out for the third straight game.

July 10: Del Unser hits his third pinch-hit home run in his last three at-bats.

July 17: Bob Boone, Steve Carlton, Pete Rose, Larry Bowa, and Schmidt represent Philly at the All-Star Game.

August 31: Danny Ozark is fired as manager and replaced by farm director Dallas Green.

September 30: The Phillies conclude September with an 18–11 record under the demanding Green—their winningest month of the season.

NOTES

Mike Schmidt clubs a team-record 45 home runs and drives in 114 runs.

Pete Rose ranks second in the NL in batting (.331) and first in OBP (.418).

Steve Carlton (18–11) once again leads the staff in wins.

Schmidt, Bob Boone, Garry Maddox, and second baseman **Manny Trillo** all win Gold Gloves. It is Maddox's fifth year in a row to be so honored.

The Phillies set a team attendance record (2,775,011).

FEELING THE PAIN
20-Plus Injuries Lead to Fourth-Place Finish

Given their status as defending division champions and the additions of free-agent star Pete Rose and slick second baseman Manny Trillo, the 1979 Phillies appeared to be the favorites to win another National League East title. That plan fell apart due to a barrage of injuries, as the Phillies finished fourth, well behind the world champion Pirates.

The Phillies started the season at 24–10 to take a 3½-game lead in the East. But injuries began to take a toll, and Philadelphia lost 23 of 34 games to fall out of the race.

The injuries, which numbered more than 20, didn't all occur on the field. Pitcher Larry Christenson fell off a bicycle and broke his collarbone. During spring training, Dick Ruthven developed bone chips. He recovered to start the season with six wins, but he eventually needed surgery. With reliever Warren Brusstar injured and closer Tug McGraw unable to keep his ERA under 5.00, the pitching staff was thin and ineffective.

Position players did not escape unscathed, either. Larry Bowa fractured his thumb while Trillo suffered a broken hand. Later on, catcher Bob Boone tore ligaments in his knee and had to undergo season-ending surgery.

Among the regulars, Rose was one of the few who stayed healthy. Playing every game, the first baseman finished with a .331 batting average, second best in the league. Along the way, Rose racked up 208 hits and led the league with a .418 on-base percentage.

Mike Schmidt also had a terrific season, bouncing back from his subpar 1978. Schmidt set a franchise record with 45 home runs while leading the league with 120 walks.

Yet, the play of Schmidt and Rose could not carry the Phillies, nor could it save the job of longtime manager Danny Ozark. The Phillies fired Ozark in late August, replacing him with minor league director Dallas Green. The seven-year Ozark era had featured plenty of winning and three division titles, but no NL pennants.

> **PHILLIES PHACT**
>
> On May 17 at Wrigley Field, the Phillies outscore the Cubs 23–22. Mike Schmidt's second homer of the game, in the tenth inning, wins it.

Mighty Mike

It's an interesting discussion—outside of Philly—over which third baseman was better, Mike Schmidt or George Brett. Well, in their only head-to-head meeting, Schmidt's Phillies beat Brett's Royals in the 1980 World Series. Schmidt hit .381 with two homers, seven RBI, four walks, and six runs to earn World Series MVP honors and finally get the Phillies a world championship after 97 years of existence.

A superb fielder, Schmidt won 10 Gold Gloves, more than any other National League third baseman. Even on the uneven AstroTurf at Veterans Stadium, hitting a ball by Schmidt was harder than sneaking a fastball past him at the plate. Schmidt led the NL in home runs eight times, more often than any other slugger in NL history. He was the 14th player to reach 500 home runs and collected 548 for his career, all as a Phillie. He owns most Phillies career offensive records, many by a wide margin.

That he reached adulthood at all was a blessing. While climbing a tree in his Ohio backyard at age five, Michael Jack Schmidt grabbed onto a power line and was knocked unconscious. The impact of hitting the ground restarted his heart.

Schmidt played shortstop at Ohio University, leading the Bobcats to the College World Series for the first time in school history in 1970. The Phillies drafted him in the second round the following year, and he was moved to third base during his brief minor league tenure. In October 1972, the Phillies traded Don Money to make room for their young slugger.

In 1973, Schmidt batted .196 for the Phillies while striking out 136 times. The next year,

he hit .282, led the NL with a .546 slugging average, and captured his first home crown with 36. It would have been 37 if a drive estimated at 500 feet hadn't hit the Astrodome roof and been ruled a single.

Schmidt became the third Phillie to hit four home runs in a game. All three achieved their homer quartets on the road, doing so 40 years apart: Ed Delahanty, 1896 in Chicago; Chuck Klein, 1936 in Pittsburgh; and Schmidt, 1976 in Chicago. Schmidt loved hitting at Wrigley Field, clubbing 50 homers there, 21 more than at any other road park.

From 1974 to 1987, Schmidt finished in the top 10 in MVP voting 10 times, won the award three times (1980, 1981, 1986), and knocked in 100 runs nine times. On 12 occasions, he made the NL All-Star team. The Phillies retired his No. 20, and he was elected to the Hall of Fame on his first try in 1995.

Pete Rose on Mike Schmidt: "To have his body, I'd trade him mine and my wife's, and I'd throw in some cash."

Team Leaders

Batting

1970: Tony Taylor, .301
1971: Tim McCarver, .278
1972: Greg Luzinski, .281
1973: Del Unser, .289
1974: Willie Montanez, .304
1975: Jay Johnstone, .329
1976: Garry Maddox, .330
1977: Greg Luzinski, .309
1978: Larry Bowa, .294
1979: Pete Rose, .331

Home Runs

1970: Deron Johnson, 27
1971: Deron Johnson, 34
1972: Greg Luzinski, 18
1973: Greg Luzinski, 29
1974: Mike Schmidt, 36
1975: Mike Schmidt, 38
1976: Mike Schmidt, 38
1977: Greg Luzinski, 39
1978: Greg Luzinski, 35
1979: Mike Schmidt, 45

RBI

1970: Deron Johnson, 93
1971: Willie Montanez, 99
1972: Greg Luzinski, 68
1973: Greg Luzinski, 97
1974: Mike Schmidt, 116
1975: Greg Luzinski, 120
1976: Mike Schmidt, 107
1977: Greg Luzinski, 130
1978: Greg Luzinski, 101
1979: Mike Schmidt, 114

Wins

1970: Rick Wise, 13–14
1971: Rick Wise, 17–14
1972: Steve Carlton, 27–10
1973: Steve Carlton, 13–20;
Wayne Twitchell, 13–9;
Ken Brett, 13–9;
Jim Lonborg, 13–16
1974: Jim Lonborg, 17–13
1975: Steve Carlton, 15–14
1976: Steve Carlton, 20–7
1977: Steve Carlton, 23–10
1978: Steve Carlton, 16–13
1979: Steve Carlton, 18–11

ERA

1970: Jim Bunning, 4.11
1971: Rick Wise, 2.88
1972: Steve Carlton, 1.97
1973: Wayne Twitchell, 2.50
1974: Jim Lonborg, 3.21
1975: Steve Carlton, 3.56
1976: Steve Carlton, 3.13
1977: Steve Carlton, 2.64
1978: Steve Carlton, 2.84
1979: Steve Carlton, 3.62

Strikeouts

1970: Dick Selma, 153
1971: Rick Wise, 155
1972: Steve Carlton, 310
1973: Steve Carlton, 223
1974: Steve Carlton, 240
1975: Steve Carlton, 192
1976: Steve Carlton, 195
1977: Steve Carlton, 198
1978: Steve Carlton, 161
1979: Steve Carlton, 213

Saves

1970: Dick Selma, 22
1971: Joe Hoerner, 9
1972: Mac Scarce, 4
1973: Mac Scarce, 12
1974: Eddie Watt, 6
1975: Gene Garber, 14;
Tug McGraw, 14
1976: Ron Reed, 14
1977: Gene Garber, 19
1978: Ron Reed, 17
1979: Tug McGraw, 16

NL Leaders

1972: Doubles—Willie
Montanez, 39;
Triples—Larry Bowa, 13;
Wins—Steve Carlton, 27;
ERA—Carlton, 1.97;
Strikeouts—Carlton, 310;
Complete Games—
Carlton, 30
1973: Complete Games—
Carlton, 18
1974: Home Runs—Mike
Schmidt, 36;
Strikeouts—Carlton, 240

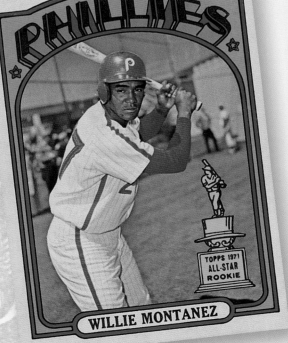

Willie Montanez knocked 30 homers and drove in 99
runs in 1971 and finished second to Atlanta's Earl
Williams in NL Rookie of the Year voting.

WILLIE MONTANEZ

1975: Hits—Dave Cash, 213;
Home Runs—Schmidt, 77;
RBI—Greg Luzinski, 120
1976: Triples–Cash, 12;
Home Runs—Schmidt, 38
1977: Wins—Carlton, 23

NL Awards

NL MVP Voting

1972: Steve Carlton, 5th
1974: Mike Schmidt, 6th
1975: Greg Luzinski, 2nd
1976: Mike Schmidt, 3rd;
Garry Maddox, 5th;
Greg Luzinski, 8th
1977: Greg Luzinski, 2nd;
Steve Carlton, 5th;
Mike Schmidt, 10th
1978: Larry Bowa, 3rd;
Greg Luzinski, 7th

NL Cy Young Winners

1972: Steve Carlton
1977: Steve Carlton

Gold Glove Winners

1972: Larry Bowa, SS
1975: Garry Maddox, OF
1976: Jim Kaat, P;
Mike Schmidt, 3B;
Garry Maddox, OF
1977: Jim Kaat, P;
Mike Schmidt, 3B;
Garry Maddox, OF
1978: Bob Boone, C;
Mike Schmidt, 3B;
Larry Bowa, SS;
Garry Maddox, OF

1979: Bob Boone, C;
Manny Trillo, 2B;
Mike Schmidt, 3B;
Garry Maddox, OF

NL All-Stars

1970: Joe Hoerner, P
1971: Rick Wise, P
1972: Steve Carlton, P
1973: Wayne Twitchell, P
1974: Larry Bowa, SS;
Steve Carlton, P;
Dave Cash, 2B;
Mike Schmidt, 3B
1975: Larry Bowa, SS;
Dave Cash, 2B;
Greg Luzinski, OF;
Tug McGraw, P
1976: Greg Luzinski, OF;
Bob Boone, C;
Larry Bowa, SS;
Dave Cash, 2B;
Mike Schmidt, 3B

1977: Greg Luzinski, OF;
Steve Carlton, P;
Mike Schmidt, 3B
1978: Larry Bowa, SS;
Greg Luzinski, OF;
Bob Boone, C
1979: Steve Carlton, P;
Bob Boone, C;
Mike Schmidt, 3B;
Larry Bowa, SS;
Pete Rose, 1B

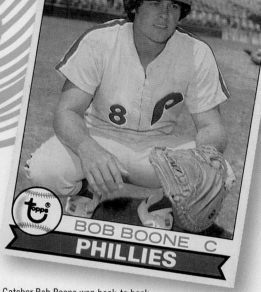

Catcher Bob Boone won back-to back
Gold Glove Awards in 1978 and 1979,
and he went on to win five more with the Angels.

PHILLIES 1970s All-Decade Team

1B	WILLIE MONTANEZ
2B	DAVE CASH
SS	LARRY BOWA
3B	MIKE SCHMIDT
C	BOB BOONE
OF	GREG LUZINSKI
OF	GARRY MADDOX
OF	JAY JOHNSTONE
SP	STEVE CARLTON
SP	JIM LONBORG
RP	TUG MCGRAW

"BASEBALL'S BEST"?

Not quite. While the Phillies open the decade with their first world title in team history, great expectations erode into perennial disappointments.

When a franchise closes one decade by winning three of the last four division titles and opens the next by capturing a World Series title, optimism reigns. So it was that the Phillies, after reaching the playoffs again in 1981, adopted as their official slogan, "Baseball's Best."

This was the expectation for the 1980s, a decade the Phillies believed they would dominate. But the promise of the decade's beginning turned sour by the middle years—and rotten by the end.

The six-game triumph over Kansas City in the 1980 World Series was a historic highlight for Phillie fans young and old. Management had assembled the core players by patiently building from within and making inspired acquisitions to supplement the homegrown talent. Then an ownership transfer signaled a change.

Ruly Carpenter went out on top in 1981, selling the team for $30 million to a group of partners led by Bill Giles. The Phillies stayed competitive for a bit, capped by a trip to the World Series in 1983. But less emphasis on scouting and player development and worse luck in trades was a recipe for disaster.

The Phillies succumbed in five games to the Baltimore Orioles in the '83 Series, looking every bit their age. With a nickname like the "Wheeze Kids," the Phillies had little staying power. By then, they had surrendered the last remaining jewels of their farm system.

When they won the 1980 World Series, the Phillies had George Bell, Julio Franco, and Ryne Sandberg in the minor league system. Bell and Sandberg would each win an MVP Award in the decade, and Franco would snare a batting title in 1991. Together, that young trio might have helped the Phillies hold their claim to being "Baseball's Best."

Instead, Philadelphia lost Bell to Toronto in the Rule 5 draft before the 1981 season. They traded Sandberg to the Cubs for Ivan DeJesus 13 months later. And they included Franco among the five players sent to Cleveland for Von Hayes in December 1982.

After recording the final out of the 1980 World Series, Tug McGraw did what Phillies fans had been waiting to do for 97 years: jump for joy!

The team also traded Willie Hernandez, a useful middle reliever for the 1983 champs, to Detroit for Glenn Wilson before the 1984 season. Hernandez immediately led the Tigers to a world title while winning the AL MVP Award.

Mike Schmidt remained a feared hitter through 1987, and he won MVP Awards in 1980, 1981, and 1986. Hayes was a better hitter than most fans remember. Juan Samuel was an electrifying talent at second base, and Wilson was reasonably productive, earning an all-star selection in 1985.

The biggest problem was pitching. The Phillies never found an ace to replace Steve Carlton, who was released in 1986. John Denny, the surprise 1983 NL Cy Young Award winner, was a one-year wonder. Marty Bystrom and Charlie Hudson—rookie sensations for the 1980 and 1983 pennant-winners, respectively—quickly fizzled out. Philadelphia might have had an ace in Dave Stewart, a scrap-heap pick-up in 1985, but he was released the next season before going on to four straight 20-win campaigns with Oakland.

The Phillies blew a chance to take slugger Frank Thomas in the 1989 amateur draft, and they went on to post their second-straight cellar-dwelling finish that year, their fifth season out of six without a winning record. Change was coming, though, with new general manager Lee Thomas moving aggressively to reshape the team for the 1990s.

The organization and its fans were looking forward to a decade of the Phillies being among the baseball elite.

1980

▶ 91-71　1st ◀

Highlights

October 4: The Phillies, beset by internal strife all season, clinch the division with an 11-inning, 6–4 victory at Montreal.

October 10: Houston nips Philly 1–0 in 11 innings to take a 2–1 lead in the NLCS.

October 11: The Phils score two in the tenth to win 5–3 at Houston.

October 12: A Garry Maddox double in the top of the tenth of Game Five gives Philly an 8–7 NLCS-clinching win.

October 15: The Phils follow a 7–6 Game One win over Kansas City in the World Series with a 6–4 triumph (thanks to four in the bottom of the eighth) in Game Two.

October 18: With the series tied, the Phillies win Game Five 4–3 with two runs in the top of the ninth.

October 21: Back in Philly, Tug McGraw saves Steve Carlton's 4–1 victory in Game Six, as the Phillies celebrate their first World Series title. Mike Schmidt is named World Series MVP.

NOTES

Mike Schmidt, the NL MVP, leads the league in HRs (48) and RBI (121).

Steve Carlton (24–9, 2.34, 286 strikeouts) wins the Cy Young Award.

Tug McGraw logs 20 saves and a 1.46 ERA.

Phinally!

Phillies Crown Royals for First World Title

At the moment of victory, when the Phillies eased the heartache of nearly a century by winning their first championship, Bob Boone could hardly move. When Tug McGraw's fastball whooshed past Willie Wilson's bat and popped into Boone's glove at 11:29 p.m. on October 21, 1980, Boone simply stood, raised his arms, and strode slowly to the mound. Years later, Boone would say, he was so relieved it was over that his weary knees could take no more.

Not McGraw, of course. He had been to the World Series before, with the Mets in 1969, but had not appeared in that Fall Classic. Here, in his moment of glory, the effervescent closer windmilled his exhausted left arm in triumph and threw both arms to the sky. Then he bounced, as if Veteran Stadium's AstroTurf were spring-loaded, and with his catcher in no hurry to hug him, he turned to third base.

Bounding toward him was the greatest player in Phillies history, Mike Schmidt, whose two-run single had given the Phillies all the runs they needed to vanquish Kansas City in Game Six of the World Series. Schmidt had hit .381 against the Royals, earning the World Series MVP trophy to go along with his regular-season NL MVP Award.

Never one for splashy displays of emotion, Schmidt let loose, leaping into McGraw's arms just as a throng of Phillies teammates stormed them from the first-base dugout. The Veterans Stadium scoreboard said it all: "WORLD CHAMPIONS," a title the Phillies had never held.

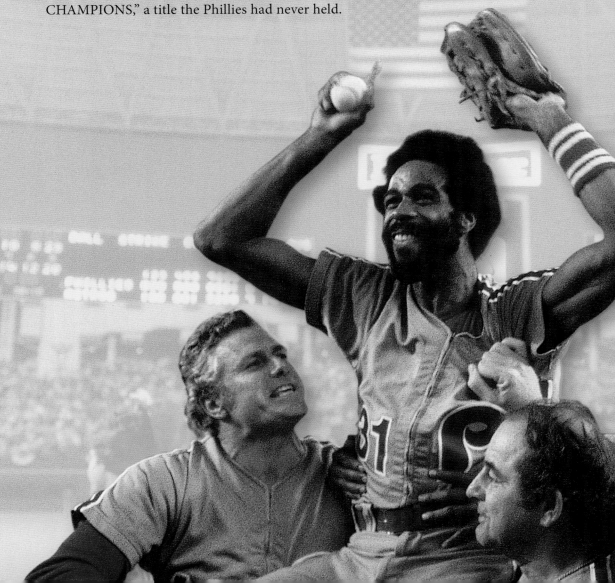

Larry Bowa high-fives Lonnie Smith after scoring in the sixth inning of Game Six of the World Series, giving Philly a 4–0 lead.

By then—actually, by 1966—each of the other 16 franchises that had comprised the major leagues in 1901 had won a World Series. Some, like the Chicago Cubs, had to reach back decades to find theirs. Another, the Baltimore Orioles, had to be relocated to break through. But all could point to a moment or two in their past and say, "That was when we ruled the game."

In 1980, it was the Phillies' turn. But in typical Phillies fashion, it did not come easily. After falling in the National League playoffs three times in the 1970s, frustration had set in. Dallas Green, the hard-driving manager who had replaced Danny Ozark in 1979, had challenged the Phillies to reach their potential. For a while in 1980, they failed his test.

"Dallas lined out his program of what Phillie baseball should be," McGraw would say after the World Series. "He told us we had to be a team with character, that we had to look in the mirror. He was just an average player at best, and where he got his 'Phillie baseball' is beyond me. But he had confidence in his ideas, and he backed his people. It took us a few months to catch on, but then we did."

The Phillies entered August in third place, and on the second weekend of the month, they dropped four in a row in Pittsburgh. Between games of a Sunday doubleheader at Three Rivers Stadium, Green unleashed a blistering tirade at the players, who fell to six games out of first when they lost the second game.

Manager Dallas Green helps carry Garry Maddox off the field after the outfielder's fantastic NLCS-ending catch in Houston.

PHILADELPHIA Phillies 1980 WORLD CHAMPS

For the first time ever, Phillies fans could finally wave a world championship pennant.

"In September and October, when we had all those close finishes, the great playoffs and the Series, the players were showing why baseball is the American pastime. I can't tell you how happy I am to be a part of it."

—Tug McGraw

But there was too much talent—and too much will—for the slump to last. With Green prodding and Schmidt hitting nearly .400 the rest of the month, the Phillies arrived in September just a half-game out of first place, which they claimed for themselves with a sweep in San Francisco.

Marty Bystrom, a 22-year-old righty, arrived from Oklahoma City to help the Phillies stay close to the top. He fired a shutout against the Mets in his first major league start, and he won all five of his starts in September. Yet the Montreal Expos would not go away.

The Expos had built a talented roster, including future Hall of Famers Gary Carter and Andre Dawson, and were seeking their first division crown. They took two of three at the Vet in late September to wrest back first place. After the Phillies swept the Cubs at home, the teams met at Olympic Stadium in Montreal, tied for the division lead with three to play.

McGraw closed out Dick Ruthven's victory on Friday with two perfect innings, striking out five. After a three-hour rain delay on Saturday, Schmidt buried a homer—to use broadcaster Andy Musser's verb—in the 11th inning to give the Phillies a 6–4 lead. McGraw secured that win, too, setting up an epic best-of-five NL Championship Series with the Houston Astros.

It was, perhaps, the most tightly contested postseason series in baseball history, with so much at stake. The Astros had never reached the World Series. The Phillies had not been in 30 years. Incredibly, the series featured just one home run, by Greg Luzinski during Steve Carlton's 3–1 victory in the opener at the Vet. After that, the teams played four consecutive extra-inning games, each thick with tension.

The Astros took Game Two with four runs in the 10th inning, and the series moved to Houston for the remaining three games. In Game Three, the Astros beat McGraw in the 11th inning when Joe Morgan led off with a triple and scored on a sacrifice fly by Denny Walling for the game's only run.

Game Four took 10 rollicking innings and nearly four hours. The game featured five double plays, including one the Astros first thought should have been a triple play. The Phillies entered the eighth inning down to their final six outs and trailing Vern Ruhle 2–0. Four straight singles tied the score, and a sacrifice fly put the Phillies ahead. After the Astros tied it in their half of the ninth, doubles by Luzinski and Manny Trillo gave the Phillies a 5–3 win.

The fifth game would go down as one of the most thrilling battles in baseball history. Down 5–2 to Nolan Ryan in the eighth inning, the Phillies stormed back with a five-run rally keyed by Del Unser and Trillo. When McGraw blew the two-run lead, Unser came through again in the tenth, doubling off Frank LaCorte with one out. He scored the go-ahead run on a double by Garry Maddox, who snared Enos Cabell's liner in the bottom of the inning to clinch the pennant.

"I sat back and watched the whole thing," said Schmidt, who struck out three times, "and it was unbelievable."

Such an emotional series could have led to a letdown against the Royals. But after the playoff misery of the '70s, the Phillies played with a sense of relief, as if the pressure had finally lifted. They overcame a four-run deficit to win Game One behind rookie Bob Walk, and they scored four in the eighth for another comeback victory in Game Two.

The Royals—who, like the Phillies, had lost in the playoffs in 1976, '77, and '78—beat McGraw in the tenth inning in Game Three and blitzed Larry Christenson for four runs in the first inning of a 5–3 win in Game Four. But the Phillies never lost their swagger, a point driven home by reliever Dickie Noles, who knocked down the great George Brett with a fastball that afternoon.

Bystrom started Game Five, making him the Phillies' fifth different starting pitcher in the World Series. The Phillies trailed 3–2 heading into the ninth. But Schmidt opened the inning with a single off Dan Quisenberry, and Unser—the epitome of a clutch role player—lashed a pinch-hit double to right to tie the game. A single by Trillo scored Unser, and after McGraw walked the bases loaded in the ninth, Jose Cardenal struck out to send the World Series back to Broad Street.

With Carlton ready for Game Six, it was all set up for the Phillies—and the team that had fizzled in 1950, folded in 1964, and come up short in the '70s finally delivered. Counting the postseason, Carlton gritted his way through 331⅓ innings in 1980, and he made the final seven count, fanning seven Royals and handing McGraw a 4–0 lead in the eighth.

With two on and none out when he entered, McGraw waded deeper into a jam but survived. One run scored, but a bases-loaded ground out ended the eighth with the Phillies ahead by three runs. In the ninth, Frank White lifted a foul near the Phillies' dugout with one out and the bases loaded. The ball popped out of Boone's mitt and landed, miraculously, in Pete Rose's. The Phillies needed just one more.

As Wilson stepped in, McGraw took a moment to savor the scene. There were 65,838 fans ready to erupt—and mounted police and dogs ringing foul territory to control them.

"All of a sudden, one of the horses makes a deposit on the turf," McGraw would say. "And I thought, 'If I don't get Wilson out, that's what I'll be in this town!' Then I noticed one of the dogs and thought, 'K-9 Corps—that's what I need, a K in the ninth!'"

He got it, and it changed baseball history forever. The Phillies, at last, had a season to call their own.

Johnny-on-the-spot, Pete Rose prepares to catch the ball after it pops out of Bob Boone's mitt for the penultimate out of the World Series.

151

1981

Highlights

June 10: The Phillies sit in first place at 34–21, but a players strike will wipe out the next two months of the season.

August 6: The MLB owners decide to divide the season into two, with the teams in first place on June 10 (including the Phillies) making the playoffs.

October 4: The Phils finish the second half-season at 25–27, but it's meaningless since they have already made the playoffs.

October 7: Eight MLB teams are in the postseason. Montreal defeats Philly 3–1 in Game One of their first-round series.

October 9: After losing Game Two 3–1, the Phillies beat Montreal at home 6–2 in front of nearly 30,000 empty seats.

October 10: The Phillies win Game Four 6–5 on a walk-off home run by George Vukovich in the tenth.

October 11: Montreal wins the series 3–0, as Steve Rogers outduels Steve Carlton.

NOTES

Mike Schmidt repeats as NL MVP. He leads the league in numerous categories, including homers (31) and RBI (91).

Pete Rose bats .325.

Steve Carlton (13–4, 2.42) and **Tug McGraw** (2.66 ERA) are the pitching standouts.

FIRST-HALF CHAMPS

Phils Make the Playoffs in Strike-Marred Season

The Phillies had reason to believe they could repeat as world champions in 1981. They shuffled their left fielders in spring training, selling Greg Luzinski to the White Sox and acquiring Gary Matthews from Atlanta for Bob Walk. Otherwise, they returned almost the entire roster that had beaten Kansas City the previous October.

After a victory on June 10, the Phillies had won 9 of 11 to lift their record to 34–21, the best in the National League East. Then came the players strike, and with it went the Phillies' momentum.

Baseball stopped for almost two months as owners and players haggled over free-agent compensation. Play resumed with the All-Star Game in Cleveland on August 9, and Mike Schmidt crunched a two-run homer off Rollie Fingers in the eighth inning, propelling the NL to a 5–4 win.

But if the Phillies thought that could be a positive portent for their second half, they were wrong. Baseball decided to start anew, with a split-season concept that awarded a playoff spot to each of the teams in first place at the time of the strike. Knowing they were already in the playoffs, the Phillies staggered to a 25–27 mark in the second half.

To be sure, there were individual highlights sprinkled through the season. Steve Carlton notched his 3,000th career strikeout when he fanned Montreal's Tim Wallach on April 29. Pete Rose broke Stan Musial's NL record for hits on August 10, with number 3,631 off the Cardinals' Mark Littell. And Schmidt captured his second consecutive Most Valuable Player Award with 31 homers, 91 RBI, and a career-high .316 average.

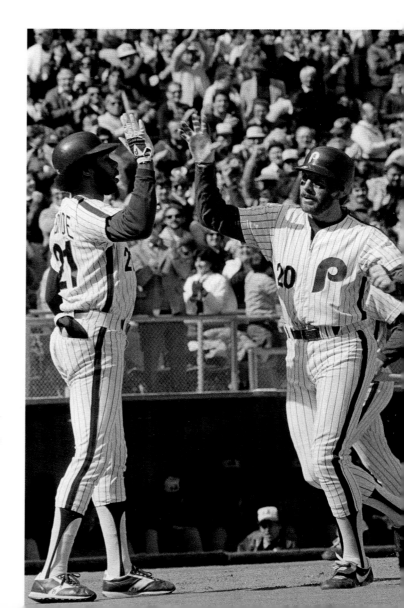

Bake McBride (left) congratulates Mike Schmidt after scoring on the latter's first-inning home run in Game Four of the NLDS. It was Schmidt's only two RBI of the five-game series.

PHILLIES PHACT

On April 29, Steve Carlton becomes the first left-hander in history to record his 3,000th strikeout.

But the best-of-five divisional playoff series against the Expos was a major letdown. The Phillies lost the first game at Olympic Stadium 3–1, with Steve Carlton walking five in six innings. They lost by the same score in Game Two before a 6–2 victory in Game Three that was witnessed by just 36,835 fans at the Vet.

The Phillies forced a decisive fifth game when George Vukovich hit the first walk-off postseason homer in franchise history with a leadoff blast off Jeff Reardon in the bottom of the tenth inning in Game Four. Alas, it was the last run the Phillies would score, as Steve Rogers blanked them 3–0 on six hits in Game Five, helping himself with a two-run single off Carlton.

That was the final game Dallas Green ever managed for the Phillies, and his departure would be even more devastating than a lost playoff series. Green left after the season to become the general manager of the Cubs, taking with him a deep knowledge of the Phillies' major league roster and minor league system.

Green proceeded to raid his old team, and his 1984 division champions would feature an array of former Phillies, including Larry Bowa, Bob Dernier, Gary Matthews, Keith Moreland, and a young second baseman who collected one hit for the 1981 Phillies and 2,385 in his Hall of Fame career for the Cubs: Ryne Sandberg, acquired with Bowa for shortstop Ivan DeJesus in one of the most lopsided deals in baseball history.

Pete Rose displaying his trademark hustle on the base paths.

Added Hustle

Pete Rose was a third baseman when he went looking for a new team following 16 seasons in Cincinnati. The Phillies had legendary third sacker Mike Schmidt, so Rose moved to first in 1979. That year, he placed second in the league with a .331 average while leading the circuit in on-base percentage (.418). The next year, Rose homered once in 162 games, but he led the National League with 42 doubles. "Charlie Hustle" batted .400 in the National League Championship Series against Houston, reaching base 13 times in the best-of-five epic.

Rose spent five years in Philadelphia, batting .291 in 745 games and amassing 826 hits toward his all-time record total, but his Philly tenure is best remembered for a single catch. With the bases loaded in the ninth inning of the 1980 World Series clincher, a foul ball popped out of catcher Bob Boone's mitt and was snagged out of the air by Rose. "I wanted to kiss him," Boone later said. Phillies fans understand.

Highlights

January 27: The Phillies trade Larry Bowa and prospect Ryne Sandberg (a future Hall of Famer) to the Cubs for shortstop Ivan DeJesus.

April 8: The Phillies begin the season with a new manager, Pat Corrales.

June 22: Pete Rose doubles against St. Louis to move into second place on the all-time hit list (3,772), surpassing Hank Aaron.

September 13: Steve Carlton shuts out St. Louis 2–0. The win allows the Phillies to move past the Cardinals into first place.

September 14–15: The Cards shut out the Phils in two straight games to take over first place for good.

December 9: The Phillies trade Manny Trillo, prospect Julio Franco (who will play until 2007), and three others to Cleveland for outfielder Von Hayes.

NOTES

Mike Schmidt jacks 35 HRs and leads the NL in OBP (.403) and slugging percentage (.547).

Catcher Bo Diaz and **outfielder Gary Matthews** drive in 85 and 83 runs, respectively.

Steve Carlton (23–11) leads the NL in wins and cops the Cy Young Award.

Mike Schmidt, Manny Trillo, and **Garry Maddox** win Gold Gloves.

September Fizzle

Carlton Keeps Them in It Until the Final Weeks

With manager Dallas Green gone, the Phillies gave his job to Pat Corrales, a former manager of the Texas Rangers who had played two games for the star-crossed Phillies of 1964. Bumper stickers played off his last name—"Corrales a pennant," they pleaded—and for a while, it seemed as if Corrales might deliver.

The Phillies had shed two of the stalwarts from the 1980 champs, trading Larry Bowa to the Cubs and selling catcher Bob Boone to the Angels after Boone had helped lead the players' negotiating team during the 1981 strike. They also shipped speedy left fielder Lonnie Smith to St. Louis in a three-way trade that brought catcher Bo Diaz to the Phillies.

Diaz did his part, hitting .288 with 18 homers, and Bob Dernier adequately replaced Smith on the bases, with 42 steals. But Smith was a sensation for the Cardinals, leading the league with 120 runs scored, finishing second in National League MVP voting, and helping St. Louis win the World Series that fall.

The Phillies, at least, had their chances to stop the Cardinals. Steve Carlton twirled a masterpiece against St. Louis at the Vet on September 13—a 2–0 three-hitter with 12 strikeouts that lifted the Phillies to a half-game lead in the NL East. But they lost five of their next six, the first two by shutout to the Cardinals, and slipped further and further from the top. In one week's time, the Phillies fell to 5½ games out of first place, and they never recovered.

Even so, at 89–73 the Phillies tied for the second best record in the league, and Carlton turned in a remarkable season to win his fourth Cy Young Award in 11 years with the team. In one stretch, from June 19 through August 9, Carlton completed 10 of 11 starts while going 9–1 with a 2.06 ERA. Overall, he went 23–11 with a 3.10 ERA, leading the majors in victories, innings (295⅔), and strikeouts (286).

In his four seasons as the Phillies' second baseman (1979–82), Manny Trillo won three Gold Gloves and two Silver Slugger Awards.

Lefty

Steve Carlton was the first pitcher to win four Cy Young Awards, but Phillies fans remember him winning on the night the team ended a 97-year world championship drought in 1980. "Lefty" retired with 329 wins, 4,136 strikeouts, a record 144 pickoffs, a statue in Philadelphia, and a plaque in Cooperstown.

Carlton signed with the Cardinals at 19 out of Miami-Dade Community College, and he debuted in relief at age 20 in 1965. He tossed six innings in his World Series debut in 1967, allowing only one unearned run but losing Game Five to Boston. In a game against the Mets in 1969, he became the first to fan 19 in a game yet lost on two Ron Swoboda home runs. The Cards sold low on Carlton after his 20–9 season in 1971, sending him to Philadelphia for Rick Wise. Lefty set about making that the greatest steal in Phillies history.

His 27 wins in '72 accounted for 46 percent of his team's total. The unanimous Cy Young winner claimed the pitching Triple Crown with a 1.97 ERA and 310 strikeouts; his 346 1/3 innings, 41 starts, and 30 complete games also led the National League. After he lost 20 in 1973, both Lefty and the Phillies stayed around .500 the next two seasons. In 1976, Philadelphia claimed its first postseason birth since 1950 and Carlton won 20 for the third time. He won 23, plus another Cy Young, in 1977.

Carlton went 24–9 in 1980, claiming his third Cy Young while becoming the last pitcher to surpass 300 innings in a season. After the Phillies clinched the division title on the penultimate day of the season, Carlton won the NLCS opener against Houston—the only game in that epic not to go extra innings. Carlton won twice in the World Series, including the Game Six clincher. He claimed his fourth Cy Young Award in 1982 and pitched in his fourth World Series in 1983.

Lefty and Houston's Nolan Ryan spent 1983 and 1984 trading ownership of the all-time strikeout mark. After numerous lead changes, Ryan grabbed the record for good. Despite a demanding martial arts regimen (he also strengthened his arm in a big bucket of rice), Lefty was slowing down. Released by the Phillies in 1986, he bounced around with the Giants (picking up his 4,000th strikeout), White Sox, and Indians, and he retired with the Twins in 1988. In 1994, he received 96 percent of the Hall of Fame vote by the writers, whom Carlton had famously refused to speak with during his career.

A master of control and focus, Steve Carlton often pitched with cotton in his ears to block out crowd noise.

Highlights

July 18: With the Phillies at 43–42, but in first place, GM Paul Owens fires Pat Corrales as manager and takes the reins himself.

September 23: Steve Carlton records his 300th win, defeating St. Louis 6–2.

September 26: The Phils win their eleventh game in a row, a streak that takes them from being tied for first place to having a 4 1/2-game lead.

September 28: The Phillies trounce the Cubs in Chicago 13–6 to clinch the NL East.

October 4: The "Wheeze Kids" enter the playoffs with three former Reds stars who are now over 40: Pete Rose, Joe Morgan, and Tony Perez. Carlton (age 38) beats L.A. 1–0 in Game One of the NLCS.

October 8: The Phils defeat the Dodgers 7–2 in Game Four to clinch the NLCS.

October 11: Philly edges Baltimore 2–1 in Game One of the World Series thanks to a Garry Maddox homer in the eighth.

October 16: Scott McGregor shuts out the Phils 5–0 in Game Five to give Baltimore the world title.

NOTES

Mike Schmidt leads the NL in home runs (40).

John Denny (19–6) wins the NL Cy Young Award.

SENIOR MOMENTS

"Wheeze Kids" Chug Their Way to World Series

For a team that would come to regret so many trades in the 1980s, this season stands out as one in which everything—until the very end—broke right. The cast supporting Mike Schmidt and Steve Carlton was drastically different, but it came together in a dizzying September sprint that pushed the Phillies into the playoffs, where they captured the fourth pennant in franchise history.

The ace of the staff was not Carlton, though he pitched very well, but John Denny, acquired from Cleveland late in the 1982 season for three prospects. Winless in four starts for the Phillies in '82, Denny became the surprise NL Cy Young Award winner in 1983, going 19–6 with a 2.37 ERA.

Tug McGraw, the merry closer of the 1980 champions, gave way to a different lefty, the menacing Al Holland, nicknamed "Mr. T" for his resemblance to the actor on *The A-Team*. The Phillies had traded starter Mike Krukow and two other players to the Giants for Holland and second baseman Joe Morgan, who was 39 years old.

Other important newcomers included reliever Willie Hernandez, outfielders Joe Lefebvre and Sixto Lezcano, and first baseman Tony Perez. Pete Rose, Morgan, and Perez—three members of Cincinnati's fearsome "Big Red Machine" from the '70s—now called the Vet home. The Phillies became known as the "Wheeze Kids," a play on their 1950 "Whiz Kids" nickname, and naturally they needed a grandfather type to lead them.

At 59 years old, Paul Owens—"The Pope," as he was known—left the front office to replace Pat Corrales in mid-July, making Corrales the first manager ever fired with his team in first place.

Then again, the Phillies were only 43–42, a sluggish start for a team clearly built to win now. Owens charted a winning course, and in September the Phillies surged to 11 victories in a row, a stretch that included Carlton's 300th win at Busch Stadium against his former team, the Cardinals. The Phillies rolled past the Cubs to clinch

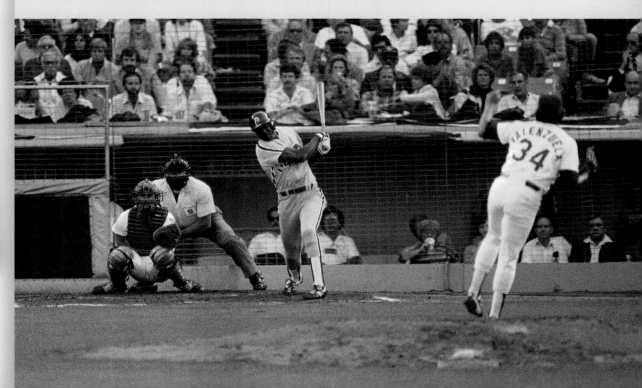

Gary Matthews hit 10 home runs in 446 at bats during the 1983 regular season. In 14 at bats during the NLCS against the Dodgers, he went deep three times, including this solo blast off Fernando Valenzuela in Game Two.

Bo Diaz beats the throw to Baltimore's Rick Dempsey in Game Four of the World Series. The Orioles won the game 5–4.

the National League East at Wrigley Field on September 28, setting up a date with the Dodgers in the NLCS.

The Dodgers had won 11 of 12 games from the Phillies in the regular season, and they seemed to hold a psychic edge after humbling the Phils in the 1977 and 1978 playoffs. But the Phillies held strong this time, returning to a frothy Veterans Stadium after splitting the first two games out West. With "Beat L.A.! Beat L.A.!" chants spurring them on, the Phillies took Games Three and Four, both by 7–2 scores, to clinch the best-of-five series.

Rookie pitcher Charlie Hudson won Game Three and Carlton took Game 4, with series MVP Gary Matthews ripping three homers and batting .429 over the four contests. Holland struck out Bill Russell on a checked swing to end the series, and he thrust his arms high as Schmidt lifted him to the sky.

The Phillies did not travel far for the World Series, just a couple of hours down I-95 to Baltimore, where Denny pitched them to a 2–1 victory in Game One. But rookie Mike Boddicker silenced the Phillies in Game Two, winning 4–1, and the Orioles never looked back.

An error by Ivan DeJesus, on a ball that skidded on a wet patch of AstroTurf, doomed the Phillies in a 3–2 loss in Game Three. Denny faltered in a 5–4 loss in Game Four, and Scott McGregor held the Phillies to five hits to close out the Series, 5–0, in Game Five. Schmidt managed just one hit—a broken-bat single—in 20 at-bats, and the Phillies hit .195 as a team.

For the Orioles, the lasting image of the Series was shortstop Cal Ripken snaring Garry Maddox's liner and shaking his glove in the air to start the celebration. For the Phillies, it was Morgan stumbling off third as he tried to tag up on a fly out in the eighth inning.

The Phillies would need a decade to get up off the ground.

The third game of the 1983 World Series saw Jim Palmer earn the win (in relief) for Baltimore while fellow Hall of Famer Steve Carlton took the loss.

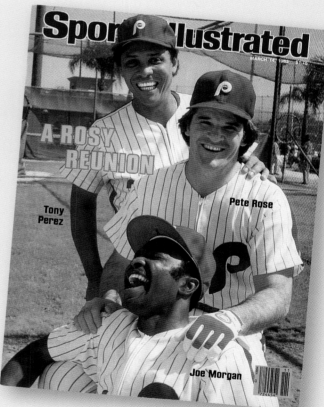

The reunion of three former (and aged) Reds greats on the Phillies in 1983 was noteworthy enough to make the cover of *Sports Illustrated*.

1984

Highlights

March 24: The Phillies trade reliever Willie Hernandez to Detroit. (He and former Phillie Ryne Sandberg will be the league MVPs in 1984.)

May 15: Against Dodgers pitcher Bob Welch in L.A., Mike Schmidt blasts his 400th career home run.

May 22: The Phillies win their tenth straight game to improve to 23–16.

July 2: A 4–0 win over Cincinnati puts the Phils in first place for the twelfth time this season.

September 30: The Phillies conclude the season with their ninth straight defeat.

NOTES

Mike Schmidt shares the NL home run (36) and RBI (106) crowns.

Outfielder **Von Hayes** steals 48 bases, and second baseman **Juan Samuel** scores 105 runs (but commits 33 errors).

Potent-hitting reserves include **Jeff Stone** (.362, 185 at-bats), **Tim Corcoran** (.341, 208 at-bats), and **Greg Gross** (.322, 202 at-bats).

Steve Carlton (13–7) and **Jerry Koosman** (14–15) headline the pitching staff.

Schmidt wins his ninth consecutive Gold Glove Award at third base.

BACK TO REALITY

Lots of Plus and Minuses Add Up to .500

Lots of Phillies enjoyed the season of their lives in 1984. Unfortunately, they were playing for the Cubs, who wrestled the National League East crown from the Phillies with a collection of players who once called Philadelphia home.

The Phillies, meanwhile, tried to get younger. They shed some of the veterans from the 1983 pennant-winners, including Pete Rose, Joe Morgan, and Tony Perez. Juan Samuel was given Morgan's second-base job, Von Hayes took a spot in the outfield, Len Matuszek got a chance at first, and Ozzie Virgil did most of the catching.

Samuel finished as the runner-up to the Mets' Dwight Gooden for the Rookie of the Year Award. Harry Kalas delighted in shouting "Watch Sammy run!" when Samuel punched a ball to the gap and tore around the bases. Samuel led the league in triples, with 19, to go with his 72 stolen bases. It would be one of the best seasons of his career.

The other young players did well enough, and Mike Schmidt led the league in homers and RBI. But another newcomer, right fielder Glenn Wilson, was a major disappointment, hitting .240 with six homers while Willie Hernandez, the reliever he was traded for, led Detroit to the World Series title.

The rotation got a boost from Jerry Koosman, 41, who went 14–15 with a 3.25 ERA, and the Phillies salvaged something for the fading Marty Bystrom by trading him to the Yankees for the much more dependable Shane Rawley. But John Denny won just 7 of 22 starts, and Carlton (13–7) started looking mortal.

The uneven performances added up to a season with an appropriate record: 81–81. The Phillies hung around the fringes of the race all summer, with Larry Andersen chipping in 33 consecutive scoreless innings, a team record for relievers. But the Phillies lost 12 of their last 14 games, including their final 9, and things soon got worse.

Von "Purple" Hayes, as ESPN's Chris Berman called him, tallied 124 homers and 202 steals in his nine seasons with the Phillies (1983–1991).

Running on Empty

"Speedy" Phils Can't Make a Playoff Run

The running game ruled baseball in the 1980s, and the Phillies wanted in on the action. They marketed their 1985 team around the slogan "Follow Us," with a silhouetted base runner serving as the centerpiece of the ad campaign.

Juan Samuel, Von Hayes, and Jeff Stone were supposed to make it happen. The three had combined for 147 stolen bases in 1984, but in '85 they combined for just 79 steals as the Phillies suffered their first losing season in 11 years.

It was not the kind of year Paul Owens had hoped for when he left the dugout and turned over the manager's job to John Felske. They lost eight of their first nine games, 34 of their first 52, and finished 75–87, fifth in the NL East.

Kevin Gross led the team in wins and strikeouts—an impressive feat for him but a bad sign for a team that had hoped to count on Steve Carlton (1–8, 3.33) and John Denny (11–14, 3.82). Shane Rawley went 13–8, but Charlie Hudson was his mirror image at 8–13.

The Phillies had no shortstop to speak of—Steve Jeltz hit .189—and the decision to move Mike Schmidt to first to clear space for Rick Schu, a rather ordinary third baseman, looks laughable now. Schmidt's sojourn is most memorable for one thing: the day he took the field wearing a wig and dark glasses after criticizing fans in the newspaper.

As a whole, an otherwise dreary season is best remembered for an offensive explosion on June 11. The Phillies, who scored just 25 runs in the first nine games of June, erupted that night in a 26–7 thrashing of the Mets. Von Hayes led off the bottom of the first with a homer and smashed a grand slam later in the inning, and the Phillies set team records for runs, hits (27), and extra-base hits (14).

In addition to his 102 RBI in 1985, rocket-armed right fielder Glenn Wilson led NL flyhawks in assists each year from 1985 to 1987.

▶ 75-87   5th ◀

Highlights

April 19: Under new manager John Felske, the Phillies jump off to a 1–8 start, putting them seven games out of first place.

June 11: In a 26–7 romp over the Mets, Von Hayes becomes the first MLB player to hit two home runs in the first inning, the second of which is a grand slam.

July 16: Outfielder Glenn Wilson and catcher Ozzie Virgil are Philly's All-Star representatives.

September 11: A 13–3 streak puts the Phillies at .500 for the first time all season, but they will never have a winning record.

October 2: The Phillies lose their eleventh straight game.

NOTES

Juan Samuel steals 53 bases and scores 101 runs, but he again leads the league in strikeouts (141).

Mike Schmidt belts 33 homers.

Glenn Wilson leads the team in RBI (102) and tops NL outfielders in assists (18).

Kevin Gross (15–13, 3.41) and **Shane Rawley** (13–8, 3.31) are the bright lights on the starting staff.

Former Pirates star **Kent Tekulve** saves 14 games, while **Don Carman** sets a team record for appearances by a left-hander (71).

1986

Highlights

April 20: Garry Maddox, who won eight Gold Gloves with the Phillies, plays his last game before retiring.

May 9: The Phillies release pitcher Dave Stewart, who will win 20 games with Oakland in each of the next four seasons.

May 22: The Phils are 14–22, 11½ games behind the high-flying Mets.

June 2: The Phillies win their seventh straight, outscoring opponents 47–13 during the stretch.

June 23: The Phils crush the Cubs 19–1, as Juan Samuel knocks in six.

June 24: Steve Carlton (4–8, 6.18) is released.

August 20: Don Carman loses a perfect game at San Francisco when Bob Brenly leads off the ninth with a double. The Phillies win 1–0 in 10 innings on a Samuel home run.

NOTES

Mike Schmidt wins his third NL MVP Award after leading the league in homers (37), RBI (119), and slugging (.547). He also wins his tenth and final Gold Glove.

Von Hayes hits .305–19–98, while **Juan Samuel** swipes 42 bases.

Kevin Gross (12–12) leads the staff in victories.

Steve Bedrosian, acquired from Atlanta, saves 29 games.

Fightin' Phillies
Team Shows True Grit in Comeback Season

It was clear from the start of this season that nobody would catch the New York Mets. They were a sure thing, and played like it, winning 108 games and the World Series.

For the Phillies, then, the storyline became self-respect. After a forgettable 1985 season, they needed to show improvement and come as close to the Mets as they could. That is exactly what happened.

There were tears along the way. Garry Maddox, the graceful center fielder, retired in May. In June, owner Bill Giles choked up as he announced the release of Steve Carlton, the proud and stubborn left-hander who would not retire despite a 6.18 ERA.

Lefty's replacement, Bruce Ruffin, made the Topps All-Rookie Team with a 9–4 record and a sterling 2.46 ERA. Steve Bedrosian and Kent Tekulve supported an ever-changing rotation with stellar relief, and Mike Schmidt led the league in homers and RBI to win his third and final MVP Award.

No Phillies pitcher exceeded 12 victories. The team got little production from its outfield, and shortstop Steve Jeltz, at .219 with no homers, continued his helpless performance at the plate. Yet somehow, the Phillies managed an 86–75 record, good for second place, and they delayed the Mets from clinching the division with an electric three-game weekend at the Vet in September.

The Mets needed one victory to formally win the National League East, and their rabid fans were ready to party. Mets fans flooded the upper deck, and the tension created a charged atmosphere not to be experienced again at the Vet until 1993.

The Phillies rose to the occasion. Schmidt bashed his 493rd career homer—tying Lou Gehrig on the career list—to propel the Phillies past Dwight Gooden on Friday and send them on their way to a sweep. The Mets would clinch soon enough, of course, but they had to leave the Phillies' turf to do it.

Mike Schmidt's eighth home run title in 1986 set an National League record, as he one-upped Ralph Kiner. Babe Ruth (12) was the only big-leaguer to win more.

500 AND .500

Schmidt Belts Milestone Homer for Mediocre Team

By 1987, Bill Giles' vision of the Phillies as the Team of the '80s was spinning out of reach. So Giles bucked his fellow owners, who were colluding to keep salaries down by not signing each other's free agents. He plucked star catcher Lance Parrish from the Detroit Tigers in hopes of building off the Phillies' strong 1986 season.

Instead, Parrish sagged to a .245 average, and manager John Felske was fired after a 29–32 start. Lee Elia went 51–50 the rest of the way, leaving the Phillies just shy of .500 at 80–82 and in fourth place.

Behind the record was a season of oddities. Kevin Gross was suspended for 10 games in August after umpires found sandpaper glued to his glove. Veteran newcomer Joe Cowley completely lost his control, walking 17 in 11⅔ innings and never pitching again. Greg Gross homered for the first time in nine seasons with the Phils, and Kent Tekulve set a club mark with 90 games pitched.

The high point of the season came on April 18, when Mike Schmidt batted in the ninth inning at Three Rivers Stadium in Pittsburgh with two outs, two on, and the Phillies trailing the Pirates 6–5. Don Robinson fell behind in the count, 3–0,

Armed with a nasty slider, closer Steve Bedrosian won the NL Cy Young Award in 1987. His 40 saves were, at the time, third most in league history.

and fired a fastball down the middle. This is what Harry Kalas said next:

"Swing and a long drive! There it is! Number 500! The career five hundredth home run for Michael Jack Schmidt!"

It was a classic Schmidt blast—a hard line drive that sliced through the air and disappeared in a hurry over the left field wall. The Phillies won 8–6, as Schmidt became the 14th player to reach the 500-home run club.

The bearded Steve Bedrosian proved to be the star of the team. He racked up 40 saves, matching his uniform number, and gave the Phillies their third Cy Young winner in six seasons.

PHILLIES PHACT

With the Phillies down 6–5 with two on and two out in the bottom of the ninth, on April 18, Mike Schmidt socks a walk-off homer against Pittsburgh. It's his 500th career home run.

Highlights

April 7: Shane Rawley is the starting pitcher on Opening Day, ending Steve Carlton's 14-year run.

April 16: The Phillies start the season at 1–8. From here, they won't come within 3½ games of first place.

June 7: Rookie Michael Jackson loses a no-hitter in the ninth against Montreal.

June 18: With the club at 29–32, Lee Elia takes over managerial duties from John Felske.

September 29: Don Carman tosses a one-hit shutout against the Mets.

NOTES

Mike Schmidt enjoys his last productive season, tallying 35 HRs and 113 RBI.

Juan Samuel raps .272–28–100 with 113 runs, 35 steals, 37 doubles, and an NL-high 13 triples.

Outfielder Milt Thompson hits .302 with 46 stolen bases.

Reliever Steve Bedrosian wins the Cy Young Award. His 40 saves are a league high and a Phillies record.

Shane Rawley (17–11) leads the staff in wins.

Kent Tekulve sets a Phillies pitching record with 90 appearances.

1988

▸ 65-96   6th ◂

Highlights

April 17: The Phillies lose their seventh straight game to fall five games back. They will not get back in the race.

June 8: New general manager Woody Woodward is fired two months into the season. Lee Thomas will replace him.

July 12: Pitcher Kevin Gross and catcher Lance Parrish make the All-Star team as reserves.

September 23: John Vukovich replaces Lee Elia as Phillies manager.

September 24: With a 1–0 loss to Montreal, the Phillies are shut out for the sixteenth time.

NOTES

Run production is down throughout the league, including Philadelphia, where Juan Samuel leads the team with just 67 RBI.

The Phils ranks near the bottom of the NL in runs scored, runs allowed, and fielding percentage.

Hampered by a rotator cuff injury, **Mike Schmidt** hits just 12 home runs.

Kevin Gross (12–14, 3.69) is the ace of the staff, as only one pitcher out of 21 has a winning record.

Steve Bedrosian saves 28 games despite missing much of the season with pneumonia.

TIME TO CLEAN HOUSE

No One's Safe After Last-Place Performance

Only the most devout Phillies fans—or those who had little else to do in 1988—remember some of the names who wore the burgundy pinstripes in this woeful last-place season. Bill Almon. Danny Clay. Jackie Gutierrez. Alex Madrid. Bob Sebra. Mike Young.

Steve Bedrosian missed the start of the season with pneumonia. Mike Schmidt missed the end with a rotator-cuff injury. New left fielder Phil Bradley was a dud. The image of pitcher David Palmer losing his balance and tumbling over third base, a staple of blooper reels for years to come, pretty much defines this sad bunch.

This was a team that gave 450 plate appearances to Steve Jeltz, the shortstop with inexplicable staying power throughout the second half of the '80s. Jeltz batted .187, again with no homers. Lance Parrish was nearly as bad, with a sickly .215 mark. Chris James led the team in homers with just 19. Three starters had at least 14 losses, and just one, Kevin Gross, earned more than 10 wins.

A new first baseman, Ricky Jordan, offered hope when he homered off Houston's Bob Knepper on July 17 in his first official major league at-bat. But even the Phillies' date with history was ultimately wiped from the record books: On August 8, they were the visitors in Chicago for the first night game ever at Wrigley Field. Bradley led off with a homer, but rain washed away the game before it could be official.

Woody Woodward, hired to run the baseball operations after the previous season, was fired in June and replaced by Lee Thomas as general manager. Thomas, who had helped build the St. Louis Cardinals, hired a new scouting director and minor league director, and he fired manager Lee Elia and some of his coaches in September. A roster overhaul was up next, and everyone knew it was needed.

Second baseman Juan Samuel cannot prevent Chicago's Andre Dawson from stealing second base—or his team from finishing in last place in 1988.

So Long, Mike

While New Stars Arrive, Schmidt Calls It Quits

The 1989 Phillies had a new manager in Nick Leyva. They had a new color for their road uniforms, with gray replacing baby blue. And on Memorial Day, they had a new third baseman, though no one could replace the man who retired that day.

Mike Schmidt decided he was no longer playing to his standards. With a .203 average, six home runs, and greatly diminished skills in the field, Schmidt called a news conference before a game in San Diego.

"Some 18 years ago, I left Dayton, Ohio, with two very bad knees and a dream to become a major league baseball player," Schmidt said, his cracking voice thick with emotion. "I thank God that dream came true."

Chris James played third base for Schmidt that night, but in less than a week he was gone, shipped to the Padres for John Kruk and Randy Ready. On June 18, Lee Thomas pulled off two more deals, sending Juan Samuel to the Mets for Lenny Dykstra and Roger McDowell and swapping Steve Bedrosian to the Giants for Dennis Cook, Charlie Hayes, and Terry Mulholland.

The Phillies finished in last place again, but the deals energized the fans. Along the way, two victories stand out. One was a 15–11 win over Pittsburgh after the Phillies trailed 10–0 in the first. The other occurred on May 15, when the Phillies and the World Series–bound Giants played scoreless ball for 11 innings at the Vet.

The Giants scored twice in the top of the 12th on back-to-back homers by Will Clark and Kevin Mitchell. With two on and two out in the bottom of the inning, Bob Dernier pulled a ball down the left-field line. It rattled around in the corner, skidding away from Mitchell. Dernier scrambled madly around the bases, sliding safely headfirst into home and pounding his palms on the dirt in celebration of a walk-off, three-run, inside-the-park home run.

Long before he penned the autobiography *I Ain't an Athlete, Lady*, John Kruk was a fan favorite in Philly. He averaged .309 in his six years there.

Highlights

April 4: The Phillies open the season with a new manager, 35-year-old Nick Leyva.

May 29: Mike Schmidt announces his retirement at age 39. He leaves as the team's all-time leader in hits (2,234), HRs (548), RBI (1,595), runs (1,506), total bases (4,404), and walks (1,507).

June 4: The Phils run their losing streak to 11 games.

June 8: The Phillies overcome a 10–0 first-inning deficit against Pittsburgh to win 15–11.

June 18: GM Lee Thomas announces two big trades: Steve Bedrosian and a minor leaguer to San Francisco for pitchers Dennis Cook and Terry Mulholland and third baseman Charlie Hayes; and Juan Samuel to the Mets for outfielder Lenny Dykstra and reliever Roger McDowell.

July 4: Phils shortstop Dickie Thon breaks up a perfect game by Reds pitcher Tom Browning with a ninth-inning leadoff double.

NOTES

Von Hayes, the team's sole All-Star, leads the Phils in home runs (26) and RBI (78).

Midseason arrival **John Kruk** rips .331 in 81 games for the Phillies.

Roger McDowell posts a 1.11 ERA and 19 saves for the Phils.

Team Leaders

Batting

1980: Bake McBride, .309
1981: Pete Rose, .325
1982: Bo Diaz, .288
1983: Garry Maddox, .275
1984: Von Hayes, .292
1985: Mike Schmidt, .277
1986: Von Hayes, .305
1987: Milt Thompson, .302
1988: Milt Thompson, .288
1989: Tommy Herr, .287

Home Runs

1980: Mike Schmidt, 48
1981: Mike Schmidt, 31
1982: Mike Schmidt, 35
1983: Mike Schmidt, 40
1984: Mike Schmidt, 36
1985: Mike Schmidt, 33
1986: Mike Schmidt, 37
1987: Mike Schmidt, 35
1988: Chris James, 19
1989: Von Hayes, 26

RBI

1980: Mike Schmidt, 121
1981: Mike Schmidt, 91
1982: Mike Schmidt, 87
1983: Mike Schmidt, 109
1984: Mike Schmidt, 106
1985: Glenn Wilson, 102
1986: Mike Schmidt, 119
1987: Mike Schmidt, 113
1988: Juan Samuel, 67
1989: Von Hayes, 78

Wins

1980: Steve Carlton, 24–9
1981: Steve Carlton, 13–4
1982: Steve Carlton, 23–11
1983: John Denny, 19–6
1984: Jerry Koosman, 14–15
1985: Kevin Gross, 15–13
1986: Kevin Gross, 12–12
1987: Shane Rawley, 17–11
1988: Kevin Gross, 12–14
1989: Ken Howell, 12–12

ERA

1980: Steve Carlton, 2.34
1981: Steve Carlton, 2.42
1982: Steve Carlton, 3.10
1983: John Denny, 2.37
1984: John Denny, 2.45
1985: Shane Rawley, 3.31
1986: Bruce Ruffin, 2.46
1987: Don Carman, 4.22

1988: Kevin Gross, 3.69
1989: Ken Howell, 3.44

Strikeouts

1980: Steve Carlton, 286
1981: Steve Carlton, 179
1982: Steve Carlton, 286
1983: Steve Carlton, 275
1984: Steve Carlton, 163
1985: Kevin Gross, 151
1986: Kevin Gross, 154
1987: Don Carman, 125
1988: Kevin Gross, 162
1989: Ken Howell, 164

Saves

1980: Tug McGraw, 20
1981: Tug McGraw, 10
1982: Ron Reed, 14
1983: Al Holland, 25
1984: Al Holland, 29
1985: Kent Tekulve, 14
1986: Steve Bedrosian, 29
1987: Steve Bedrosian, 40
1988: Steve Bedrosian, 28
1989: Roger McDowell, 19

NL Leaders

1980: Doubles—Pete Rose, 42;
Home Runs—
Mike Schmidt, 48;
RBI—Schmidt, 121;
Wins—Steve Carlton, 24;
Strikeouts—Carlton, 286
1981: Runs—Schmidt, 78;
Hits—Rose, 140;
Home Runs—Schmidt, 31;
RBI—Schmidt, 91
1982: Wins—Carlton, 23;
Strikeouts—Carlton, 286;

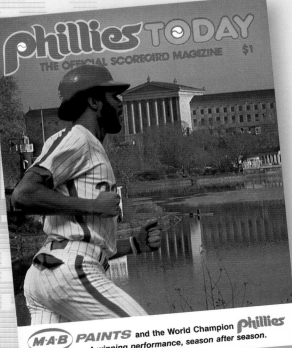

Like Rocky Balboa, Bake McBride gets a workout on the streets of Philadelphia, as depicted on this *Phillies Today* cover from 1981.

M·A·B PAINTS and the World Champion *Phillies*
A winning performance, season after season.

Complete Games—
   Carlton, 19;
   Shutouts—Carlton, 6
1983: Home Runs—Schmidt, 40;
   Wins—John Denny, 19;
   Strikeouts—Carlton, 275
1984: Triples—Juan Samuel, 19;
   Home Runs—Schmidt, 36;
   RBI—Schmidt, 106
1986: Runs—Von Hayes, 107;
   Doubles—Hayes, 46;
   Home Runs—Schmidt, 37;
   RBI—Schmidt, 119
1987: Triples, Samuel, 15;
   Saves—Steve Bedrosian, 40

NL Awards

MVP Voting

1980: Mike Schmidt, 1st;
   Steve Carlton, 5th,
   Bake McBride, 10th
1981: Mike Schmidt, 1st,
   Steve Carlton, 9th,
   Pete Rose, 10th
1982: Mike Schmidt, 6th;
   Steve Carlton, 9th
1983: Mike Schmidt, 3rd;
   Al Holland, 9th
1984: Mike Schmidt, 7th
1986: Mike Schmidt, 1st;
   Von Hayes, 8th

This 1980 Cy Young Award was Steve Carlton's third. Two years later, he would become the first pitcher to win four.

Cy Young Winners

1980: Steve Carlton
1982: Steve Carlton
1983: John Denny
1987: Steve Bedrosian

Gold Glove Winners

1980: Mike Schmidt, 3B;
   Garry Maddox, OF
1981: Steve Carlton, P;
   Manny Trillo, 2B;
   Mike Schmidt, 3B;
   Garry Maddox, OF
1982: Manny Trillo, 2B;
   Mike Schmidt, 3B;
   Garry Maddox, OF
1983: Mike Schmidt, 3B
1984: Mike Schmidt, 3B
1986: Mike Schmidt, 3B

NL All-Stars

1980: Steve Carlton, P;
   Pete Rose, 1B;
   Mike Schmidt, 3B

1981: Pete Rose, 1B;
   Mike Schmidt, 3B;
   Steve Carlton, P;
   Dick Ruthven, P;
   Manny Trillo, 2B
1982: Pete Rose, 1B;
   Manny Trillo, 2B;
   Mike Schmidt, 3B;
   Steve Carlton, P
1983: Mike Schmidt, 3B
1984: Mike Schmidt, 3B;
   Al Holland, P;
   Juan Samuel, 2B
1985: Ozzie Virgil, C;
   Glenn Wilson, OF
1986: Mike Schmidt, 3B;
   Shane Rawley, P
1987: Mike Schmidt, 3B;
   Steve Bedrosian, P;
   Juan Samuel, 2B
1988: Kevin Gross, P;
   Lance Parrish, C
1989: Von Hayes, OF;
   Mike Schmidt, 3B

Mike Schmidt used this bat in 1988 to belt his 536th career home run, tying him with Mickey Mantle for seventh on the all-time list.

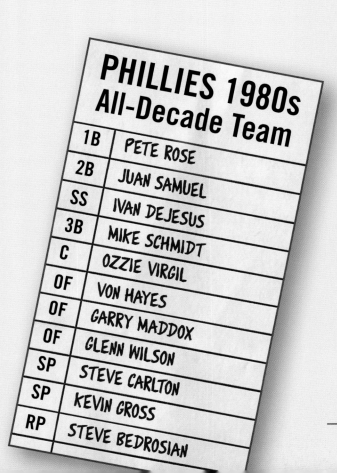

PHILLIES 1980s All-Decade Team

1B	PETE ROSE
2B	JUAN SAMUEL
SS	IVAN DEJESUS
3B	MIKE SCHMIDT
C	OZZIE VIRGIL
OF	VON HAYES
OF	GARRY MADDOX
OF	GLENN WILSON
SP	STEVE CARLTON
SP	KEVIN GROSS
RP	STEVE BEDROSIAN

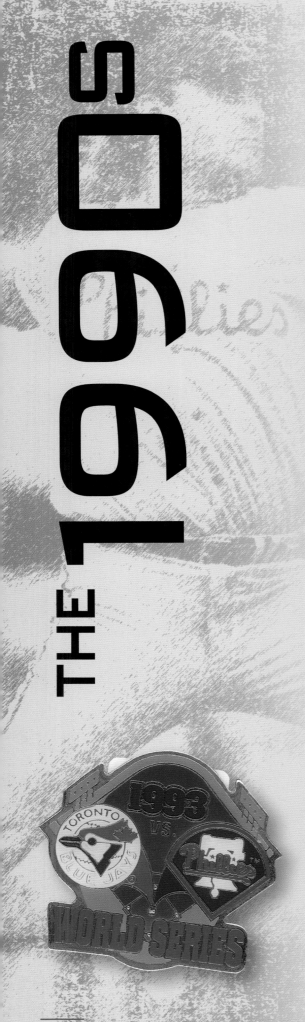

TASTE OF GLORY

The Phillies romp to the World Series in 1993 with a motley crew, but they otherwise fail to reach the postseason during the decade.

With one stunning and exhilarating exception, the decade of the 1990s was one to forget for the Phillies. They rose from last place in 1992 to the World Series in 1993, but that would be the only winning season of the decade. In fact, from 1984 to 2006, that '93 season was the only one in which the Phillies reached the playoffs.

Just as frustrating, in some ways, was the sense that the game was passing them by. The revolution in ballpark building was going on all around, and the Phillies could not get in the game. The Baltimore Orioles opened their sparkling Camden Yards in 1992, showing fans how fun it could be to watch baseball in an old-style setting with modern amenities. Envy spread quickly up I-95 to Philadelphia.

Veterans Stadium, the Philadelphia's dual-purpose, AstroTurf structure, had been progressive when it opened in 1971, but by the 1990s it had become a relic. A venue with more than 60,000 seats was impractical for regular-season baseball, and the sterile atmosphere stifled any real sense of community in the stands.

Fans could look past the Vet's drawbacks when the Phillies were winning—the team drew 3.1 million fans in 1993, and it was on pace to top 3 million again before the strike in 1994—but too often the team was a loser. As much as Phillies management wanted the financial boon of a new ballpark, it struggled to find a suitable financing plan and location.

The first three years of the '90s were a buildup to 1993. General manager Lee Thomas added to the core of Darren Daulton, Lenny Dykstra, John Kruk, and Terry Mulholland by cobbling together veterans and castoffs—Mitch Williams, Jim Eisenreich, Danny Jackson—and plucking a young pitcher or two in almost every deal.

It was a shrewd strategy borne largely out of necessity; the Phillies had a threadbare farm system and needed to look elsewhere for young talent. Mulholland, Curt Schilling, and Tommy Greene, who formed the top of the '93 rotation, all came from other teams in trades.

Mulholland started the last game of the 1993 season—the infamous Game Six of the World Series in Toronto—and Williams finished it. Neither was back for 1994, with Mulholland traded to the Yankees to save money and Williams exiled to Houston. Injuries ruined Greene, who made just 15 more starts over the rest of his career, and derailed Schilling, who was 9–13 in 30 starts over the 1994 and '95 seasons.

The Phillies flirted with contention in 1995 but finished 69–75. Although he batted .306, heralded free agent Gregg Jefferies was a disappointment. In hindsight, the Phillies should have gone all-out for the other free agent they considered that offseason: future MVP Larry Walker.

Fans loved the team's joyride to the 1993 World Series, but it was the only season of the decade in which the Phils had a winning record.

Jim Fregosi was fired after the 1996 season, which was notable only for the All-Star Game the Phillies hosted that July. They had just one representative, reliever Ricky Bottalico, and finished last in the standings. Terry Francona took over as manager in 1997, when third baseman Scott Rolen won the NL Rookie of the Year Award and Schilling notched 319 strikeouts. But that team, too, landed in the basement.

Rolen, Schilling, and Bobby Abreu gave fans reason to cheer the next two seasons, but Francona could not lift the team above third place. Francona and Schilling would go on to win two championships together in Boston, and Rolen would win a title with St. Louis. But the Phillies' time would come.

Lenny Dykstra and his teammates high-five each other after winning Game Five of the 1993 World Series against Toronto. "Nails" and company would lose the series in dramatic fashion two nights later.

Highlights

May 25: The Phillies win to go 24–16 and move into first place. They will drop out of first for good the next day.

June 4: After his third straight three-hit game, outfielder Lenny Dykstra is hitting .418.

June 10: Dykstra's average drops to .401 after his 23-game hitting streak is snapped.

July 10: Dykstra leads off for the NL in the All-Star Game. He is the Phillies' sole representative.

August 3: The Phils acquire two-time NL MVP Dale Murphy from the Braves in a multiplayer deal.

August 15: Terry Mulholland no-hits the Giants, becoming the first Phillies pitcher to achieve the feat at home in the twentieth century.

September 23: Hayes cracks a walk-off hit to defeat Montreal in the sixteenth inning.

November 23: Former Phillies catcher Bo Diaz, 37, is crushed to death by a satellite dish.

NOTES

Lenny Dykstra hits .325 and leads the league in hits (192) and OBP (.418).

Von Hayes paces the team in homers (17) and RBI (73).

Pat Combs leads the staff in wins (10–10), but **Terry Mulholland** (9–10, 3.34) is the most effective starter.

CHARACTERS WITH CHARACTER

Dykstra, Kruk, Mulholland Lead the Way

When he played for the Mets, the cocky, fidgety Lenny Dykstra was a player whom Phillies fans loved to hate. But with a full-season look at Dykstra as one of their own, Philadelphia fell in love. Dykstra helped spark the team to a 21–13 start in 1990, and by June 10 he was hitting .407. *Sports Illustrated* made him the first Phillies cover boy in five years.

Though he faded in the second half, Dykstra still hit .325. John Kruk, also acquired in a midseason trade in '89, hit .291 and showed a keen eye at the plate. Catcher Darren Daulton finally emerged as a solid hitter, and the Phillies shrewdly retained the rights to young third baseman Dave Hollins by keeping him in the majors all season.

Dykstra, Kruk, and Hollins had all been acquired by general manager Lee Thomas, whose vision for the team—characters with character—was taking shape. Thomas also reached for veteran outfielder Dale Murphy, landing the Atlanta Braves icon in a trade for a package of middling prospects.

But the season's high point came from left-hander Terry Mulholland, who anchored the staff for the first four years of the decade. On August 15 against his old team, the Giants, Mulholland spun the Phillies' first no-hitter at home in the twentieth century.

More important than his 1990 no-hitter, starter Terry Mulholland was remarkably consistent for Philly, with 33 complete games and a cumulative ERA of 3.52 from 1990 to 1993.

Mulholland faced the minimum 27 batters, the only blemish coming when a wild throw by third baseman Charlie Hayes allowed Rick Parker to reach first base in the seventh inning. Parker was erased on a double play, and Mulholland was perfect the rest of the way. Hayes made up for his miscue by snaring the game-ending out, stretching for a liner by Gary Carter before Mulholland tossed his glove and wrapped Daulton in embrace.

The Phillies did not contend—just one pitcher, Pat Combs, reached 10 victories—but this was their most interesting team in years.

PLAYING WITH AN EDGE

Manager Fregosi Demands a New Attitude

The Phillies improved by just one game in 1991, from 77 wins to 78. But they continued to add to their nucleus and create a culture that would eventually help them rise to the top of the National League.

Thirteen games into the season, with a 4–9 record, Lee Thomas hired his old Angels teammate, Jim Fregosi, to replace the fired Nick Leyva. A gruff but personable character who had managed in the majors since 1978, Fregosi demanded that his team play hard, and with an edge. They responded, winning 13 games beginning July 30 to tie a modern club record, although the season, by then, had been lost.

The Phillies' fortunes went awry in May, when Lenny Dykstra and Darren Daulton suffered injuries when Dykstra crashed his Mercedes after John Kruk's bachelor party. Dykstra broke his collarbone and was charged with drunk driving. He reinjured the collarbone in August and played in only 63 games. Daulton played in 89 games and hit just .196.

But a season that could have easily represented a step back was not. John Kruk became an All-Star with a terrific year, leading the team with a .294 average, 21 homers, and 94 RBI. Terry Mulholland was a horse, logging 232 innings to go with a 16–13 record. Dave Hollins showed promise with a .298 average in limited work.

Thomas found a closer in Mitch "Wild Thing" Williams, obtained from the Cubs in a trade, and held his breath as Williams collected 30 saves and 12 victories.

Righty Tommy Greene broke out with a 13–7 record and 3.38 ERA. Greene was not part of the rotation at the start of the season, but he established himself in his second start on May 23 in Montreal. He walked seven but was unhittable, striking out 10 and tossing the Phillies' second no-hitter in two years with a 2–0 victory over the Expos.

In August 1991, Mitch "Wild Thing" Williams went 8–1 with five saves and four blown saves. He posted a 1.21 ERA for the month despite earning his nickname by walking 16 batters in 22 1/3 innings.

1991

▶ 78-84   3rd ◀

Highlights

April 23: After the Phillies' 4–9 start, Jim Fregosi replaces Nick Leyva as manager.

April 28: Second baseman Randy Ready is at the center of a triple play against San Diego.

May 23: Tommy Greene no-hits the Expos in Montreal, walking seven in a 2–0 victory.

August 9: Reliever Mitch "Wild Thing" Williams wins his fifth game of the month. He will win eight games total in the month—an MLB record for a reliever.

August 12: The Phils win their thirteenth straight game, although they are still under .500 (53–58).

October 6: David Cone of the Mets ties an NL record for strikeouts when he fans 19 Phillies in the season finale.

NOTES

Lenny Dykstra twice fractures his collarbone, once while driving drunk and then by crashing into a wall. MLB also places him on probation for gambling.

John Kruk bats .294 and leads the team in homers (21) and RBI (92).

Terry Mulholland (16–13, 3.61) and **Tommy Greene** (13–7, 3.38) anchor the staff.

Mitch Williams goes 12–5 while posting a 2.34 ERA, notching 30 saves, and allowing 6.3 walks per nine innings.

169

THE FINAL PIECES

Phils Add Schilling, Jackson to Promising Mix

To signal a new direction in 1992, the Phillies unveiled new uniforms on Opening Day at the Vet. They ditched their burgundy color scheme and the familiar baseball-in-P logo for the traditional red of the old days, with a script "Phillies" wordmark across the pinstripes, little blue stars dotting the i's, and a liberty bell as part of the logo.

As a fashion statement, it looked sharp. As a positive omen, it didn't work. On the second pitch of the season, the Cubs' Greg Maddux shattered Lenny Dykstra's wrist with a pitch. Future general manager Ruben Amaro Jr. made a brief splash as a replacement, but without Dykstra, who played only 85 games, the Phillies lacked a spark.

Other injuries piled up, and the decimated pitching staff needed 15 different starters to make it through a 70–92, last-place season. But Darren Daulton led the league in RBI, John Kruk hit .323, and Dave Hollins erupted for 27 homers while driving in 93. Second baseman Mickey Morandini even turned the first unassisted triple play in the National League in 65 years one afternoon in Pittsburgh.

> ### PHILLIES PHACT
> On September 20, Mickey Morandini becomes the first second baseman in NL history to turn an unassisted triple play.

Meanwhile, Lee Thomas continued to find useful parts. Thomas inherited a barren farm system, and he did not draft well to add to it. But he made the most of his marginal prospects. In April, he shipped Jason Grimsley (who was 5–12 in 27 career starts) to Houston for Curt Schilling, a hard-throwing, underachieving reliever.

Inspired by an offseason lecture from Roger Clemens, Schilling started taking baseball more seriously, and when the Phillies got him, he was ready to take off. Under the guidance of pitching coach Johnny Podres, Schilling went 14–11 with a 2.35 ERA in 1992, holding opponents to a league-low .201 average.

After the season, Thomas made another steal when he dealt two forgettable pitching prospects to the expansion Florida Marlins for veteran lefty Danny Jackson. Few knew it then, but that move gave the Phillies all the pieces they needed for a strong rotation that would turn the team around in 1993.

Opposite: Curt Schilling blossomed after coming to Philadelphia in 1992, completing 10 of his 26 starts and hurling 4 shutouts. His 1,554 strikeouts in nine years with the Phillies left him fifth on the franchise all-time list.

Highlights

April 2: The Phillies trade Jason Grimsley to Houston for Curt Schilling.

April 7: The team opens the season with new uniforms, as the P is replaced on both the home and road jerseys with Phillies. In the opening game at Chicago, the second pitch of the season breaks Lenny Dykstra's wrist.

June 24: A loss at Montreal drops the Phillies into last place—for good.

July 6: Starting pitcher Kyle Abbott loses to drop to 0–11. He'll finish at 1–14.

July 14: Outfielder John Kruk and catcher Darren Daulton represent Philly at the All-Star Game.

NOTES

John Kruk finishes third in the NL in batting (.323) after leading for most of the year.

After six sub-.210 seasons, catcher **Darren Daulton** stuns the league with 27 home runs and an NL-high 109 RBI while batting .270.

Third baseman **Dave Hollins** emerges with 27 homers and 93 RBI.

After starting the season in the bullpen, **Curt Schilling** becomes the ace of the staff, going 14–11 with a 2.35 ERA (fourth in the NL).

Terry Mulholland (13–11) tops the league with 12 complete games.

1993

Highlights

May 10: The Phillies beat Pittsburgh to improve to 23–7.

July 3: A Mitch Williams walk-off single beats San Diego at 4:40 a.m.

July 7: Philly defeats the Dodgers 7–6 in 20 innings on a two-run, walk-off double by Lenny Dykstra.

September 28: The Phils win 10–7 in Pittsburgh to clinch the NL East.

October 13: The Phillies beat the Braves 6–3 in Game 6 of the NLCS. Curt Schilling, with two pitching gems, is named series MVP.

October 20: Toronto scores six in the eighth to defeat the Phils 15–14 in Game 4 of the World Series.

October 21: Schilling shuts out the Blue Jays 2–0 in Game 5.

October 23: Toronto's Joe Carter belts a three-run walk-off homer off Mitch Williams in the ninth inning of Game 6 to clinch the world title.

NOTES

Lenny Dykstra (143 runs, 37 SBs), Darren Daulton (105 RBI), Kevin Stocker (.324), and John Kruk (.316) power the NL's best offense.

Curt Schilling and Tommy Greene lead the staff with 16 wins apiece.

Mitch Williams is fourth in the league with 43 saves.

What a Ride!

The Fun Lasts Until Carter's Series Blast

You knew it would end sometime. It had to, right? The Phillies had spent nine full seasons in the wilderness. Injuries haunted them. They had no championship pedigree, and they certainly did not look the part. The adventure of the zany 1993 Phillies, it seemed, would simply be fun while it lasted, a giddy little diversion for a woebegone franchise.

In the end, that was indeed their epitaph. The Phillies rose for one glorious season and then slipped right back to mediocrity and misfortune. But few could have expected the trip to last all the way to the sixth game of the World Series. Even at the very end, these Phillies were no fluke. They rose for one final, frantic comeback that Saturday night in Toronto before an unforgettable crash-and-burn on Joe Carter's epic home run. Typically for the 1993 Phillies, they did not simply limp off the stage. They blew it up.

A heartbreaking finish? In the moment, sure. But in hindsight, not really. To come so close to a championship and lose is wrenching. But to look back bitterly at the 1993 Phillies is to miss the whole point of sports. That Phillies team kept fans riveted to their radios, sent them streaming into the Vet, made them queasy when Mitch Williams wobbled on his tightrope, and made them proud with each rollicking victory.

More than that, the players connected with the fans as few teams have. They had scraggly mullets and scruffy beards and spit so much tobacco that they were mocked for it on *Saturday Night Live*. They flexed their muscles—nobody asked about steroids back then—and stayed late in the clubhouse, drinking beer and bonding. They hustled all the time.

We knew they could hit. As John Kruk told David Letterman the previous summer—quoting Williams—"the best thing about our pitching is that we hit good." But in 1993, the pitching awoke. Night after night, Jim Fregosi would start his postgame press conference with: "You can't say enough good things about Curt Schilling." Or Terry Mulholland. Or Tommy Greene. Or Danny Jackson. Or even Ben Rivera.

All five made at least 28 starts, giving the rotation the consistency it had lacked for years. Schilling, Jackson, and Greene each logged at least 200 innings, and Mulholland's 3.25 ERA was the best of the bunch. Lefty David West and righty Larry Andersen dependably set up Williams, who earned 43 saves.

Jackson, West, and Andersen were all brought in after the 1992 debacle. They were typical of the moves made by general manager Lee Thomas, who banked on better health in 1993 and focused on complementary pieces to fill specific roles.

Thomas imported three veteran outfielders: Pete Incaviglia and Milt Thompson, who formed a platoon in left, and Jim Eisenreich, who teamed with Wes Chamberlain in right. All four had productive seasons flanking Lenny Dykstra, the runner-up to Barry Bonds for the NL MVP Award.

Dykstra, who had so often struggled to stay on the field, played 161 games and made 773 plate appearances, a major league record that would stand until the next

Dave Hollins goes deep against Greg Maddux to put the Phillies up 4–1 in the fifth inning of Game 6 of the NLCS. Philly went on to win 6–3 to clinch the series.

time the Phillies made the playoffs—in 2007, when another leadoff man, Jimmy Rollins, broke it with 778. Dykstra pulled off the nifty trick of leading the league in both at-bats and walks, while also leading in hits. His 143 runs scored was the highest NL total since the Phillies' Chuck Klein in 1932.

The Phillies simply wore down opposing pitchers, grinding out walks and hammering strikes. Six regulars had an on-base percentage over .360, including Dykstra, Kruk, Eisenreich, Darren Daulton, Dave Hollins, and shortstop Kevin Stocker, who was promoted on July 7 to stabilize the one weakness in the lineup.

By then, the Phillies had established themselves as a team that not only won, but did so in thrilling and creative style.

On April 29 in San Diego, Thompson scaled the fence in the eighth inning to save a grand slam and preserve a win. On May 9, down by three runs to St. Louis with two

Built Tough

Lenny Dykstra arrived in Philadelphia in June 1989 with supreme self-confidence and the ability to back it up. A 1986 postseason hero with the Mets, "Nails" was traded to Philly— along with prized reliever Roger McDowell—for Juan Samuel, an infielder-turned-outfielder whose star was slipping. For Philadelphia that summer, Dykstra hit just 222 in 90 games.

While the Mets quickly ditched Samuel, Dykstra stayed put . . . and batted 103 points higher in 1990. His .325 average ranked third in the National League, and his 192 hits and .418 on-base percentage topped the circuit.

Injuries, including a broken collarbone in a drunk-driving accident, hampered his next two seasons, but he rallied in 1993. Dykstra led the league in runs (143), hits (194), and walks (129) while clubbing 19 homers and stealing 37 bases. He was second in NL MVP voting, and his team claimed the pennant by beating Atlanta in the National League Championship Series.

Beset by injuries, Dykstra never played another full season, and his missteps in finance later landed him in serious legal trouble. In Philly, however, Dykstra will always be remembered for being as tough as nails.

Even this Topps card showcases "Nails" in his down-and-dirty best.

outs in the bottom of the eighth, Mariano Duncan drilled a grand slam off Lee Smith for a one-run victory. On May 30 at Colorado, Greene homered and pitched a complete game, improving to 7–0 in an 18–1 laugher.

On and on it went. At the end of June, the Phillies were 52–25, the best record in the majors, with a 6½ game lead in the NL East. After starting July with two losses, they hosted the Padres in the second game of a doubleheader. After hours of rain had delayed the first game, the nightcap actually started in the early morning—1:28 a.m., to be precise. The Padres built a 5–0 lead, and as the local bars let out, night-crawlers descended on the Vet and stumbled in for free. This was the Phillies' kind of crowd, and the hometown team came back to tie it in the eighth.

The game dragged to the tenth inning—more baseball, why not?—before Williams, of all people, stroked a game-winning single to left off Trevor Hoffman. On the air, a delirious Harry Kalas gave Williams a new nickname—"Mitchie Poo"—and the scoreboard clock read 4:40, the latest a major league game had ever ended.

By late August, the Phillies' lead had grown to 11 games. It shrunk to four by September 19, but nine days later the division was theirs, with Kalas singing "High Hopes" in the clubhouse in Pittsburgh.

Schilling opened the NL Championship Series with five strikeouts in a row against the Atlanta Braves before a frothy crowd at the Vet. A Kim Batiste throwing error let the Braves tie the game in the ninth, but Batiste won it with a game-ending double in the tenth.

The Braves took the next two convincingly, drubbing Greene and Mulholland, but then things turned bizarre. The Phillies left 15 runners on base in Game Four, but Jackson was brilliant, working into the eighth and driving in the go-ahead run in a 2–1 victory. Williams blew another Schilling masterpiece in Game Five, but Dykstra homered in the tenth to send the series back to Philadelphia with the Phillies leading three games to two.

From there, it was bedlam. Mickey Morandini lined a ball off Greg Maddux's leg in the first inning of Game Six, and Maddux allowed six runs. That was plenty for Greene, who worked seven strong innings. Williams clinched the pennant with a 1-2-3 save, firing a fastball past Bill Pecota to win it and leaping to the sky.

The World Series would end much differently, of course, and the Phillies played catch-up from the start. The Blue Jays—who boasted future Hall of Famers Rickey Henderson, Roberto Alomar, and Paul Molitor—knocked around Schilling in Game One, but a three-run homer by Eisenreich helped even the series in Game Two.

Back at the soggy Vet, Toronto mauled Jackson in Game Three, then prevailed through the rain and mist in Game Four, scoring six in

"Going home and sulking isn't going to bring that ball back over the fence. It ain't coming back. That ball is out of the park."

—Mitch Williams, on Joe Carter's World Series–ending home run

the eighth off Andersen and Williams for a backbreaking 15–14 victory. Schilling's Game Five shutout took the World Series back to Canada, where a three-run blast by Dykstra sparked a five-run rally in the seventh that gave the Phillies a one-run lead.

Roger Mason, a nondescript righty, had retired seven in a row when Fregosi replaced him with one out in the eighth. West and Andersen survived a rocky inning, but they turned over the lineup so that Henderson—the greatest leadoff hitter in baseball history—would start the ninth against Williams.

Naturally, Henderson drew a walk. Molitor singled him to second, and Williams, distracted by the game's all-time leading base stealer, tried a slide-step delivery for the first time in his career. With a 2-2 count, he shook off Daulton's call for a slider and tried to throw a fastball up and away. Instead, it was down and in.

He might have gotten away with it, except Carter was expecting the slider. Because of that, he was able to stay back on the fastball and keep it fair. The ball sailed over the left-field wall, Carter soared into history, fireworks burst inside the SkyDome, and the Phillies were finished.

"They did what they had to do to win this series, and I let us down in big situations," Williams said. "I carry that burden. No excuses. I didn't get the job done."

It was the last pitch Williams ever threw for the Phillies. The fun was over, but the ride was a blast.

Philly fans—and reliever Mitch Williams (right)—were delivered a devastating blow in Game 6 of the 1993 Fall Classic, when Joe Carter (background) clubbed the second World Series–ending homer in history.

1994

▶ 54-64   4th ◀

Highlights

April 4: The reigning NL champions begin the season without Terry Mulholland and Mitch Williams (both traded). John Kruk is coming off preseason treatment for testicular cancer.

May 7: A fourth straight loss drops Philly to 11–18, 7½ games back. The team will go the whole season without making a charge.

July 12: Lenny Dykstra and second baseman Mariano Duncan are selected as All-Star starters, and pitchers Danny Jackson and Doug Jones join them.

July 31: Steve Carlton is inducted into the Baseball Hall of Fame.

August 12: Major league players go on strike. No games will be played over the rest of the season.

NOTES

John Kruk (.302), **Darren Daulton** (.300), and outfielder **Jim Eisenreich** (.300) lead the team in hitting.

Danny Jackson goes for 14–6 and 3.26 in 25 outings.

Doug Jones, a veteran pickup, posts a 2.17 ERA and saves 27 games.

Former Dodgers phenomenon **Fernando Valenzuela** starts seven games for Philadelphia (1–0, 3.00 ERA).

The Phils draw 2,290,971 fans despite the abbreviated season.

SHORT BUT NOT SWEET

A Players' Strike Means No Return to Series

Coming off their pennant-winning 1993 season, the Phillies aimed for a return trip to the World Series. In 1994, however, they not only didn't make it back to the Fall Classic, but no one did. An ongoing labor dispute came to a head, and on August 12 the players went on strike. When a resolution was not forthcoming, the rest of the season was canceled, and for the first time since 1904, there was no World Series.

The Phillies welcomed back nearly all of the key players from the pennant-winning 1993 club. They also welcomed new teams into a realigned National League East, including the expansion Florida Marlins and the Atlanta Braves, who would come to dominate the division in the years to come. Meanwhile, Mitch Williams, who had coughed up the 1993 Series-winning homer, was swapped to Houston for closer Doug Jones.

The season started with a bang. In sweeping the Colorado Rockies, the Phillies became the first team ever to open the season by winning back-to-back road games while trailing in the eighth. However, that would be about it. John Kruk missed the start of the season due to testicular cancer, which was just the first in a series of problems for the team. For example, Andy Carter, a young reliever who had grown up in Philly, was tossed from his May 3 big-league debut after hitting two of the first three batters he faced. The ballclub hovered around .500 until dipping below it to stay on July 5.

The Phillies' pitching woes certainly contributed to the team's tough year. Injuries, particularly to aces Curt Schilling and Tommy Greene, wrecked the staff so much that Philly had to dip into the Mexican League for a past-his-prime Fernando Valenzuela.

Perhaps the only highlight of the season came in a game that didn't count. As the defending NL champ, Jim Fregosi led the NL All-Stars to victory. His own Doug Jones was the winning pitcher.

With the decline of the Phillies and the distaste from the 1994 players' strike, the team suffered at the gate over the rest of the decade.

THE PHILLY ROLLERCOASTER

A Hot Start Fades in the Heat of the Summer

Though the Phillies' 1995 season didn't begin until April 26 due to the players' strike, the team started the year like gangbusters. The Phils jumped to a 37–18 start and had a 4½ game lead on June 25. They didn't lose back-to-back games until June 2 and 3. Their ace pitcher, Curt Schilling, was having another great season. The season's initial closer, Norm Charlton, failed in the role, but they found an All-Star replacement in Heathcliff Slocumb. They were on a roll. Of course, Phillies fans knew to brace themselves. Due up next: the inevitable downfall.

A late-June homestand against the Reds and Braves was a disaster, as the Phillies' lost six of seven. That began a streak in which the Phils would lose 34 of 46 and disappear from contention. They won at a .574 clip in the first half, .395 in the second. Remember that division lead? They ended up 21 games behind the Braves.

When Mickey Morandini and Jim Eisenreich are your key offensive contributors, you know your team is not built on power. Three players tied with 11 homers for the team lead (a season that was only 144 games long due to the delayed start). Injuries played a role, too, knocking out Darren Daulton, Lenny Dykstra, and David West for long periods.

The Phillies did pull it together to make a run at the newly created wildcard spot. Led by a pair of midseason pickups—Sid Fernandez, who had five wins in August, and Mark Whiten, who ended up one of that trio with 11 bombs—the Phils were five games over .500 in late August. But they won only four games from September 13 through 29, and that was that. An injury-wracked and confidence-shaken Phillies team slunk into the offseason, at least sure that 1996 would start on time.

Jim Eisenreich, at 36 years old, was one of the Phillies' most productive offensive contributors in 1995. He hit .316 that season and a combined .324 in his four seasons with the team (1993–1996).

Highlights

April 26: The new season begins late due to the players strike.

May 30: The Phillies jump out of the gate with a surprising 23–8 record.

July 4: After nearly two months in first place, the Phils drop out of the top spot for good.

July 11: Lenny Dykstra, Darren Daulton, Mickey Morandini, Tyler Green, and Heathcliff Slocumb make the All-Star team, but only Slocumb (32 saves) will finish the year with exceptionally good numbers.

July 30: A large throng of Phillies fans flocks to Cooperstown, as Mike Schmidt and Richie Ashburn are inducted into the Baseball Hall of Fame.

August 10: A 13–32 drought drops the team below .500.

August 25: The Phillies beat the Dodgers 17–4, as Gregg Jefferies hits for the cycle.

NOTES

Outfielders Jim Eisenreich (.316) and **Gregg Jefferies** (.306) lead the team in batting.

Third baseman Charlie Hayes tops the club in RBI (85), while he and two others lead in homers with just 11.

Paul Quantrill (11–12) is the only pitcher to win in double digits.

1996

▶ 67-95   5th ◀

Highlights

May 3: The Phillies beat Atlanta to move to 16–11, just one game out.

June 18: With their 11th loss in 12 games, the Phils fall into the cellar, where they will remain for the rest of the season.

July 9: Veterans Stadium hosts the All-Star Game. Ricky Bottalico is the team's sole All-Star representative.

August 4: Jim Bunning is inducted into the Hall of Fame.

September 30: Terry Francona replaces Jim Fregosi as Phillies manager.

NOTES

The injury-riddled Phillies tie an NL record by fielding 54 players during the season. Darren Daulton and Lenny Dykstra miss most of the year with injuries.

Catcher Benito Santiago tops the club in homers (30) and RBI (85).

Jim Eisenreich raps .361 in 338 at-bats.

Curt Schilling (9–10) leads the league in complete games (8) and his team in wins.

Ricky Bottalico logs 34 saves, helping the team go 25–22 in one-run games.

The team's attendance (1,801,677) is its lowest for a full season since 1973.

JUNE SWOON

Ghastly Month Compounds Phillies' Woes

Only two seasons before this one, Major League Baseball stopped play in August. Some Phillies fans probably were hoping for a repeat after a dismal June dropped the team far out of playoff contention.

The season had started out with some hope. Added power from free-agent acquisitions Benito Santiago, Todd Zeile, and Pete Incaviglia figured to give some pop to the team's light-hitting '95 lineup. Only Santiago truly paid off, hitting 30 homers, by far a career high for the five-time All-Star catcher. Rookie pitcher Mike Grace was a revelation, going 6–0 to start the season. (In a sign of things to come, he missed the second half of the year with an elbow injury.) Grace was a big part of the Phillies' decent jump out of the gate that saw them at 16–11, even without the services of ace Curt Schilling until late May. They didn't really make a big move in either direction for several weeks after that.

And then came June.

Starting with a June 5 loss to the Cubs, the Phillies won only four games in their next 23. Goodbye, playoffs.

Unfortunately, the biggest highlight of the summer in Philly was one that most of their fans could only watch on TV. The All-Star Game was played at Veterans Stadium for the second time. Adding to a summer of misery, Phillies fans watched Dodgers catcher Mike Piazza, a native son who got away, slug a homer to help the National League win.

July and August signaled the end of the line for a lot of Phillies, as the team looked to dump salaries. Zeile, Incaviglia, and pitcher Terry Mulholland all turned in their red-and-white uniforms.

In one hopeful, yet still injury-tinged sign, rookie third baseman Scott Rolen joined the club on August 1. However, a wrist injury knocked him out for September. The silver lining? He remained in line for the big award he would win in 1997.

Coming off an All-Star campaign in 1995, Mickey Morandini struggled at the plate in 1996—along with many of his teammates. He did nab a career-high 26 bases, however.

SLUMP RIDDEN

Another Horrible June Dooms the Phils

The Phillies improved in 1997 under new manager Terry Francona, but only by one game. They also didn't wait until June to hit bottom, getting that out of the way in April. They did have another swoon, though, losing 19 of 20 from June 14 to July 4. In fact, their 4–22 mark in the month was the worst June in franchise history—and with their history, that's saying something.

The Phillies couldn't even win against amateurs. They selected Golden Spikes Award–winning outfielder J. D. Drew, No. 2 overall in the June draft, but he wouldn't sign with the team. Philadelphia even had to pull a starter, Scott Ruffcorn, from a no-hitter in the sixth inning because he was too wild. And in a tragic note, popular broadcaster and fan favorite Richie Ashburn died of a heart attack in September, not long after covering a game in New York against the Mets.

But even with all that, believe it or not, the Phillies ended the 1997 season hopeful and excited about the future. That's what you get when you rise from the depths of a 30–72 record in late July to a finishing record of 38–22 (only the Yankees matched that record in all of baseball . . . and the Phils swept the Yanks to open September). How did that happen?

Scott Rolen, the NL Rookie of the Year, was a big reason, with a club-leading 92 RBI. Turnarounds by catcher Mike Lieberthal and first baseman Rico Brogna also helped. Waiver-wire acquisition Midre Cummings hit .303. Having an ace like Curt Schilling never hurts, either, and his 17 wins led an improving staff. Rookie Garrett Stephenson chipped in with eight wins. Ricky Bottalico (34 saves) was also terrific.

After having chased the 1962 Mets for the first half of the season, the Phillies' resurrection turned some heads. Fifth place never looked so good.

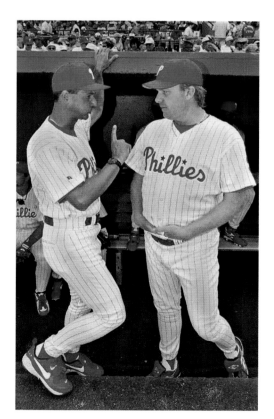

With a franchise-record 319 strikeouts in 1997, Curt Schilling (right) needed little advice from rookie manager Terry Francona (left) at that season's spring training.

Highlights

April 1: Free-agent acquisition Danny Tartabull, who drove in 101 runs for the White Sox in 1996, breaks his foot on Opening Day and will go 0-for-7 as a Phillie.

April 23: The Phils drop to 6–13 and fall into last place for good.

June 3: The team drafts super-prospect J. D. Drew, but they won't be able to meet his considerable financial demands.

July 4: The Phillies suffer their 11th straight loss and 19th defeat in 20 games. Their record is 24–62.

September 1: Curt Schilling rings up 16 strikeouts against the Yankees.

September 28: The Phillies conclude the season having won 38 of their last 60 games thanks to much-improved hitting.

December 9: New team president David Montgomery replaces GM Lee Thomas with Ed Wade.

NOTES

Third baseman Scott Rolen leads the club in homers (21) and RBI (92) and is named NL Rookie of the Year.

Curt Schilling goes 17–11 and leads the league with 319 strikeouts, a team record.

Attendance drops again, to 1,490,638, due to the team's poor start and aging stadium.

1998

▶ 75-87   3rd ◀

Highlights

March 31: The Mets defeat the Phillies 1–0 in 14 innings, the longest 1–0 Opening Day game in NL history.

April 5: Curt Schilling strikes out 15 against Atlanta.

May 19: Cardinals slugger Mark McGwire, en route to 70 home runs, belts three against the Phillies.

July 7: Schilling is the Phillies' sole All-Star.

July 12: A sixth straight win pushes the team's record to 46–42.

August 30: The Phillies pull off a triple play against the Giants.

September 8: Marlon Anderson becomes the first Phillie to slug a pinch-hit home run in his first big-league at-bat.

NOTES

Lenny Dykstra retires before the season.

Scott Rolen leads the team in HRs (31), RBI (110), and runs (120) and becomes the first Phillie in 12 years to win a Gold Glove Award.

First baseman Rico Brogna drives in 104 runs.

Outfielder Bobby Abreu, picked up in a preseason trade, leads the team in hitting at .312.

Curt Schilling goes 15–14 and leads the NL in complete games (15) and strikeouts (300). He is the fifth MLB pitcher to record back-to-back 300-K seasons.

180

ALL THE RIGHT MOVES

Phils Ascend to Third Place in Rebuilding Year

A batch of new faces brought fresh hope to Veterans Stadium in 1998. The momentum of 1997 kept rolling, as most of the team's offseason player moves paid off. The Phillies weren't really in contention, but they weren't in the cellar, either. Onward and upward.

With Scott Rolen now firmly anchored at third and continuing his outstanding play, the other infielders upped their games, too. New shortstop Desi Relaford shined defensively, while Mark Lewis held the second-base spot until Marlon Anderson got ready in the minors (and then hit .326 during a September call-up). Over at first, Rico Brogna's run-producing skills finally reached their potential. In the outfield, a pair of newcomers quickly became Phillies favorites. Bobby Abreu showed the first inklings of his power-speed combination, while Doug Glanville flashed leather and speed.

The pitching was again anchored by Curt Schilling. His workhorse ability (15 complete games) was key because the bullpen was shaky. The return of Mark Portugal from injury (he missed nearly all of 1997) and his 10 wins gave the rotation a bit of depth. Midseason pickup Paul Byrd contributed a few big wins, too. Ricky Bottalico's injury forced Al Leiter into the closer role, and he contributed 23 saves.

Put it all together, and the revamped club managed to stay above .500 entering the month of August. Highlights included a few improbable comebacks, which showed that the team had some heart to go with its new talent. Particularly memorable was a win over the Pirates on June 16, when the Phillies scored seven runs in the bottom of the ninth to prevail 8–7. They overcame a 7–0 deficit to defeat the Florida Marlins on July 26.

In the middle of a string of seasons (1987–2000) that saw the Phillies finish over .500 just once, the 1998 campaign was a bright spot despite the team's overall 75–87 record.

In addition hitting .290 with 31 homers and 110 RBI in 1998, 23-year-old Scott Rolen ranked among NL leaders in runs (120), doubles (45), and walks (93).

FUN WHILE IT LASTED

Great Start Ends with September Implosion

You could almost see Phillies general manager Ed Wade cackling with glee during the summer of 1999. He had spent the previous year shuffling the Phillies' deck, adding free agents, nursing along young players, patching, filling, and building. It all seemed to come together in 1999, as the Phillies made a run at the playoffs.

And then came September, when cackling turned to cursing. But we'll get to that in a moment.

The reasons for the team's success in the first three-quarters of the season were numerous. Bobby Abreu had the best season of his young career with his first 20-20 campaign (20 homers, 27 stolen bases). He and third baseman Scott Rolen were the heart of a heavy-hitting lineup. Speedy Doug Glanville hit .325 and became the first Phillies player since Pete Rose in 1979 to amass 200 hits. Newly added Ron Gant helped give the Phillies one of the top outfields in the National League. Even catcher Mike Lieberthal finally lived up to his offensive prowess.

In 1999, Mike Lieberthal and Texas' Ivan Rodriguez became the first catchers to hit .300, knock 30 homers, and win a Gold Glove all in the same season.

The offense drove the show, but the pitching staff improved as well. Curt Schilling once again led the way with 15 wins, and Paul Byrd, Robert Person, and Randy Wolf were terrific—for a while.

Put it all together and you got a team that beat the Padres 15–1 on August 25 to move to eight games over .500. Then the roof fell in.

Schilling's shoulder injury was the first straw, knocking him out after August 7. Rolen then went on the shelf with a back injury. The rest of the team imploded at the same time, and the Phillies lost 18 of their next 19 games. Wolf went from 5–0 to 6–9. Starter Chad Ogea ended up at 6–12. It wasn't 1964, but a season that had been going along pretty well quickly turned to another walk into loser land.

Highlights

May 15: Shortstop Alex Arias starts a triple play for the Phillies against the Mets.

July 3: The Phils crush the Cubs 21–8, as Marlon Anderson goes 5-for-6.

August 6: The Phillies beat Arizona in 11 innings to improve to 61–48, but subsequent injuries will take them out of the playoff race.

August 24–25: The Phils crush the Padres 18–2 and 15–1, with Rico Brogna going 8-for-10 with nine RBI over the two games.

September 4: The Reds set an NL record with nine home runs in a 22–3 shellacking of the Phillies.

September 14: The team suffers its 11th consecutive defeat and its 18th loss in 19 games.

NOTES

Catcher Mike Lieberthal hits .300 with 31 homers and 96 RBI and wins a Gold Glove Award.

Bobby Abreu cracks .335–20–93 with 27 stolen bases and 118 runs.

Outfielder Doug Glanville raps .325 with 204 hits, 101 runs, and 34 steals.

Ron Gant (107) gives the team three outfielders with 100 runs scored.

Curt Schilling (15–6) and **Paul Byrd** (15–11), both All-Stars (along with Lieberthal), lead the team in victories.

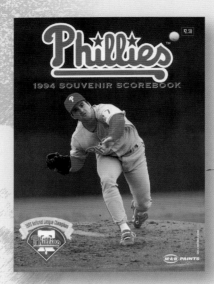

Danny Jackson (14–6, 3.26 ERA) was on pace for a 20-win campaign before the strike ended the 1994 season.

Team Leaders

Batting

1990: Lenny Dykstra, .325
1991: John Kruk, .294
1992: Darren Daulton, .323
1993: Jim Eisenreich, .318
1994: John Kruk, .302
1995: Jim Eisenreich, .316
1996: Jim Eisenreich, .361
1997: Mickey Morandini, .295
1998: Bobby Abreu, .312
1999: Bobby Abreu, .335

Home Runs

1990: Von Hayes, 17
1991: John Kruk, 21
1992: Darren Daulton, 27;
Dave Hollins, 27
1993: Darren Daulton, 24;
Pete Incaviglia, 24
1994: Darren Daulton, 15
1995: Charlie Hayes, 11;
Gregg Jefferies, 11;
Mark Whitten, 11

1996: Benito Santiago, 30
1997: Scott Rolen, 21
1998: Scott Rolen, 31
1999: Mike Lieberthal, 31

RBI

1990: Von Hayes, 73
1991: John Kruk, 92
1992: Darren Daulton, 109
1993: Darren Daulton, 105
1994: Darren Daulton, 56
1995: Charlie Hayes, 85
1996: Benito Santiago, 85
1997: Scott Rolen, 92
1998: Scott Rolen, 110
1999: Rico Brogna, 102

Wins

1990: Pat Combs, 10–10
1991: Terry Mulholland, 16–13
1992: Curt Schilling, 14–11
1993: Curt Schilling, 16–7
1994: Danny Jackson, 14–6
1995: Paul Quantrill, 11–12
1996: Curt Schilling, 9–10
1997: Curt Schilling, 17–11
1998: Curt Schilling, 15–14
1999: Paul Byrd, 15–11;
Curt Schilling, 15–6

ERA

1990: Terry Mulholland, 3.34
1991: Tommy Greene, 3.38
1992: Curt Schilling, 2.35
1993: Terry Mulholland, 3.25
1994: Bobby Munoz, 2.67
1995: Paul Quantrill, 4.67
1996: Curt Schilling, 3.19
1997: Curt Schilling, 2.97
1998: Curt Schilling, 3.25
1999: Curt Schilling, 3.54

Strikeouts

1990: Pat Combs, 108
1991: Tommy Greene, 154
1992: Curt Schilling, 147
1993: Curt Schilling, 186
1994: Danny Jackson, 129
1995: Curt Schilling, 114
1996: Curt Schilling, 182
1997: Curt Schilling, 319
1998: Curt Schilling, 300
1999: Curt Schilling, 152

Saves

1990: Roger McDowell, 22
1991: Mitch Williams, 30
1992: Mitch Williams, 29
1993: Mitch Williams, 43
1994: Doug Jones, 27
1995: Heathcliff Slocumb, 32
1996: Ricky Bottalico, 34
1997: Ricky Bottalico, 34
1998: Mark Leiter, 23
1999: Wayne Gomes, 19

NL Leaders

1990: Hits—Lenny Dykstra, 192
1992: RBI—Darren Daulton, 109;
Complete Games—
Terry Mulholland, 12
1993: Runs—Dykstra, 143;
Hits—Dykstra, 194
1996: Complete Games—
Curt Schilling, 8
1997: Strikeouts—Schilling, 319
1998: Strikeouts—Schilling, 300;
Complete Games—
Schilling, 15
1999: Triples—Bobby Abreu, 11

1993 National League Champions™

Philadelphia Phillies™
Limited Edition
9618 of 30,000

NL Awards

NL MVP Voting
1990: Lenny Dykstra, 9th
1992: Darren Daulton, 6th
1993: Lenny Dykstra, 2nd; Darren Daulton, 7th

NL Rookie of the Year Winners
1997: Scott Rolen

Gold Glove Winners
1998: Scott Rolen, 3B
1999: Mike Lieberthal, C

NL All-Stars
1990: Lenny Dykstra, OF
1991: John Kruk, 1B
1992: Darren Daulton, C;
John Kruk, 1B
1993: Terry Mulholland, P;
Darren Daulton, C;
John Kruk, 1B;
Dave Hollins, 3B

1994: Mariano Duncan, 2B;
Lenny Dykstra, OF;
Danny Jackson, P;
Doug Jones, P
1995: Lenny Dykstra, OF;
Darren Daulton, C;
Tyler Greene, P;
Mickey Morandini, 2B;
Heathcliff Slocumb, P
1996: Ricky Bottalico, P
1997: Curt Schilling, P
1998: Curt Schilling, P
1999: Curt Schilling, P;
Paul Byrd, P;
Mike Lieberthal, C

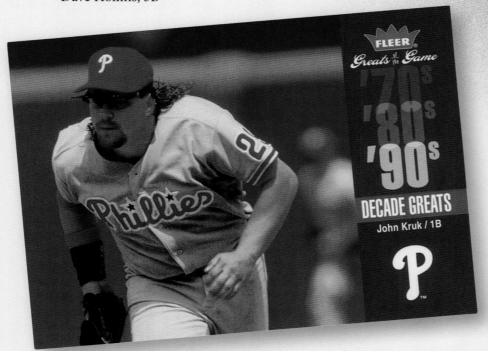

FLEER
Greats of the Game
'70s
'80s
'90s
DECADE GREATS
John Kruk / 1B

Fleer tabbed first baseman John Kruk as one of the decade's greats. From 1991 to 1993, he made the All-Star team each year for the Phillies.

PHILLIES 1990s All-Decade Team

1B	JOHN KRUK
2B	MICKEY MORANDINI
SS	KEVIN STOCKER
3B	SCOTT ROLEN
C	DARREN DAULTON
OF	LENNY DYKSTRA
OF	JIM EISENREICH
OF	GREG JEFFERIES
SP	CURT SCHILLING
SP	TERRY MULHOLLAND
RP	MITCH WILLIAMS

RISE TO THE TOP

With a new ballpark, dynamic sluggers, and some of the best pitchers in baseball, the Phillies evolve into a perennial contender, winning it all in 2008.

Throughout the years, the Phillies promised fans that they would start spending more on talent if and when they secured a new stadium. That proved to be a major legislative undertaking, and the Phillies lagged far behind their cross-state counterparts, the Pittsburgh Pirates, who opened a new park in 2001, some three months before the Phillies even broke ground on theirs.

But it all proved worth the wait, because management lived up to its word. The team signed Jim Thome, the strapping slugger from the Cleveland Indians, who took a six-year, $85 million deal before the 2003 season, the final one at Veterans Stadium. With Citizens Bank Park rising in the parking lot beyond right field, Thome blasted 47 homers, one shy of Mike Schmidt's franchise record, and pitcher Kevin Millwood hurled a no-hitter.

In the 2000s, shortstop Jimmy Rollins (left) and first baseman Ryan Howard (right)—both NL MVPs during the decade—powered the Phillies to unprecedented success.

Unfortunately for Larry Bowa, the favorite son who was finally hired as Phillies manager for the 2001 season, that '03 team finished 15 games out of first place, with 86 wins. That seemed to be the ceiling for Bowa's teams, who won 86, 80, 86, and 86 games in his four seasons.

The core of the Bowa teams—Bobby Abreu, Pat Burrell, Mike Lieberthal, Randy Wolf—simply could not knock the Atlanta Braves off their perch atop the National League East. Even adding an elite closer, Billy Wagner, did not work. After two seasons, Wagner fled to the New York Mets and promptly helped them take down the Braves in 2006, ending Atlanta's run of 14 consecutive playoff appearances.

By then, Bowa was gone from Philly, replaced by Charlie Manuel, who had come to the club in a front-office role in 2003. After two productive seasons in Philadelphia, Thome broke down physically in 2005, and his presence was keeping a superior power prospect, Ryan Howard, trapped in the minors.

General manager Pat Gillick, who succeeded Ed Wade after the 2005 season, traded Thome to the White Sox for hard-nosed center fielder Aaron Rowand, who helped change the culture in the clubhouse. Gillick added several more important pieces, including starter Jamie Moyer, outfielder Jayson Werth, and closer Brad Lidge. Most importantly, though, the farm system was finally growing its own superstars.

Under the supervision of Mike Arbuckle, the Phillies drafted and developed a bumper crop of talent, including Howard, Jimmy Rollins, Chase Utley, Carlos Ruiz, Cole Hamels, Brett Myers, and Ryan Madson. They also produced the prospects needed to trade for Lidge.

In 2007, the Phillies stormed back to the playoffs for the first time since 1993, overcoming a deficit of seven games with 17 to play to upend the Mets for the NL East title. After a sweep by Colorado in a Division Series that October, the Phillies went all the way in 2008, marching past the Milwaukee Brewers, Los Angeles Dodgers, and Tampa Bay Rays to claim the franchise's second World Series championship.

Just five days after Lidge dropped to his knees upon fanning Eric Hinske to clinch the title, Gillick announced he was turning over the general manager job to Ruben Amaro. Amaro, who proved to be aggressive and resourceful, dipped into the still-rich prospect pool in July 2009 to trade for Cliff Lee. The former Cy Young Award winner helped the Phillies back to the World Series, where they lost in six games to the Yankees.

Amaro dealt Lee to Seattle after the season, but he sent another batch of prospects to Toronto for Roy Halladay, who won the 2010 NL Cy Young Award for Philadelphia while tossing a perfect game and a playoff no-hitter. Amaro also dealt homegrown players to the Astros for Roy Oswalt, and after an NLCS loss to the San Francisco Giants, he snared Lee again as a free agent in the offseason.

The Phillies' rotation was the envy of baseball in 2011, and fans responded by scooping up every available ticket to every game at Citizens Bank Park. The Phillies were a phenomenon, enjoying a sustained run of excellence that would have been hard to imagine just a decade before.

The Phillies breezed past Milwaukee (three games to one), L.A. (four to one), and Tampa Bay (four to one) en route to their 2008 world title.

Highlights

May 2: The Phillies open at 7–18, 12½ games out of first place.

May 4: The Phils crack four consecutive doubles in the first inning, and Doug Glanville collects five hits, in a 14–1 rout of the Reds.

July 11: Mike Lieberthal is the team's sole All-Star representative.

July 26: Curt Schilling (6–6) is traded to Arizona for four players.

October 1: Manager Terry Francona is fired. He will be replaced by Larry Bowa.

NOTES

Due largely to injuries, the Phillies finish with their worst record since 1972.

Scott Rolen hits .298–26–89 in 128 games, and he also wins a Gold Glove.

Bobby Abreu bats .316 with 25 homers and 28 stolen bases.

Doug Glanville swipes 31 bases and scores 89 runs.

Rookie first baseman **Pat Burrell**, the No. 1 overall pick in the 1998 draft, contributes 18 homers and 79 RBI.

Randy Wolf (11–9) is the only Phillies pitcher to win in double digits.

AN UGLY SEASON

Nothing Goes Right in Injury-Wracked Campaign

While America survived the dreaded Y2K bug on the first day of the millennium, some other type of virus seemed to plague the Phillies' bats. They finished last in the league in runs scored.

Hopes were high enough before the campaign started that "Bring It On!" was adopted as the team's marketing slogan. New hires such as pitcher Andy Ashby, along with the return of familiar face Mickey Morandini and the return from injury of several regulars, presaged a bit of hope. 'Twas not to be. Ashby was gone by July, missed by none (especially the fans with whom he argued after a game). Morandini was a shadow of his former Phillie self and was gone by August.

He wasn't alone. As the team plummeted down the standings, the front office made like a fantasy team, dumping players left and right at the trade deadline. Schilling, after so many magnificent seasons, was sent to Arizona (where he would win a World Series the following year). The team also bid farewell to less-heralded but still useful players such as Desi Relaford, Ron Gant, and Rico Brogna.

PHILLIES PHACT

With the Phillies and Giants tied 1–1 on August 27, Bobby Abreu ends the game in thrilling fashion in the bottom of the tenth, lacing a game-ending inside-the-park home run.

Along with all the injuries and player moves, those who stuck around showed perfect timing . . . by having rotten seasons themselves. Doug Glanville's average dropped by 50 points. The team used 27 pitchers, who combined for a team ERA of 4.77.

Bright spots? Amid the disaster, a few players shone relatively brightly. Scott Rolen and Mike Lieberthal delivered, though both of their seasons were shortened by injuries. Pat Burrell played well in his first full season, while a September call-up named Jimmy Rollins took the first steps in his remarkable Philly career.

Not around to watch that career? Manager Terry Francona and his coaching staff, who were given their walking papers after the season. If this was how the 2000s were going to be, thought Phillies fans, let's turn back the clock.

Opposite: Third baseman Scott Rolen won four Gold Glove Awards with the Phillies thanks to his consistent and often spectacular play.

Highlights

April 6: The Phillies retire Jim Bunning's No. 14.

June 1: In first place since April 13, the Phillies are now 35–18, eight games up in the NL East.

June 27: The Braves sweep the Phils and take over first place.

July 15: The Phillies draw 59,470 for a game against the Yankees.

August 26: Rookie Jimmy Rollins is finally caught stealing after 35 consecutive swipes.

September 11–16: The Phillies are idle as MLB shuts down due to the 9/11 terrorist attacks.

September 26: The Phils are one game out after Randy Wolf shuts out the Reds on one hit.

October 2–4: The Phillies defeat Atlanta 3–1 behind pitcher Wolf to pull within one game of the first-place Braves. However, they then lose the next two to Atlanta to fall three games back with three to play.

NOTES

Bobby Abreu amasses 31 homers, 36 steals, 110 RBI, and 118 runs.

Jimmy Rollins leads the NL in triples (12) and steals (46).

Robert Person (15–7) tops the staff in wins, while **Jose Mesa** records 42 saves.

Larry Bowa is named NL Manager of the Year.

Bowa Fires 'Em Up

But Team Falls Short After 9/11 Shutdown

After a long dry spell, the Phillies put it all together in 2001. They ended up on the cusp of the playoffs for the first time since 1993. Though they once again missed the postseason—after being in first place as late as September 24—2001 kicked off a series of winning seasons that carried them to their next championship. Unfortunately, the season and the nation were marred by the tragic events of September 11.

Almost exactly the same Phillies team that had won a mere 65 games in 2000 busted out of the gate in 2001. Their success might have resulted from the simple fear of fiery new manager Larry Bowa. But it also could have been the result of a maturing young team coming into its own (and staying healthy).

Bowa, the team's longtime shortstop and a key contributor to the 1980 world champions, had managed briefly in San Diego. His style was considered too abrasive for the Padres, but in Philadelphia his tough love definitely worked. Fans and players alike appreciated his intensity. A local newspaper ran a contest to see how soon he would be ejected from a game, and a coach got a swollen hand after high-fiving the fired-up skipper.

"He's always pacing and cheerleading and trash-talking, as if he's itching to get out on the field," said center fielder Doug Glanville. "It works. We're all focused from the first pitch of the game. He gets everybody's attention."

That attention must have wandered in late spring, however. By June 1, the Phillies were the best team in the National League (35–18), but then they lost 16 of 23 games. The final three came at the hands of the Atlanta Braves, who leapfrogged Philly for first place. The Phils recaptured the lead not long after the All-Star break, but they couldn't create enough separation from the Braves.

Bowa kept at his charges, however, and churned them back to the top of the division in August, setting up a furious charge to the end of the season.

Suddenly, on September 11, baseball just didn't seem to matter anymore. The stunning events shut down the game for

Patriotism flourished at the Vet and other big-league ballparks after 9/11. At each park, "God Bless America" was sung during the seventh-inning stretch.

a week as Americans reeled and fought to keep their balance. By September 17, baseball was back.

The Phillies were within a game soon after their return. However, a key series with Atlanta proved decisive in early October. The Braves won two of three to give themselves a three-game lead with three to play. Bowa's boys had fallen short.

It was a frustrating end to a positive season, but the signs pointed to a solid future. Abreu became the first 30-30 Phillie ever. Rollins developed into an All-Star. Rolen belted 25 homers and won another Gold Glove. Pat Burrell and first baseman Travis Lee were other key sluggers.

And, of course, Bowa would be back to kick some more tail in 2002.

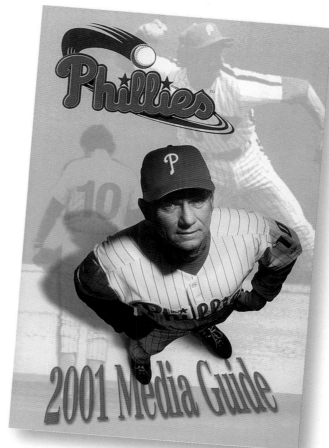

Hard-driving manager Larry Bowa had the Phillies in first place as late as September 1.

Mr. Consistency

The Tampa Bay Devil Rays suffered their first loss five months before they played their very first game. In November 1997, they foolishly traded Venezuelan Bobby Abreu to Philadelphia for shortstop Kevin Stocker.

The powerfully built Abreu was amazingly consistent during his nine years in a Phillies uniform. For seven straight seasons, he drew 100 or more walks. More importantly, he displayed a superior mix of speed (254 steals as a Phillie) and power (195 homers and 585 extra-base hits), resulting in the highest wins above replacement number (46.6) for a Phillie since Mike Schmidt. In 2005, he won the Home Run Derby with a record-shattering 41 big flys.

Abreu was a 30-homers/30-steals player in 2001 and 2004, but the Phillies sent Abreu and Cory Lidle to the Yankees at the 2006 trading deadline for four nondescript prospects. The trade seemed to signal a rebuilding phase, but that never happened. The Phils went on a tear over the last two months, missing the wildcard by three games. There would be no missing the postseason after that.

In 2001, Bobby Abreu became the first Phillies player to hit 30 homers and steal 30 bases in the same season.

2002

Highlights

April 10: Pat Burrell belts his second eleventh-inning, walk-off homer in four days.

April 29: The Phillies start 9–19 and are 8½ games out of first place.

June 2: In an 18–3 rout of Montreal, pitcher Robert Person socks two home runs and knocks in seven runs.

July 9: Vicente Padilla, Scott Rolen, and Jimmy Rollins represent Philadelphia in the All-Star Game.

July 15: The Phillies erupt for eight runs in the top of the ninth to overtake Montreal 11–8.

July 28: Phillies announcer Harry Kalas is inducted into the broadcasters' wing of the Baseball Hall of Fame.

July 29: The Phils trade star third baseman Rolen, a free agent-to-be, to St. Louis.

December 6: The team signs slugger Jim Thome as a free agent.

NOTES

Pat Burrell clubs 37 homers and ranks third in the NL in RBI (116).

Bobby Abreu leads the team in batting (.308), runs (102), and steals (31).

Vicente Padilla (14–11, 3.28) and **Randy Wolf** (11–9, 3.20) are the only effective starting pitchers.

Jose Mesa sets a franchise record with 45 saves.

A STEP BACKWARD
Too Many Players Fail to Meet Expectations

With the thrill of the 2001 pennant chase still fresh in their minds, Phillies fans were ready for the club to rock and roll in 2002. Unfortunately, for the first two months of the season, they got rocked or got rolled over. The Phils were 9–18 in April, lost 22 of their first 27 road games, and were eight games out when May turned into June. Manager Larry Bowa could push a lot of buttons, but he didn't have a button on a time machine.

The biggest problem was that the team's pitching, a strength in 2001, went south in 2002. Robert Person won only four games, Brandon Duckworth flopped, and the bullpen (aside from record-setting closer Jose Mesa) was underwhelming. The team's offense was adequate, with Pat Burrell and Bobby Abreu leading the way. However, Doug Glanville, Travis Lee, Marlon Anderson, and Jeremy Giambi underperformed.

The left side of the National League All-Star starting infield was manned by Phillies, as both third baseman Scott Rolen and shortstop Jimmy Rollins were voted in by the fans. Rolen, however, would not have gotten a lot of votes from his teammates. His feisty relationship with manager Larry Bowa and with the team's management as he headed toward a free-agent offseason caused numerous problems. In July, the Phillies dealt this potential franchise player to St. Louis. Did watching him leave buoy the club? They did win 25 of 37 in late July and August. However, even that successful streak was not enough to overcome their disastrous beginning. They couldn't even reach .500. A loss to Florida on the final day of the season left them one game short.

In a season of lowlights, one highlight was the solid return from injury of popular catcher Mike Lieberthal. He won the NL Comeback Player of the Year Award. Phillies fans hoped that "comeback" would be the theme for 2003.

Mike Lieberthal congratulates Pat Burrell (right) after one of his 37 home runs—most by a Philllie since Mike Schmidt in 1986.

GOODBYE TO THE VET

Last Season in Old Ballpark Is Topsy-Turvy

A promising 2001 had devolved into a frustrating 2002. And though the team would improve by six games in 2003, the season left fans even more exasperated. The Vet should have been renamed Six Flags Over Philly for its last season hosting the ball club. The players took fans on more roller-coaster rides this year than a dozen amusement parks. An example: On April 5, thanks in part to free-agent pickup Jim Thome's mighty bat, the Phillies whomped the Pirates 16–1. The next day? They got shut out by the same Pittsburgh team. The team couldn't put together any consistency from day to day or week to week. They started out pretty well, sitting in first place on April 28. A no-hitter by another free-agent pickup, Kevin Millwood, gave them the W that put them there. However, they would lose three of the next five, fall out of first, and never return.

They had a shot at the wildcard, however. By August 17, they led the standings for the bonus playoff spot. Then that old devil *inconsistency* struck, as they dropped 9 of 10 to disappear from the playoff radar. Their two longest losing streaks of the season (six games each) happened to come as they were chasing the wildcard spot late in the season.

After blasting 101 home runs for Cleveland in 2001–2002, first baseman Jim Thome launched 89 for the Phillies in 2003–2004.

In the steamy heat of late August, tempers boiled over. First, pitcher Randy Myers jawed with pitching coach Joe Kerrigan after taking a pasting from the Expos. Then Pat Burrell snubbed Larry Bowa in the dugout. Key pinch hitter Tyler Houston was cut after egging on Burrell. Patience was as thin as the fading artificial turf at the Vet.

The final series at the ballpark was bittersweet, as Philly lost two of three, including the finale, to Atlanta. Though fans enjoyed visits from past stars including Steve Carlton, Mike Schmidt, and Tug McGraw, they were probably wishing those guys were still playing instead of just watching.

2003

▸ 86-76   3rd ◂

Highlights

April 5: Jimmy Rollins goes 5-for-6 with three doubles in a 16–1 trouncing of Pittsburgh.

April 13: In the top of the fourth, the Phillies score a team-record 13 runs in one inning (thanks largely to seven walks). They win 13–1.

April 27: Offseason acquisition Kevin Millwood no-hits the Giants 1–0. He walks three and fans 10.

April 28: The Phils shut out the Dodgers 3–0 to hold onto first place. They will fall out of first for good the next day.

September 9: The Phillies crush Atlanta 18–5, as Tomas Perez and Jason Michaels belt grand slams.

September 8: The team finishes five games behind Florida in the wildcard chase.

November 3: The Phillies trade for All-Star closer Billy Wagner.

NOTES

Jim Thome leads the league in homers (47) and drives in 131 runs.

Bobby Abreu hits .300 with 101 RBI.

Mike Lieberthal and outfielder **Marlon Byrd** bat .313 and .303, respectively.

Randy Wolf (16–10) leads the team in wins, while **Kevin Millwood, Vicente Padilla,** and **Brett Myers** win 14 each.

Jose Mesa logs 24 saves, but his ERA is 6.52.

Home of Champions

Baseball in Philadelphia has been different since the Phillies moved into Citizens Bank Park in 2004. But for many entering the ballpark for the first time, there's an uncanny feeling that they've been there before.

Citizens Bank Park is a National League version of Camden Yards. It mimics the Baltimore park's redbrick exterior, ivy growing on the batter's eye, and a wide concourse that makes for good strolling, shopping, and eating. In fact, each has a barbeque joint named after a sizeable slugger from years past (Boog Powell in B'more and Greg "The Bull" Luzinski in Philly). Also like the Orioles, the first decade in the new digs coincided with a renewed fan following.

After the ballpark opened, the Phillies became a perennial winning team. At first, the offense carried the load. With a left-field power alley at 369 feet that actually was about 10 feet closer when measured with computer maps, balls tended to fly out of CBP—even after the fence was moved back by five feet. Despite decades of aiming at cozy Baker Bowl's sub-300-foot right-field fence, the Phils had never had a 200-homer season. They reached that plateau each of their first six years at Citizens Bank.

After Veterans Stadium (1971–2003), the new park was like a gift to Phillies fans. There were no more jokes about the worst AstroTurf in sports or "concrete doughnut" cracks. Sunk 23 feet below street level, the crown jewel of the South Philadelphia Sports Complex is surrounded by stadia and no shortage of parking. A Philadelphia Wall of Fame along with statues of Richie Ashburn, Steve Carlton, Harry Kalas, Robin Roberts, and Mike Schmidt—plus legendary Philadelphia Athletics manager Connie Mack—remind fans of the city's days of yore.

Built at a cost of $458 million—some $100 million over budget—the park was just what the Phillies and their fans needed. A million more fans came the first year at CBP than the last year of the Vet, despite the latter's capacity being 20,000 higher. The first-year park outdrew the previous franchise record of 3.14 million in 1993. By 2010, the new record was 3.77 million, as Citizens Bank Park sold out game after game. And why wouldn't they come? The food is great—from cheese steaks to Old Bay fries to the Bull's turkey leg—and the baseball is even better.

DREAMS ON HOLD

Big Bats Can't Overcome Pitchers' Injuries

On April 12, 2004, the Phillies welcomed 41,626 fans to their new home in hitting-friendly Citizens Bank Park—but couldn't score more than one run. That loss to Cincinnati dropped them to 1–6, putting the fans' preseason World Series dreams on ice.

Pitchers Kevin Millwood, Vicente Padilla, and Randy Wolf were the anchors of the starting rotation, but each of them spent time on the disabled list. They were joined there by closer Billy Wagner, and in all four cases the replacements couldn't get the job done effectively.

PHILLIES PHACT

On July 2, Phillies batters amass 18 walks and 19 strikeouts in a 7–6, 16-inning loss to Baltimore that lasts 6 hours and 15 minutes.

Fortunately, the Phillies boasted the third most potent offense in the league, with Jim Thome topping 40 home runs, Jimmy Rollins exceeding 40 doubles, and Bobby Abreu recording 40 steals (and 30 homers). The Phils bounced back to grab the division lead in late June and held it for most of July, but it was an illusion. The team's pitching staff was in disarray, the players were barking at manager Larry Bowa and his staff, and the Phils were not creating separation from the onrushing Braves. They fell out of first on July 23, never to return.

Speaking of fighting, the Phillies had one more shot to battle their way back into contention—a 10-game homestand at their new park in August. However, they managed to win only one of those 10 games. Goodbye, pennant race. A three-game sweep by the Astros sealed the deal, dropping the team to third place, 10½ games back. After that, they never got closer than within eight games of the first-place Braves. The wildcard was out of the picture, too, as four non-division winners won more than the Phillies' 86 games. Houston grabbed the wildcard with 92 triumphs.

In the end, Bowa proved to be too much for Phillies management to handle. Yes, he had led the team to some winning seasons. But the baggage of his personality and his deteriorating relations with players got too heavy. In came the more mild-mannered Charlie Manuel, and with him came good times aplenty.

Opposite: Citizens Bank Park seats 43,500 fans. As long as the Phillies are in playoff contention, it's assured that the house will be packed for virtually every game.

2004

▸ 86-76   2nd ◂

Highlights

April 12: The Phillies play their first game at their new home, Citizens Bank Park, losing to the Reds 4–1.

June 14: Against Cincinnati, Jim Thome belts his 400th career home run.

June 28: Third baseman David Bell hits for the cycle and drives in six runs as the Phillies trounce Montreal 14–6. The win puts them in first place, where they will remain for three weeks.

July 16: Bobby Abreu becomes the fourth MLB player to record six straight 20-homer, 20-steal seasons.

July 23: With a loss to the Cubs, the Phillies fall out of first for good.

August 11: Pitcher Randy Wolf homers twice and beats Colorado 15–4.

October 2: Manager Larry Bowa is fired. He will be replaced by Charlie Manuel.

NOTES

Jim Thome amasses 42 homers and 105 RBI.

Bobby Abreu rips .301–30–105 with 40 steals.

Jimmy Rollins tallies 119 runs, 43 doubles, and an NL-high 12 triples.

Eric Milton (14–6) leads the club in wins.

Billy Wagner and **Tim Worrell** close out games, recording 21 and 19 saves, respectively.

2005

▶ **88-74   2nd** ◀

Highlights

April 4: The Phillies open the season with a win over the expansion Washington Nationals.

June 12: The Phils win for the 15th time in 17 games to improve to 36–28.

September 17: Down 2–0 at Florida, the Phillies score 10 runs in the top of the ninth to win 10–2.

October 2: The Phils conclude the season with their 14th win in their final 20 games, finishing two games out of first (behind Atlanta) and one game out in the wildcard chase (behind Houston). Jimmy Rollins ends the season with an intact 36-game hitting streak.

November 9: Ugueth Urbina, a Phillies reliever in 2005, is charged with attempted murder in Venezuela.

NOTES

Pat Burrell slugs 32 homers and ranks second in the NL with 117 RBI.

Bobby Abreu notches 24 homers and 31 steals while again topping 100 runs and RBI.

Outfielder **Kenny Lofton** bats .335.

Ryan Howard is named NL Rookie of the Year after hitting .288–22–63 in just 88 games.

Jon Lieber (17–13) leads the team in victories, while **Billy Wagner** posts 38 saves and a 1.51 ERA.

A PROBLEM WITH HOUSTON

Astros Sweep Phils, Edge Them for Wildcard

After their strong late-season run at a wildcard playoff berth in 2004, the Phillies entered 2005 under new manager Charlie Manuel with high hopes—hopes that appeared to be quashed while the team foundered in last place in the National League East on Memorial Day. But the Phillies eventually made another spirited run at a postseason berth. They finished just two games in back of Atlanta in the East and just one game behind Houston in the wildcard chase.

The Phillies overcame their sluggish start with a near-perfect, 13-game homestand that began with a 5–2 victory over San Francisco on the last day of May. Two days later, veteran right-hander Jon Lieber—a free-agent signee who won 17 games in 2005—helped complete a three-game sweep of the Giants. Then came three victories in four games against the Arizona Diamondbacks, including a 7–6 thriller highlighted by catcher Mike Lieberthal's controversial three-run homer; a three-game sweep of the Texas Rangers; and a three-game sweep of the Milwaukee Brewers. Suddenly, the Phillies were in second place in the division, only 1½ games out.

After that, Philadelphia remained in contention until the final day of the regular season. Not even an elbow injury that ended slugger Jim Thome's year on June 30 could slow the Phillies. Instead, Thome's injury merely paved the way for young Ryan Howard to crack the starting lineup. Howard belted 21 of his 22 home runs after July 1 and was an easy choice as NL Rookie of the Year.

With Howard blossoming into a star, the Phillies scored more runs in 2005 than any other National League team except Cincinnati. Right fielder Bobby Abreu drove in more than 100 runs for the third consecutive year, earned his second All-Star berth, and won a Gold Glove. Second baseman Chase Utley plated 105 runs in his first full season as a starter, and left fielder Pat Burrell belted 32 homers.

Kenny Lofton slides into Atlanta's Rafael Furcal to break up a double play on September 13. The Phillies nearly caught the Braves down the stretch.

Harry the K

For 38 years—more than half his life—Harry Kalas' baritone voice boomed over the airwaves of Pennsylvania. He was the voice of Phillies baseball and beloved by generations of fans. "He was a lovely guy," said fellow broadcaster Vin Scully upon Harry the K's death in 2009. "I mean, everybody liked Harry."

A baseball broadcaster for 43 of his 73 years, and also a distinctive voice of NFL Films, Kalas began broadcasting Phillies games in 1971, the year they moved into Veterans Stadium. He thrilled fans with his "Outta here!" call whenever a Phillies hitter cracked a home run. He was so revered, he was named Pennsylvania Sportscaster of the Year 18 times.

Inducted into the broadcaster's wing of the National Baseball Hall of Fame in 2002, Kalas concluded his speech with a poem he had written for Phillies fans. "We feel your passion through and through," he intoned. "Philadelphia fans, I love you."

Harry Kalas, in 1992.

In the end, the Phillies were done in by a five-game losing streak in early September, with three of the defeats coming at home to Houston. In fact, Philadelphia dropped all six games to the Astros—their main competition for the wildcard berth—in 2005.

"We just came up a game short," Manuel said at season's end. "I'm very proud of our guys. We fought hard."

Although a 9–3 victory over the Washington Nationals on the final day was rendered moot by the Astros' playoff-clinching victory over the Cubs, it was still significant for the two hits registered by Phillies shortstop Jimmy Rollins. He extended his hitting streak to 36 games, equaling the ninth longest mark ever. (Rollins eventually stretched the mark to 38 games, No. 8 on the all-time list, before it was stopped early in the 2006 season.)

Despite the individual accomplishment, no one on the roster lost sight of the ultimate goal. "I told them, 'Don't ever be satisfied until we win the World Series,'" Manuel said.

That day was getting closer.

Armed with a 100-mph fastball, Billy Wagner saved 59 games with a 1.86 ERA in his two seasons with the Phillies (2004–2005).

▶ 85-77   2nd ◀

Highlights

April 6: Jimmy Rollins' 38-game hitting streak ends against St. Louis.

June 20: Ryan Howard tallies two homers, a triple, and seven RBI in a 9–7 loss to the Yankees.

July 10: Howard wins the Home Run Derby a year after Philly's Bobby Abreu won it.

July 30: The Phillies move into second place for good. On this day, they deal Bobby Abreu and pitcher Cory Lidle to the Yankees for prospects.

August 4: Chase Utley's 35-game hitting streak comes to an end against the Mets.

October 1: The Phils finish three games behind the Dodgers in the NL wildcard chase after closing the gap to a half game in the final week.

October 11: Lidle dies while crashing his airplane into a New York City building.

NOTES

Ryan Howard wins the NL MVP Award after leading the league in homers (a team-record 58), RBI (149), and total bases (383).

Chase Utley (.309–32–102) and **Pat Burrell** (29 HRs, 95 RBI) provide ample power.

Jimmy Rollins posts 127 runs and 36 steals.

Brett Myers (12–7) leads the staff in victories, while **Tom Gordon** saves 34 games.

TOO LITTLE, TOO LATE
Phillies Fall Just Short After Late-Season Run

Each summer, there are buyers and sellers in Major League Baseball's trading market. The buyers are teams that want that one final ingredient for a playoff push. The sellers are teams that are out of the race and playing for the next year. The Phillies were clearly sellers in 2006.

Manager Charlie Manuel's club stumbled at the start, losing six of its first seven games. A nine-game winning streak in late April and early May raised hopes, but a disastrous June—including 13 losses in a 15-game stretch—appeared to doom the team's chances. By the All-Star break, the Phillies were just 40–47 and languishing 12 games behind the Mets, who would coast to the division championship.

And so, veteran outfielder Bobby Abreu and starting pitcher Cory Lidle were shipped to the Yankees shortly before the July 31 trading deadline. Reliever Rheal Cormier was traded to the Reds, and third baseman David Bell was sent to Milwaukee.

But then a funny thing happened. With second baseman Chase Utley reeling off hits in 35 consecutive games during the summer and league MVP Ryan Howard blasting home runs at a club-record pace, the Phillies began winning. On August 1, the day after the trading deadline, they beat the Cardinals 5–3 in St. Louis to begin a four-game winning streak. From that point on, they went 36–22. Among National League teams, only the Dodgers had more victories (38) over the final two months.

Howard finished his first full season in the big leagues with 58 home runs, easily shattering Mike Schmidt's 26-year-old club record of 48. Utley batted .309 with 32 homers and made the All-Star Game for the first of five years in a row. Eventually, the Phillies (85–77) fell three games short of the Dodgers in the NL wildcard race.

However, with an exciting nucleus of Howard, Utley, and spectacular shortstop Jimmy Rollins, the Phillies were primed for a championship run in 2007.

PHILLIES PHACT

On September 3 against Atlanta, Ryan Howard becomes the first Phillies slugger to bash 50 homers in a season—then adds numbers 51 and 52 later in the game.

Raw Power

It is hard to imagine that no team was interested in Ryan Howard when he was a high school ballplayer. But no team was. That was all right with his father, Ron, who wanted him to go to college. Big-time college programs, however, were likewise uninterested, so Ryan stayed close to his suburban St. Louis home and played at Southwest Missouri State—as a walk-on. His 19 homers as a junior at that school finally caught someone's eye. The Phillies chose Howard in the fifth round in 2001.

Howard crushed the ball in the minors, but first base in Philadelphia was occupied by Jim Thome, who led the league with 47 homers during his first year in Philadelphia in 2003 and hit 42 the following year. After Howard's agent hinted that the Phillies should trade the young slugger, and after Thome injured his elbow, the team summoned the 25-year-old to Philly in mid-2005. Howard crushed the ball with such authority that he claimed Rookie of the Year honors after playing just 88 games—and clubbing 22 homers. Imagine what he could do for a full season! People soon saw.

Thome wound up being traded, and Howard proved that the move was a wise one. He rocketed 58 home runs during his sophomore season, not counting 10 spring training homers and the 23 he hit while winning the 2006 All-Star Game Home Run Derby. He was voted the National League MVP after batting .313 and leading the NL in homers and RBI (149). Howard drove in at least 136 runs in four straight seasons. He claimed the RBI crown three times and won another home run title with 48 in '08.

Howard came through in the postseason as well. He homered three times and drove in six in the 2008 World Series to help the Phillies claim

From 2006 through 2009, Ryan Howard averaged 50 home runs and 143 RBI per season—one of the greatest four-year power stretches in history.

their first world championship since 1980. The next year, he clubbed two homers and knocked in eight in the NLCS and helped the Phillies reach the World Series for a second straight year.

Though prone to strikeouts and his defense is sometimes shaky, the 6-foot-4, 240-pound lefty can clear fences to all fields—and frequently does. Howard, who had his contract renewed after his MVP season, signed a three-year, $54 million contract in 2009. A five-year, $125 million extension followed, ensuring that the quickest major leaguer in history to reach 100 and 200 homers—to break Ralph Kiner's marks—would remain in a Phillies uniform for years to come.

2007

▶ 89-73   1st ◀

Highlights

June 27: Ryan Howard reaches his 100th home run in his 325th game, becoming the fastest in MLB history to do so.

July 15: The Phillies become the first major league team to lose its 10,000th game.

September 30: Concluding a 13–4 season finish, the Philles beat Washington 6–1 on the last day of the season to edge out the slumping Mets for the NL East title.

October 3–4: Colorado defeats the Phillies 4–2 and 10–5 in the opening games of the NLDS, both in Philadelphia.

October 6: The Rockies clinch the series with a 2–1 victory in Colorado.

NOTES

Jimmy Rollins wins the NL MVP Award while becoming the first player in major league history to amass 200 hits, 30 homers, 20 triples, and 40 steals in a season.

Rollins also sets an NL record for a shortstop with 139 runs scored and sets an MLB record with 716 at-bats.

Ryan Howard tallies 47 homers, 136 RBI, and an MLB-record 199 strikeouts.

Chase Utley rips .332–22–103, and **Pat Burrell** logs 30 homers and 97 RBI.

Cole Hamels (15–5, 3.39) shines on the hill.

Jamie Moyer (left) and Carlos Ruiz (right) both joined the Phils in 2006, Moyer as a 44-year-old veteran and Ruiz as a 27-year-old rookie. In 2007, both had key roles in bringing Philadelphia its first division title since 1993.

198

THE TEAM TO BEAT

Phils Reach Playoffs After Bold Proclamation

"I think we are the team to beat in the NL East—finally," shortstop Jimmy Rollins said as the calendar turned to 2007. That proclamation drew howls of protest from the defending NL East champion Mets and their fans. Protest soon turned to derision when the Phillies began the season with just three victories in their first 13 games. Meanwhile, the Mets bolted out of the gate at 10–4 to move into first place.

Hey, Rollins never said it would be easy.

In fact, while the Phillies quickly righted the ship after their terrible start, it took them until the final day of the season to outlast the Mets in an epic comeback for the division title.

Rollins' optimism had been fueled by the offseason acquisitions of a pair of big-time starting pitchers: Freddy Garcia, who had been a 17-game winner for the White Sox the previous year, and Adam Eaton, who had gone 18–9 over the previous two seasons. Rollins believed that those players gave the Phillies the arms to go with the team's already-explosive bats.

As it turned out, neither Garcia (who won only once in 11 starts) nor Eaton (he won 10 games but with a 6.29 ERA) made a difference. Instead, it was 23-year-old Cole Hamels (15 wins) and 44-year-old Jamie Moyer (14 wins) who carried the pitching staff.

Handy with the glove, second baseman Chase Utley was a terror with the bat, reaching 40 doubles, 100 runs, and 100 RBI in each season from 2006 to 2008.

The Phillies boasted the most potent lineup in the National League. While Rollins won the NL MVP Award, Ryan Howard finished fifth in the voting and Chase Utley placed eighth. Pat Burrell again put up big power numbers, and hard-nosed center fielder Aaron Rowand (acquired from the White Sox for Jim Thome) contributed with a .309 average and a career-best 27 home runs.

Still, things looked bleak when the visiting Colorado Rockies blasted the Phillies 12–0 at Citizens Bank Park on September 12. The loss dropped Philadelphia to 76–69, seven games behind the Mets with just 17 to play.

The next day, though, the Phillies turned the table on the Rockies, winning 12–4. Then came a crucial three-game series at New York. Greg Dobbs' pinch-hit sacrifice fly in the 10th inning delivered a 3–2 victory in the opener. Two wins later, the Phillies trailed the Mets by just 3½ games.

The Phillies won 13 of 17 games down the stretch, while the Mets went just 5–12. On the final day of the season, they were deadlocked atop the standings. While pitcher Tom Glavine and the Mets were roughed up by the Marlins, Moyer pitched the Phillies past the Washington Nationals. The 6–1 home victory gave Philadelphia 89 wins, one more than the devastated Mets. The Phillies were division champs for the first time since 1993.

In the National League Division Series, the Phillies were swept by a white-hot Colorado team that would enter the World Series on a phenomenal 21–1 run. In the Game Three finale, the Rockies cracked three straight singles in the eighth inning to push across the winning run in a 2–1 triumph.

Jimmy Rollins at the plate.

Phenom and Prophet

In January 2007, when Jimmy Rollins boldly predicted that the Phillies were the team to beat in the division that year, he irritated Mets and Braves fans up and down the East Coast. In the end, however, Rollins proved to be prophetic—thanks largely to his own phenomenal play.

Drafted out of high school in Oakland, the switch-hitting rookie shortstop led the National League in steals and triples in 2001. He enjoyed the year of his life at 28 in 2007, scoring a league-high 139 runs. He also clubbed 30 home runs and 20 triples, becoming the first NL player to do that since Willie Mays in 1957. Rollins won his first Gold Glove and Silver Slugger Awards, but more importantly his much-maligned prediction came to pass. The Phillies *were* the team to beat, pulling off a 13–4 finish after trailing the Mets by seven games with 17 games remaining. Rollins was rewarded with the NL MVP Award. The next year, his team would not be beaten, claiming the world championship.

▶ 92-70   1st ◀

Highlights

May 16: Jayson Werth tallies three homers and eight RBI in a game against Toronto.

September 27: The Phillies clinch the NL East with a 4–3 win over Washington.

October 4: The Phils defeat Milwaukee 6–2 in Game Four of their NLDS to clinch the series.

October 15: NLCS MVP Cole Hamels defeats the Dodgers 5–1 in Game Five to clinch that series.

October 22: Hamels also wins the World Series opener, a 3–2 triumph at Tampa Bay.

October 25: After losing Game Two 4–2, Philly wins Game Three 5–4 on a bases-loaded single by Carlos Ruiz in the bottom of the ninth.

October 26: Ryan Howard belts two homers in a 10–2 rout in Game Four.

October 27: The Phillies win their second world title with a 4–3 win in Game Five, with Pedro Feliz singling in the winning run in the seventh inning. Hamels (1–0, 2.77) is named Series MVP.

NOTES

Ryan Howard leads the NL in HRs (48) and RBI (146).

Chase Utley and **Pat Burrell** each bash 33 homers.

Jamie Moyer (16–7) and **Brad Lidge** (41 saves in 41 attempts) star on the mound.

WORLD CHAMPS!

City Celebrates First Sports Title in 25 Years

The NLCS and World Series MVP in 2008, Cole Hamels went 4–0 with a 1.80 ERA in five postseason starts that year.

Pitcher Brad Lidge was at the bottom of a dog pile . . . and the Phillies were at the top of the baseball world.

Lidge, the Phillies' closer, had just slammed the door on the Tampa Bay Rays in the fifth and final game of the 2008 World Series. With Philadelphia leading 4–3 and the potential tying run on second base, Lidge struck out Rays pinch-hitter Eric Hinske, then fell to his knees in jubilation. He soon was swarmed by a host of teammates, who celebrated the Phillies' first World Series victory since 1980.

It was only fitting that Lidge was in the middle of it all. Because while most of the players on the roster were the same as those who carried the team to the division title in 2007, Lidge was the missing piece to the championship puzzle. He had been acquired from the Astros in a five-player deal following the '07 season.

General manager Pat Gillick, who swung that trade, also brought in veteran Pedro Feliz to play third base, and he eventually dealt for starting pitcher Joe Blanton. But Lidge, who had saved 122 games for Houston the previous four seasons, was the key.

Lidge's arrival gave the Phillies the true closer that the team had lacked in 2007. Erstwhile starter Brett Myers had filled that role in '07, but the right-hander was more suited to the early innings than the later ones. With Lidge on board, Myers moved back into the starting rotation, where he teamed with lefties Cole Hamels and Jamie Moyer to give the team a solid top of the rotation.

With center fielder Aaron Rowand off to San Francisco as a free agent, Shane Victorino moved over from right field. That allowed veteran Jayson Werth to become a full-time starter, in right field, for the first time in his career. He responded with a career-best 24 home runs and teamed with left fielder Pat Burrell (33 home runs) to give the Phillies plenty of pop in the outfield.

The core of Philadelphia's pennant-winning infield returned in 2008, with superstars Ryan Howard at first base, Chase Utley at second, and Jimmy Rollins at shortstop. Still, the Phillies got off to a slow start, going 15–13 in April. Then, on the first day of May, Howard's eighth-inning home run keyed a 3–2 victory over the Padres at Citizens Bank Park and lifted the Phillies into first place for the first time.

Howard entered that game batting a paltry .172. But he soon found his power stroke—he would go on to lead the league with 48 homers and 146 RBI—and the rest of the Phillies' bats came alive. On May 25–26, they clobbered Houston (15–6) and Colorado (20–5). Much of the offense was supplied by Utley, who homered seven times in eight games beginning with the rout of the Astros. He would be named to the All-Star team for the third season in a row.

The only other Philadelphia player to join him on that squad was Lidge, who was busy saving games when the Phillies weren't blowing out opponents. Lidge certainly wasn't needed when the club blasted the Cardinals 20–2 in St. Louis on June 13 to move a season-high four games ahead in the NL East standings.

For all of their hitting prowess, though, the Phillies could not hide their starting pitching woes. Hamels (14–10, 3.09) and Moyer (16 wins, his most since 2003) were solid, but Myers struggled in his return to the rotation and was sent to the minors to work things out. Adam Eaton faltered, too. Young Kyle Kendrick surprisingly won 11 games, but he had an ERA of 5.49.

To shore up the staff, Gillick acquired Blanton from the A's in exchange for three minor-leaguers. The deal came on the same day in mid-July that the Mets caught the idle Phillies for the division lead.

Blanton made his first start on July 22, and the Phillies beat the Mets 8–6 to move back in front by a game. The next day, Myers made his first start after being recalled from the minors. The Mets won 6–3, but Myers was a new man. Over the rest of the season, he went 7–4 with a 3.06 ERA.

The Phillies and Mets took turns atop the standings over the final two months of the season until a 7–3 loss to visiting Florida left Philadelphia a season-high 3½ games back on September 10. And then came a repeat of 2007. The Mets faltered the rest of the way while the Phillies caught fire. Howard hit his 43rd homer to jumpstart a 6–3 victory over Milwaukee on September 11. It was the first of seven wins in a row and 13 victories in 16 games until the close of the season. Meanwhile, the Mets were losing 10 of their last 17. With a 4–3 win over Washington on the next-to-last day—with Lidge logging his 41st save in 41 tries—the Phillies were NL East champions again.

Unlike 2007, however, manager Charlie Manuel and his club would not exit early from the postseason in '08. "I always thought we'd win the World Series," Manuel said. "I knew we could beat anyone in the league."

Each of the Phillies' 2008 championship rings is encrusted with 103 diamonds, totaling 3.84 karats.

Hamels and Myers pitched brilliantly in the opening two games of the National League Division Series against visiting Milwaukee, and Lidge saved the 3–1 and 5–2 victories. The Brewers rebounded to win Game Three 4–1 in front of their home fans, but Burrell homered twice the next day, and Blanton, who had gone 4–0 in his 13 regular-season starts for Philadelphia, won 6–2 to send the Phillies to the next round.

Philadelphia's five-game rout of the Dodgers in the NLCS was nearly a carbon copy of the NLDS. Hamels and Myers got things off to a great start with back-to-back victories at home, with both wins (3–2 and 8–5) saved by Lidge. Then, after the Dodgers tagged Moyer for five first-inning runs in a 7–2 victory in Game Three, the Phillies closed out the series in Los Angeles. Shane Victorino and Matt Stairs each hit two-run homers in a four-run eighth inning for a 7–5 win in Game Four. Hamels, the series MVP, pitched seven strong innings to win Game Five 5–1. When Lidge got Dodgers infielder Nomar Garciaparra on a foul pop to end the ninth, the Phillies were in the World Series for the first time since 1993.

The Phillies were on a roll, with 20 wins in 25 games dating back to September, and the Tampa Bay Rays— surprising champions in the American League— could not stop them in the Fall Classic.

Phillies closer Brad Lidge celebrates with catcher Carlos Ruiz after striking out Tampa Bay's Eric Hinske for the final out of the World Series.

> "I think when you high-five the cops, and you're hugging the grounds crew, and you just see the jubilation in everybody out there, it really kind of hits you that wow, you just won the whole damn thing."
>
> —Outfielder Geoff Jenkins

In Game One in Florida, Utley socked a first-inning home run to put the Phillies ahead for good. Hamels went seven strong innings for his fourth postseason victory in as many starts, and Lidge closed out the 3–2 victory. Tampa Bay evened the series by winning Game Two 4–2, but the Phillies took the next three at home to end it.

The tipping point came in Game Three, when the teams entered the bottom of the ninth tied at 4–4. The Phillies, who had bashed a league-high 214 home runs during the regular season, forged the winning rally in unlikely fashion: a hit batsman, a wild pitch, an error, two intentional walks, and catcher Carlos Ruiz's infield single gained a 5–4 victory.

The big bats were back in Game Four, when Howard smashed two of the Phillies' four home runs (one by Blanton) in a 10–2 rout. Then came the decisive 4–3 victory in Game Five, though it was hardly conventional. The game started on October 27, was suspended because of rain after 5½ innings, and concluded on October 29. The game was tied at 2–2 when it was suspended. It was 3–3 in the bottom of the seventh inning when Feliz delivered the go-ahead run on a ground-ball single.

After Lidge struck out Hinske for the final out, long-suffering Philadelphia fans celebrated the city's first championship in any major sport in a quarter-century—since the 76ers won the NBA title in 1983.

The championship also marked a fitting end for Gillick's 27 years as a big-league general manager (with the last three coming in Philadelphia). The man who had helped build the Phillies' World Series winner would be inducted into the National Baseball Hall of Fame in 2011.

Highlights

Highlights

April 13: Phillies broadcaster Harry Kalas dies of a heart attack.

August 23: Second baseman Eric Bruntlett turns an unassisted triple play.

September 30: The Phillies clinch the NL East with a 10–3 win over Houston.

October 12: The Phillies rally for three in the ninth of Game Four to defeat Colorado 5–4 and clinch their NLDS.

October 19: Following an 11–0 Cliff Lee victory in Game Three, the Phillies defeat L.A. 5–4 in Game Four of the NLCS. Jimmy Rollins wins it with a two-run double in the bottom of the ninth.

October 21: Philly clinches the NLCS with a 10–4 home victory.

October 28: Lee cruises to a 6–1 road win over New York in Game One of the World Series.

November 2: After 3–1, 8–5, and 7–4 losses, the Phillies win Game Five 8–6 thanks to Chase Utley's fourth and fifth homers of the Series.

November 4: Hideki Matsui knocks in six in the Yankees' 7–3 Series-clinch win.

NOTES

Ryan Howard compiles 45 homers and an NL-high 141 RBI.

Chase Utley, Raul Ibanez, and **Jayson Werth** all top 30 HRs and 90 RBI.

Joe Blanton, J. A. Happ, and **Jamie Moyer** each win 12 games.

THE CLASS OF THE NL

Star-Studded Phils Repeat as League Champs

The 2009 Phillies enjoyed the perks of being the defending World Series winner, including a championship ring ceremony before a game against the Braves in April and a visit with President Barack Obama in May. At the White House, manager Charlie Manuel and shortstop Jimmy Rollins presented Obama, the 44th president of the United States, a Phillies jersey—number 44, of course.

As the defending world champions, the Phillies' own jerseys had a target on their backs in 2009. But they handled all comers in the National League easily while cruising to their second consecutive pennant. They were denied a second straight World Series victory, however, when the Yankees won the Fall Classic.

With almost the entire everyday lineup from their formidable 2008 team back intact, the Phillies figured to score a lot of runs in 2009. Yet they even surpassed expectations, leading the league with 224 home runs and 820 runs scored—a robust 5.06 runs per game. Hulking first baseman Ryan Howard belted 45 homers (his fourth season in a row with more than 40) and drove in 141 runs (tops in the league for the third time in four years).

Howard was one of four Phillies to club 30 home runs in 2009, making Philadelphia just the 12th big-league team ever with a quartet of such sluggers. Howard was joined by right fielder Jayson Werth (36 homers), left fielder Raul Ibanez (34), and second baseman Chase Utley (31).

Ibanez was the lone newcomer to the starting lineup. Pat Burrell had manned left field for most of the previous nine seasons, but new general manager Ruben Amaro Jr. (a Phillies player himself in the 1990s) opted to let Burrell go in free agency and bring in the 36-year-old Ibanez instead.

Ibanez, who had amassed more than 100 RBI each of the previous three seasons for the Mariners, got off to a torrid start in his new digs. When he rapped a pair of hits at St. Louis on May 5, he stood at .351 with eight home runs and 21 RBI, and the club stood in first place for the first time. On May 30, Howard blasted two homers and drove in five runs in a 9–6 victory over the Nationals, and the Phillies did not spend another day out of first place after that.

Still, the Phillies' hitting prowess did not entirely mask the club's pitching troubles. Brett Myers suffered a torn labrum and missed much of the season. Forty-six-year-old Jamie Moyer struggled. Chan Ho Park, signed to be the club's fifth starter, didn't cut it in the rotation and was sent to the bullpen. Even Cole Hamels (10–11, 4.32 ERA), the postseason star from 2008, was not immune. But the most drastic falloff came from Brad Lidge. One of the heroes of the club's championship run the previous season, Lidge saved 31 games in 2009. But he lost all eight of his decisions, blew 11 saves, and saw his ERA soar to 7.21.

So Amaro got some help. First, he signed three-time Cy Young Award winner Pedro Martinez in mid-July. Then he dealt for the Indians' Cliff Lee, the American League Cy Young Award winner in 2008, shortly before the trading deadline.

Lee (7–4) and Martinez (5–1) lived up to expectations, and the Phillies took command in the National League East. They were four games up and riding a five-game winning streak when they signed Martinez at the All-Star Break. Then they proceeded to win five more in a row and increase the margin to 6½ games. The lead grew to 8½ before the Braves made a brief run, closing the margin to four games in the final week. But the Phillies' back-to-back victories over visiting Houston sealed the deal, with a 10–3 win on September 30—Ibanez homered and drove in three runs—being the clincher.

When the postseason opened, Philadelphia had a score to settle with Division Series opponent Colorado. Two years earlier, the Rockies had knocked out the Phillies in three games. This time, the clubs split the first two games at Citizens Bank Park—Lee was masterful in a 5–1 victory in the opener—before the series shifted to Colorado.

Shane Victorino welcomes home Carlos Ruiz after Jimmy Rollins' two-run, walk-off double in the ninth inning defeated the Dodgers 5–4 in Game Four of the NLCS.

There, the Phillies exacted their revenge by winning a pair of games in their final at-bat. In Game Three, Howard broke a 5–5 tie with a ninth-inning sacrifice fly for a 6–5 win. The next night, Philadelphia was down to its last out, trailing 4–2 in the ninth against Rockies closer Huston Street. But Howard doubled in two to tie the game, and Werth followed with a go-ahead single. Lidge nailed down the final out for the second night in a row, and the Phillies advanced.

The Championship Series was a rematch of the 2008 NLCS against the Dodgers, and the result was the same: Philadelphia needed only five games to clinch the pennant. After the teams split the first two games in Los Angeles, the Phillies moved ahead with an 11–0 rout in Game Three at Citizens Bank Park. Series MVP Howard and Werth provided a potent one-two punch again, with the big first baseman tripling in two runs and Werth following with a home run for a 4–0 lead in the first inning. Lee tossed eight shutout innings while allowing a meager three hits.

The critical blow, though, came the next night. The Dodgers led 4–3 in the ninth inning and had closer Jonathon Broxton on the mound. But with two on and two out, Jimmy Rollins ripped a double to right to score Eric Bruntlett with the tying run and Carlos Ruiz with the winning run. The Phillies had a three-games-to-one lead in the series. A 10–4 rout the next night—keyed by two more home runs from Werth—was almost anticlimactic. When Lidge set the Dodgers down 1-2-3 in the ninth, the celebration was on. The Phillies were back in the World Series. Their opponent: the venerable New York Yankees.

In the World Series, Lee turned in another gem when he went all the way in a 6–1 victory in the opener. And Utley was brilliant, hitting five homers and driving in eight runs in the six games. But the Yankees dominated after Game One and won four games to two. New York slugger Hideki Matsui punctuated his team's victory with a home run and six RBI in a 7–3 victory in the finale.

Although Philadelphia finished short of its ultimate goal, the season was still an unqualified success. Before 2008 and 2009, the Phillies had never won back-to-back pennants in their long history. Enthusiasm for the club was at all-time high: a record 3,600,693 fans watched the team play at Citizens Bank Park in '09, with 73 of the 81 home dates selling out.

Chase Utley belts his fifth home run of the 2009 World Series in Game Five. The five bombs tied Reggie Jackson's fabled World Series record of 1977.

What Up, Doc?

Halladay Unhittable as Phils Win the East

It was getting to be routine. In 2010, the Phillies won the Eastern Division for the fourth year in a row and played deep into October again. However, manager Charlie Manuel's club was foiled in its bid for a third consecutive trip to the World Series by the pitching-rich Giants in a taut and exciting National League Championship Series.

The Phillies' offense featured the usual cast of characters, led by power-hitting first baseman Ryan Howard and second baseman Chase Utley. But in a classic case of the rich getting richer, the Phillies added to their wealth by trading for six-time All-Star pitcher Roy "Doc" Halladay in December 2009.

Halladay, the 2003 Cy Young Award recipient in the American League, won 148 games for Toronto from 1998 to 2009. If there were any doubts about Halladay's ability to adjust to the National League, he quickly put them to rest. On Opening Day, Halladay struck out nine Nationals in seven innings of the Phillies' 11–1 rout. He won each of his next three starts, too, capped by a 2–0 shutout at Atlanta on April 21.

Still, that was nothing compared to what he did in Florida on May 29. Halladay faced 27 Marlins batters and retired all of them in the Phillies' 1–0 victory. He struck out 11 while fashioning just the 20th perfect game in major league history.

That victory raised Philadelphia's record to 28–20, good for a 1½-game lead over the Braves in the East. But the team played middling baseball for nearly two months after that, and a post–All Star Game slump left the Phillies at 48–46 on July 21. At the time, they were seven games behind the Braves.

Then came the key week of the season. On July 22, five Phillies pitchers combined on a one-hitter to beat the Cardinals 2–0 in 11 innings in St. Louis, launching an eight-game winning streak that trimmed 4½ games off the Braves' lead. On July 29,

Outfielder Jayson Werth finished eighth in NL MVP voting in 2010 after ripping .296–27–85 with 106 runs and a league-high 46 doubles.

2010

▶ 97-65   1st ◀

Highlights

May 29: Roy Halladay pitches a perfect game at Florida, striking out 11.

July 9: The Phillies overcome a 7–1 deficit to the Reds with six in the bottom of the ninth and a Ryan Howard homer in the tenth.

September 24: The Phillies win their eleventh straight game.

September 27: The Phils clinch the NL East on a Roy Halladay shutout of Washington.

October 6: In Game One of their NLDS, Halladay no-hits the visiting Reds 4–0.

October 10: The Phillies clinch their NLDS with a 2–0 Cole Hamels shutout in Game Three.

October 20: The Giants defeat the Phils 6–5 in Game Four of the NLCS on a walk-off sacrifice fly by Juan Uribe in the ninth. They take a three-games-to-one lead.

October 21: Halladay outduels Tim Lincecum 4–2 in Game Five.

October 23: San Francisco clinches in Game Six after Uribe breaks a 2–2 tie with a homer in the top of the eighth.

NOTES

Ryan Howard (31 HRs, 108 RBI) and **Jayson Werth** (.296–27–85) pace the offense.

Roy Halladay (21–10) wins the Cy Young Award.

The Phillies draw an MLB-high and team-record **3,777,322 fans.**

Philadelphia's star-studded pitching staff prepares for the opener of the NLCS at Citizens Bank Park. From left to right are Cole Hamels, Roy Halladay, Roy Oswalt, Kyle Kendrick, and Jamie Moyer (in the bullpen).

general manager Ruben Amaro Jr. sent two minor leaguers and starting pitcher J. A. Happ to the Astros for three-time All-Star pitcher Roy Oswalt. Along with Halladay and Cole Hamels, Oswalt gave the Phillies arguably the best top of the rotation in baseball.

The Phillies were nearly unbeatable after that. They went 18–10 in August and won 21 of 27 games in September. On September 12, Oswalt tossed a complete-game four-hitter to beat the Mets 3–0 in New York and give Philadelphia sole possession of first place. The Phillies reeled off 11 consecutive victories, then clinched the division when Halladay two-hit the Nationals in an 8–0 romp at Washington in game No. 157.

Right fielder Jayson Werth was a key contributor to the NL's second best offense, belting 27 homers and leading the Phillies with 106 runs scored. Howard's numbers fell a bit from prior years, but he still finished with 31 homers and 108 RBI. Catcher Carlos Ruiz batted a team-best .302.

But for once, Philadelphia's pitchers overshadowed the hitters. Halladay went 21–10 and won the NL Cy Young Award. Oswalt won seven of his eight decisions for the Phillies while posting a 1.74 ERA. Cole Hamels rebounded from a subpar 2009 season to win 12 games and lower his ERA to 3.06. Brad Lidge saved 27 games.

The rotation's Big Three had the Phillies well positioned for a postseason run toward a third straight NL pennant. And, predictably, Philadelphia steamrolled the Central Division–champion Reds in three games in the NLDS—although no one could have predicted what Halladay did in the opening game.

Don Larsen's perfect game for the Yankees against the Dodgers in the 1956 World Series was the only postseason no-hitter in major league history before Halladay took the mound against the Reds that afternoon at Citizens Bank Park. Halladay threw his own no-hitter while allowing only one base runner—a walk in the fifth inning.

"It's surreal, it really is," Halladay said after the game. "I just wanted to pitch here [with the Phillies], to pitch in the postseason. To go out and have a game like that, it's a dream come true."

The rest of the series was a formality, although the Reds did jump to a 4–0 lead midway through Game Two. The Phillies chipped away with two runs in the fifth and another in the sixth before taking the lead with three unearned runs in the seventh. The final score was 7–4. In Cincinnati for Game Three, Hamels quickly put an end to the series. He scattered five hits and struck out nine in a clinching 2–0 victory. The Phillies scored an unearned run in the first, and Utley gave Hamels some cushion with a home run in the fifth.

That set up an arms showdown with the Western Division–champion Giants in the NLCS. With two-time Cy Young Award winner Tim Lincecum, Jonathan Sanchez, and Matt Cain, the Giants featured one of the few starting staffs that could rival the Phillies'.

Lincecum outdueled Halladay 4–3 in Game One at Citizens Bank Park before Oswalt bested Sanchez 6–1 in Game Two. At AT&T Park, the Giants won Game Three 3–0 behind Cain and Game Four 6–5 with a run in the ninth. However, the Phillies forced a return to Philadelphia when Halladay rebounded to beat Lincecum 4–2 in Game Five.

Back home for Game Six, the Phillies had Sanchez on the ropes early, but they could not score again after getting two runs in the first inning. Jose Uribe's eighth-inning solo homer for San Francisco broke a 2–2 tie, and Philadelphia's last chance ended when Giants closer Brian Wilson struck out Howard with the potential tying and winning runs aboard in the ninth inning.

It was a disappointing finish for Phillies fans, who had expected to see their team make a third consecutive trip to the World Series. But the league-leading (and club-record) 3,777,322 spectators who had cheered them on during the regular season knew that the Phillies had built one of the premier teams in baseball.

Not only that, but the club seemed destined to remain a championship contender. After the 2010 season, the Phillies announced that they had reacquired Cliff Lee, signing the free agent to a five-year contract. Earlier in the year, the club had inked Howard to a deal through 2016. To dreamy-eyed Phillies fans, the value of the two contracts, $245 million, was money well spent.

Perfection and Then Some

In Florida on May 29, 2010, Roy Halladay tossed the 20th perfect game in major league history, and the second in Phillies annals after Jim Bunning's 1964 perfecto. But come October, Halladay moved into even more rarified territory.

Acquired the previous winter from Toronto, Halladay had never pitched in the postseason before the NLDS opener against the Reds at Citizens Bank Park on October 6, 2010. Cincinnati hadn't been to the postseason in 15 years, but the Central Division champs had led the National League in home runs, batting, and scoring. Harry Leroy Halladay would have none of it.

The 21-game winner retired the side in order in all but the fourth inning, when he issued a full-count walk to Jay Bruce. No ball left the infield for the last three innings. With Philly up 4–0 in the ninth, Cincinnati's Brandon Phillips hit a squib in front of the plate that Carlos Ruiz gunned to first to complete baseball's second postseason no-hitter and the first since Don Larsen's perfect game way back in 1954.

Roy Halladay's playoff no-hitter.

Highlights

May 25: The Phils outlast the Reds 5–4 in 19 innings in a game that lasts more than six hours. Second baseman Wilson Valdez throws a hitless 19th frame to become only the third position player to win a game since 1968.

August 6: Cole Hamels beats San Francisco 2–1 for Philadelphia's ninth consecutive victory.

September 17: In their 150th game of the season, the Phils clinch a fifth straight NL East title with a 9–2 victory over the visiting Cardinals.

September 28: The Phillies eliminate the Braves from postseason contention with a 4–3, 13-inning win in Atlanta in the season finale. It's the Phillies' 102nd win, a team record.

October 7: After splitting the first four games with the Cardinals, the Phils drop the decisive game of the NLDS when St. Louis ace Chris Carpenter outduels Roy Halladay in a 1–0 final.

NOTES

Ryan Howard powers the offense with 33 homers and 116 RBI.

Roy Halladay (19–6) and **Cliff Lee** (17–8) front the most dominant starting staff in the majors.

The Phillies again lead the majors in attendance, drawing 3,680,718 fans.

Somewhere in the middle of that celebration is John Mayberry, whose bases-loaded, walk-off single on Opening Day provided a dramatic start to the season.

ARMED AND DANGEROUS

Phils Set Franchise Record with 102 Wins

From their inspired, ninth-inning comeback in the season opener to their record-setting victory in the finale, the 2011 Philadelphia Phillies produced the greatest 162-game season in franchise history. As memorable as that epic campaign was, however, the Phils and their fans will also never forget the physical and emotional agony with which the season ended: star slugger Ryan Howard collapsing with a ruptured Achilles tendon while making the final out of an upset loss to St. Louis in the National League Division Series. It was the ultimate example of injury added to insult.

The Phillies began making news long before the first pitch of spring training. In December 2010, ace Cliff Lee stunned the sports world when he decided to sign with the Phillies instead of taking a more lucrative offer from the Yankees or returning to the defending AL champion Texas Rangers. His addition gave the Phillies one of the greatest starting rotations in baseball history, with Lee joining fellow Cy Young Award winner Roy Halladay, Roy Oswalt, and Cole Hamels.

Few Opening Days in Phillies history came with the anticipation of April 1, 2011. A parade down Broad Street preceded Halladay's start against the visiting Astros in front of a sellout Citizens Bank Park crowd. That first win didn't come easy, however, requiring a three-run rally in the bottom of the ninth to secure the 5–4 triumph, capped by John Mayberry's bases-loaded single. It was Philadelphia's first walk-off Opening Day win since Mike Schmidt's two-run homer beat the Mets in 1974.

Not every win would be that exciting, of course, but victories followed in droves. The Phillies completed a three-game sweep of the Astros to open a campaign in which they would spend all but one day in first place in the National League East. The best pitching rotation in baseball paved the way to the best record in the majors by the All-Star break (57–34).

Still, the team was not going to ride out the season relying solely on its pitching. Just before the trade deadline at the end of July, the Phillies sent a package of prospects to Houston for hot-hitting right fielder Hunter Pence. Pence had hit .308 for the Astros through the season's first 100 games, and he seemed to like his new surroundings even better, batting a sizzling .324 in 54 games with Philadelphia.

Spurred by the addition of Pence, the Phillies kicked off a torrid stretch in late July, winning nine straight from July 29 to August 6 and going 18–7 in the month of August. The team's 4.8 runs per game from July 1 through the season's end was tops in the National League, and the improved run support for the dominant pitching staff sent Philadelphia soaring to a fifth consecutive division title.

The rotation proved to be everything it was cracked up to be. Though Oswalt missed much of the year with a bad back, Halladay, Hamels, and Lee combined for 50 victories, and 23-year-old rookie Vance Worley chipped in with an 11–3 mark.

Howard enjoyed another banner year at the plate, belting 33 home runs and driving in 116—his sixth straight 30–100 slate. Health issues among regular infielders Jimmy Rollins, Placido Polanco, and Chase Utley forced manager Charlie Manuel to carry three utility men on the roster and contributed to his penciling 105 different combinations on the lineup card during the season—a staggering number for a squad that ran away with a division title.

With a postseason seat secured, the Phillies let their foot off the gas in September, dropping eight straight as the playoffs approached. But they put it back together in time for a season-ending three-game sweep of Atlanta that knocked the Braves out of the playoffs and allowed the Cardinals to earn the wild-card berth. The final victory—a 4–3, 13-inning classic—gave the club its franchise record for wins with 102, and Manuel secured his 646th career triumph as Phillies manager, surpassing Gene Mauch as the biggest winner in club history.

Even with the record-setting regular season, the Phillies knew they would be judged by one standard—a World Series title—and they would have to go through those red-hot Cards in the NLDS to get there.

After the teams alternated wins through the first four games, Halladay and Cardinals ace Chris Carpenter faced off in a true pitchers' duel in the finale. Although Halladay yielded only one run on six hits, that single run was enough for Carpenter, whose three-hit, complete-game shutout left the Phillies and their fans in disbelief. Howard, who made the final out, was carried off the field with an Achilles injury and exited the stadium on crutches, in need of offseason surgery.

In the end, the best pitching staff in baseball was not enough to carry a team that went scoreless over 31 of their last 34 playoff innings and hit a mere .226 in the series. "I feel very empty," Manuel said.

With that sentiment, Philadelphia fans could relate.

In the ultimate symbol of the team's disappointing finish, Ryan Howard not only made the final out of the Phillies' postseason but also suffered an Achilles injury on the play that would require surgery.

"I remember when we lost 10,000 games and some people acted like I was there for all 10,000. Now that I'm the winningest manager, I might let someone else brag, but I'll definitely smile and take credit for it."

—Manager Charlie Manuel, upon winning his 646th game as Phillies manager

The Phillies dugout was stacked with aces in 2011 with (left to right) Cole Hamels, Cliff Lee, Roy Oswalt, and Roy Halladay.

Kings of the Hill

The Phillies fell nine postseason wins short in their quest for a 2011 World Series. Their pitching staff, which was hyped as one of the best in baseball history before even throwing a ball, was certainly not the reason.

Philadelphia's 3.02 ERA was the best in the major leagues in 2011. The starting rotation's 2.86 ERA was the best in baseball since 1985, when the Dodgers put up a 2.71 mark and the Mets were just behind at 2.84. In a five-game NLDS loss to St. Louis, the Phillies notched a respectable 3.89 ERA against a Cardinals team that would go on to average more than seven runs per game in the NLCS.

As expected, former Cy Young Award winners Roy Halladay and Cliff Lee led the way at the top of the rotation.

The former went 19–6 with a 2.35 ERA and led the NL with eight complete games, while Lee went 17–8 with a 2.40 ERA. Cole Hamels added a 14–9 mark and 2.79 ERA. And though Roy Oswalt (9–10) struggled with back pain, rookie Vance Worley stepped in to contribute 11 wins in 14 decisions.

Even a shoulder injury to closer Brad Lidge did not derail this staff. Ryan Madson moved to the back of the bullpen and racked up 32 saves in that role.

So, was the hype on the mark? Said shortstop Jimmy Rollins matter-of-factly: "It really wasn't hype."

NATIONAL CALAMITY

Washington Reigns While Phillies Fall Flat

Prior to the 2012 season, *Sports Illustrated* laid out its predictions for the upcoming MLB campaign. The Phillies, according to *SI's* crystal ball, would finish with 94 wins, tops in the National League. Questions surrounded the health of some of their star hitters, but the magazine pooh-poohed those concerns. "Philadelphia will only need to score so many runs," wrote Joe Lemire, "given its stellar starting pitching and underappreciated defense."

Those who thought the Phils would coast to their sixth straight NL East crown, however, were smacked with a cold reality. By April 17, they were 7–10 and 5½ games behind the division's upstart, the Washington Nationals.

In what was a frustrating season for the former Cy Young winner, Cliff Lee earned no decision despite striking out 10 Astros and allowing just one run during a May 15 Phillies victory.

A rivalry between the two teams was heating up. Tired of Philadelphia fans filling up their park in previous years, the Nationals in 2013 took efforts to keep them out. For example, the Nats' February presale of tickets to Phillies games was restricted to customers with addresses in Virginia, Maryland, and Washington, D.C. Phillies fans responded by driving en masse to Nationals Park.

The Phils would spend most of the season not aiming to catch the young Nats but simply trying to reach .500. They succeeded, but it took them until September. Philadelphia finished at 81–81, 17 games behind Washington, 13 behind Atlanta, and 7 games out of the wildcard hunt.

The 2012 Phillies were poster children for mediocrity. The league scoring average was 4.22 runs per game, and 4.22 is what the Philly batters produced. The team's 3.86 ERA was only 0.08 below the league norm.

Injuries and ineffectiveness plagued the Phillies' biggest stars. Ryan Howard needed until July to recover from offseason Achilles surgery. Playing in just 71 games, he batted .219 with 99 strikeouts, although he did amass 14 homers and 56 RBI. Chase Utley, who also missed the first half of the season (knees), rapped just .256 in 83 games. Outfielder/first baseman John Mayberry Jr. did not develop into the slugger that the team expected.

Highlights

April 5: Roy Halladay and closer Jonathan Papelbon combine for a 1–0 Opening Day shutout over Pittsburgh.

April 9: The Phillies lose their third game in a row to fall to 1–3. They will not come within a game and a half of first place the rest of the season.

July 4: In his 14th start, Cliff Lee wins his first game.

July 13: After 11 losses in 12 games, the Phillies are 37–51 and 15 games out.

July 25: Pitcher Cole Hamels signs a six-year, $144 million contract extension.

July 31: The Phils trade starting outfielders Shane Victorino and Hunter Pence for prospects.

August 6: The team's NL-record streak of 257 consecutive sellouts comes to an end.

September 12: With their seventh straight win, the Phillies pull within three games of the final wildcard spot. They will not get closer.

September 22: Ryan Howard clouts his 300th career home run.

NOTES

All-Star catcher Carlos Ruiz leads the team with a .325 average and 68 RBI.

Jimmy Rollins paces the club in home runs (23) and runs (102) and shares the RBI lead (68) with Ruiz.

Outfielder Juan Pierre, signed as a free agent before the season, strokes .307 and nabs a team-high 37 steals.

Cole Hamels leads the staff in wins (17–6), ERA (3.05), and strikeouts (216).

The Phillies' bats were especially cold when Cliff Lee took the hill. Through his first 10 starts—including one in which he threw 10 scoreless innings—Lee owned a 3.18 ERA and zero wins. The former Cy Young Award winner finished ninth in the league with a 3.16 ERA, yet ended with a 6–9 record in 30 starts. Roy Halladay, after ranking in the top five in Cy Young voting for six consecutive years, battled a shoulder injury throughout the season before finishing at 11–8, with his highest ERA (4.49) in 12 years.

A handful of Phillies enjoyed quality seasons. Cole Hamels had almost identical numbers to Lee except in the won-loss column. He went 17–6 behind a 3.05 ERA. Closer Jonathan Papelbon, who signed a four-year, $50 million free agent deal with the club in November 2011, fulfilled expectations with 38 saves. And catcher Carlos Ruiz, who joined Hamels and Papelbon in the All-Star Game, ripped a career-high .325 while sharing the team lead (with Jimmy Rollins) in RBI with 68.

With his team out of contention in late July, GM Ruben Amaro traded outfielders Shane Victorino and Hunter Spence as well as starting pitcher Joe Blanton—all for prospects. While manager Charlie Manuel, a favorite in Philadelphia, kept his job, his coaching staff was gutted. After the season, hitting coach Greg Gross, first base coach Sam Perlozzo, and bench coach Pete Mackanin were all sent packing.

Long-time Phillies fans cracked bemused smiles when Ryne Sandberg, the team's Triple-A manager, was added to the coaching staff in October. In 1981—in one of the worst trades in history—the Phils had dealt Ryno to the Cubs, where he enjoyed a Hall of Fame career. Management hoped he could improve the team's defense, which was one of the league's shoddiest in 2012.

The Phillies' best commodity in 2012 was its fans. The team set an NL record with its 257th consecutive sellout (streak broken in August), and it led the league in attendance for the third straight year (3,565,718). With such fan loyalty, the Phils were able to sport a payroll that was $56 million higher than that of any other NL team in 2012. But with almost all of the club's core players in their 30s, and some battling chronic injuries, the Phillies brass would have to start spending its money in creative ways.

Despite the disappointing season, fans came out to Citizens Bank Park in droves in 2012. Newcomer Juan Pierre, seen here at bat during a September 22 game against Atlanta, was one of the bright spots.

THE 2000s RECORD BOOK

Team Leaders

Batting

2000: Bobby Abreu, .316
2001: Marlon Anderson, .293
2002: Bobby Abreu, .308
2003: Mike Lieberthal, .313
2004: Bobby Abreu, .301
2005: Kenny Lofton, .335
2006: Ryan Howard, .313
2007: Chase Utley, .332
2008: Shane Victorino, .293
2009: Shane Victorino, .292
2010: Carlos Ruiz, .302
2011: Carlos Ruiz, .283
2012: Juan Pierre, .307

Home Runs

2000: Scott Rolen, 26
2001: Bobby Abreu, 31
2002: Pat Burrell, 37
2003: Jim Thome, 47
2004: Jim Thome, 42
2005: Pat Burrell, 32
2006: Ryan Howard, 58
2007: Ryan Howard, 47
2008: Ryan Howard, 48
2009: Ryan Howard, 45
2010: Ryan Howard, 31
2011: Ryan Howard, 33
2012: Jimmy Rollins, 23

RBI

2000: Scott Rolen, 89
2001: Bobby Abreu, 110
2002: Pat Burrell, 116
2003: Jim Thome, 131
2004: Jim Thome, 105;
Bobby Abreu, 105
2005: Pat Burrell, 117
2006: Ryan Howard, 149
2007: Ryan Howard, 136
2008: Ryan Howard, 146
2009: Ryan Howard, 141
2010: Ryan Howard, 108
2011: Ryan Howard, 116
2012: Carlos Ruiz, 68;
Jimmy Rollins, 68

Wins

2000: Randy Wolf, 11–9
2001: Robert Person, 15–7
2002: Vicente Padilla, 14–11
2003: Randy Wolf, 16–10
2004: Eric Milton, 14–6
2005: Jon Lieber, 17–13
2006: Brett Myers, 12–7
2007: Cole Hamels, 15–5
2008: Jamie Moyer, 16–7
2009: Joe Blanton, 12–8;
J. A. Happ, 12–4;
Jamie Moyer, 12–10
2010: Roy Halladay, 21–10
2011: Roy Halladay, 19–6
2012: Cole Hamels, 17–6

ERA

2000: Robert Person, 3.63
2001: Randy Wolf, 3.70
2002: Randy Wolf, 3.20
2003: Vicente Padilla, 3.62

2004: Eric Milton, 4.75
2005: Brett Myers, 3.72
2006: Brett Myers, 3.91
2007: Cole Hamels, 3.39
2008: Cole Hamels, 3.09
2009: J. A. Happ, 2.93
2010: Roy Halladay, 2.44
2011: Roy Halladay, 2.35
2012: Cole Hamels, 3.05

Strikeouts

2000: Robert Person, 164
2001: Robert Person, 183
2002: Randy Wolf, 172
2003: Randy Wolf, 177
2004: Eric Milton, 161
2005: Brett Myers, 208
2006: Brett Myers, 189
2007: Cole Hamels, 177
2008: Cole Hamels, 196
2009: Cole Hamels, 168
2010: Roy Halladay, 219
2011: Cliff Lee, 238
2012: Cole Hamels, 216

Saves

2000: Jeff Brantley, 23
2001: Jose Mesa, 42
2002: Jose Mesa, 45
2003: Jose Mesa, 24
2004: Billy Wagner, 21
2005: Billy Wagner, 38
2006: Tom Gordon, 34
2007: Brett Myers, 21
2008: Brad Lidge, 41
2009: Brad Lidge, 31
2010: Brad Lidge, 27
2011: Ryan Madson, 32
2012: Jonathan Papelbon, 38

These are the spikes of speedster Jimmy Rollins, who, from 2001 through 2008, topped 40 steals four times and led the NL in triples four times.

NL Leaders

2001: Triples—Jimmy Rollins, 12;
Stolen Bases—Rollins, 46

2002: Doubles—Bobby Abreu, 50;
Triples—Rollins, 10
2003: Home Runs—Jim Thome, 47;
Shutouts—Kevin Milwood, 3
2004: Triples—Rollins, 12
2006: Runs—Chase Utley, 131;
Home Runs—Ryan Howard, 58;
RBI—Howard, 149
2007: Runs—Rollins, 139;
Triples—Rollins, 20
2008: Home Runs—Howard, 48;
RBI—Howard, 146
2009: Triples—Shane Victorino, 13;
RBI—Howard, 141;
Shutouts—J. A. Happ, 2;
Cole Hamels, 2
2010: Doubles—Jayson Werth, 46;
Wins—Roy Halladay, 21;
Complete Games—Halladay, 9;
Shutouts—Halladay, 4
2011: Triples—Victorino, 16;
Complete Games—Halladay, 8;
Shutouts—Lee, 6

Shane Victorino, showcased on an Upper Deck card, shined as a hitter, base stealer, and Gold Glove–winning center fielder during the decade.

NL Awards

NL MVP Voting

2003: Jim Thome, 4th
2005: Pat Burrell, 7th;
Jimmy Rollins, 10th
2006: Ryan Howard, 1st;
Chase Utley, 7th
2007: Jimmy Rollins, 1st;
Ryan Howard, 5th;
Chase Utley 8th
2008: Ryan Howard, 2nd;
Brad Lidge, 8th
2009: Ryan Howard, 3rd;
Chase Utley, 8th
2010: Roy Halladay, 6th;
Jason Werth, 8th;
Ryan Howard, 10th
2011: Roy Halladay, 9th;
Ryan Howard, 10th

NL Cy Young Winners

2010: Roy Halladay

NL Rookie of the Year Winners

2005: Ryan Howard

Gold Glove Winners

2000: Scott Rolen, 3B
2001: Scott Rolen, 3B
2005: Bobby Abreu, OF
2007: Jimmy Rollins, SS;
Aaron Rowand, OF
2008: Jimmy Rollins, SS;
Shane Victorino, OF
2009: Jimmy Rollins, SS;
Shane Victorino, OF
2010: Shane Victorino, OF
2011: Placido Polanco, 3B

NL All-Stars

2000: Mike Lieberthal, C
2001: Jimmy Rollins, SS
2002: Scott Rolen, 3B;
Jimmy Rollins, SS;
Vicente Padilla, P
2003: Randy Wolf, P
2004: Bobby Abreu, OF;
Jim Thome, 1B
2005: Bobby Abreu, OF;
Jimmy Rollins, SS;

Billy Wagner, P
2006: Chase Utley, 2B;
Tom Gordon, P;
Ryan Howard, 1B
2007: Chase Utley, 2B;
Cole Hamels, P;
Aaron Rowand, OF
2008: Chase Utley, 2B;
Brad Lidge, P
2009: Chase Utley, 2B;
Raul Ibanez, OF;
Shane Victorino, OF;
Ryan Howard, 1B;
Jayson Werth, OF
2010: Ryan Howard, 1B;
Roy Halladay, P;
Chase Utley, 2B
2011: Placido Polanco, 3B;
Shane Victorino , OF;
Roy Halladay, P;
Cole Hamels, P;
Cliff Lee, P
2012: Cole Hamels, P;
Jonathan Papelbon, P;
Carlos Ruiz, C

PHILLIES 2000s All-Decades Team

1B	RYAN HOWARD
2B	CHASE UTLEY
SS	JIMMY ROLLINS
3B	SCOTT ROLEN
C	MIKE LIEBERTHAL
OF	BOBBY ABREU
OF	SHANE VICTORINO
OF	PAT BURRELL
SP	ROY HALLADAY
SP	COLE HAMELS
RP	BRAD LIDGE

PHOTO AND ILLUSTRATION CREDITS

We wish to acknowledge the following for providing the illustrations included in the book. Every effort has been made to locate the copyright holders for materials used, and we apologize for any oversights. Individual photographers and collections are listed for photographs when known. All other items not credited below are from the MVP Books collection.

AP/Wide World Photos: p. 77, 80, 92 (Bill Ingraham), 94, 117 top left (Harry Harris), 136 (Bill Ingraham), 141 top, 152, 156, 162 (John Swart), 173 (George Widman).

Getty Images: p. 2 (Rob Tringali/ Sportschrome), 6 (Al Tielemans/ *Sports Illustrated*), 13 (Mark Rucker/Transcendental Graphics), 18 (Chicago History Museum), 19 (Chicago History Museum), 45 (NY Daily News), 66 (Mark Rucker/Transcendental Graphics), 68 (Mark Rucker/ Transcendental Graphics), 81 (MLB Photos), 86 (Mark Rucker/ Transcendental Graphics), 87 (Hulton Archive), 105 (Rogers Photo Archive), 110 (Walter Iooss Jr./*Sports Illustrated*)), 112 (Rogers Photo Archive), 113 (Louis Requena/MLB Photos), 116 (Walter Iooss Jr./*Sports Illustrated*)), 119 (Diamond Images), 121 (Charles Bonnay/ Time & Life Pictures), 123 (Charles Bonnay/Time & Life Pictures), 126 (Focus on Sport), 128 (Herb Scharfman/*Sports Illustrated*)), 132 (Louis Requena/ MLB Photos), 133 (John Iacono/ Sports Illustrated), 134 (Al Messerschmidt), 137 top (James Drake/*Sports Illustrated*)), 138 (Walter Iooss Jr./*Sports Illustrated*)), 140 (John Iacono/ *Sports Illustrated*)), 146 (Walter Iooss Jr./*Sports Illustrated*)), 148 (Andy Hayt/*Sports Illustrated*)), 149 top (Walter Iooss Jr./ *Sports Illustrated*)), 151 (Heinz Kluetmeier/*Sports Illustrated*)), 153 (Ronald C. Modra/Sports Imagery), 154 (Focus on Sport), 157 top (John Iacono/*Sports Illustrated*)), 158 (Rick Stewart), 159 (Rick Stewart), 160 (John Williamson/MLB Photos), 161 (George Gojkovich), 163 (Ron Vesely/MLB Photos), 167 (Rick Stewart), 168 (Rick Stewart), 169 (Ron Vesely/MLB Photos), 170 (Andrew D. Bernstein), 175 (MLB Photos), 176 (Brad Mangin/ *Sports Illustrated*)), 177 (Mitchell Layton), 178 (Tom Mihalek/ AFP), 179 (Carlo Allegri/AFP), 180 (Chuck Solomon/*Sports Illustrated*)), 181 (Tom Mihalek/ AFP), 187 (Jed Jacobsohn), 188 (Tom Mihalek/AFP), 189 (Tom DiPace/*Sports Illustrated*)), 190 (Lee Celano/AFP), 191 (Jonathan Daniel), 194 (Jamie Squire), 195 top (David E. Klutho/ *Sports Illustrated*)), 198 (Len Redkoles), 200 (Gene J. Puskar), 202 (Jeff Zelevansky), 205 (Chris McGrath), 206 (Jed Jacobsohn), 208 (Jeff Zelevansky), 209 (Rob Tringali/SportsChrome), 210 (Miles Kennedy), 211 (Drew Hallowell), 212 (Miles Kennedy), 213 (Miles Kennedy), 214 (Rich Schultz).

Heritage Auctions: p. 37 left, 59 top, 65, 91 right, 107, 109 top right, 117 top right, 124, 125 right, 150, 157 bottom left.

Library of Congress, Prints and Photographs Division: p. 9, 10 top left and right, 11 both, 15, 20, 22, 23, 24, 25, 27, 28, 30, 31, 32, 34, 35, 36, 39, 42, 43, 46.

National Baseball Hall of Fame Library, Cooperstown, N.Y.: p. 10 bottom left, 12, 16, 17, 29, 33, 37 right, 41, 47, 48, 50, 51, 53, 54, 55, 56, 57, 61, 62, 63, 67, 69, 70, 71, 78, 79, 85, 88, 95 bottom, 97, 98, 99, 100, 102, 103, 104, 106, 109 bottom left, 114, 115, 118, 122, 125 left, 129, 143, 155, 165 both, 216.

Shutterstock.com: p. 139 (Aspen Photo), 184, 192, 195 bottom, 197, 198 both, 207.

Index

Aaron, Hank, 77, 100, 120, 132

Abreu, Bobby, 167, 180–181, 184–186, 189, 191, 193–194, 196

Adams, Buster, 83

Alexander, Grover Cleveland "Pete," 14–15, 26, 30–40, 62, 101

Allen, Ethan, 67–69

Allen, Richie "Dick," 111, 118–120, 122–123, 134, 137–138

Amaro, Ruben Jr., 185, 204, 207, 214

Anderson, George Lee "Sparky," 107

Anderson, Harry, 106

Anderson, Marlon, 180–181

Arias, Alex, 181

Arizona Diamondbacks, 186, 194

Arlett, Buzz, 63

Arnovich, Morrie, 70–71, 73

Ashburn, Richie, 72, 77, 87–88, 93, 95–97, 99–100, 102–104, 106, 109–110, 112, 115, 134, 177, 179, 192

Atlanta Braves, 116, 121, 134, 167, 175–177, 185, 188–189, 191, 193–194, 196, 199, 205, 207, 211, 213. *See also* Boston Braves.

Baker Bowl (a.k.a. Philadelphia Baseball Grounds), 8, 13–14, 16, 22–23, 27, 37, 39–40, 44–45, 48, 50, 52, 55, 57, 60, 62–66, 70–73, 130, 192
collapse, 20, 26, 44

Baker, William F., 32–35, 38, 44, 47, 50–51, 55, 57, 62–63

Baldschun, Jack, 114–115

Baltimore Orioles, 7, 146, 149, 156–157, 166, 193

Bancroft, Dave "Beauty," 34, 37, 44, 46, 50–51

Banks, Ernie, 77

Barrett, Dick, 81, 84

Barry, Shad, 18

Bartell, Dick, 61, 63–64, 66–68

Bates, Johnny, 28

Beck, Boom-Boom, 73

Becker, Beals, 33

Bedrosian, Steve, 160–163

Bell, David, 193, 196

Bell, George, 146

Benge, Ray, 56–57, 63, 66

Bennett, Dennis, 114

Blanton, Joe, 200–204, 214

Boone, Bob, 126, 132, 134, 136, 139–140, 142, 145, 148, 151, 153, 154

Boozer, John, 122

Boston Braves, 15, 20, 35, 37, 49, 51, 55–56, 64, 68–69, 81, 107. *See also* Atlanta Braves.

Boston Red Sox, 14–15, 35, 81

Bottalico, Ricky, 166, 178–180

Bowa, Larry, 126–127, 129, 132–134, 136, 138, 140–142, 149, 153–154, 184–186, 188, 190–191, 193

Bowman, Joe, 69

Bouchee, Ed, 104, 106

Bragan, Bobby, 81

Bransfield, Kitty, 25

Brogna, Rico, 180

Brooklyn Dodgers (a.k.a. Robins), 56, 63, 68–69, 71, 77, 79, 86, 88, 92, 94–95, 99. *See also* Los Angeles Dodgers.

Brooklyn Tip-Tops, 33, 36–37, 49

Bruntlett, Eric, 204

Brusstar, Warren, 140–142

Buffington, Charlie, 11

Buhl, Bob, 111, 119

Bunning, Jim, 111, 116–120, 122, 125, 128–129, 178, 188

Burgess, Smoky, 100, 102

Burrell, Pat, 185–186, 189–191, 194, 196, 198–202, 204

Butcher, Max, 73

Buzhardt, John, 112

Byrd, Marlon, 191

Byrd, Paul, 181

Bystrom, Marty, 147, 150–151, 158

Caballero, Ralph "Putsy," 81

Callison, Johnny, 107, 111, 114–116, 118–119, 122

Camilli, Dolph, 68–71

Camnitz, Howie, 33

Campbell, Bill, 110

Carlson, Hal, 54

Carlton, Steve, 6–7, 126–127, 131–133, 135–136, 138–142, 147–148, 150–158, 160–161, 165, 176, 191–192

Carman, Don, 159–161

Carpenter, Bob Jr., 76, 82–83, 92

Carpenter, Robert R. M., 83, 85, 87, 93, 107, 122–123

Carpenter, Ruly, 146

Cash, Dave, 127, 133–134, 136, 138

Chapman, Ben, 77, 84–88

Chicago Cubs, 11, 19, 23, 25, 31, 38–39, 46, 49, 52, 60, 69, 73, 77–78, 87–89, 97–98, 111–113, 136, 142, 146, 149–150, 153, 156, 158, 214

Chicago White Sox, 41, 107, 135, 155

Christenson, Larry, 127, 138–142

Church, Bubba, 95

Cincinnati Reds, 8, 16, 30, 34, 40–41, 67, 83, 112, 116–117, 127, 137, 177, 196, 208–209

Citizens Bank Park, 7, 14, 97, 130, 135, 184–185, 192–193, 199, 201, 205, 208–210

Cleveland Indians, 17–18, 99, 147, 184

Cohen, Andy, 112

Coleman, John, 8–9

Collins, "Fidgety" Phil, 64

Colorado Rockies, 176, 185, 199, 201, 205

Columbia Park, 19–20, 26

Combs, Pat, 168

Conley, Gene, 107

Connie Mack Stadium, 49, 72, 103, 121, 126, 128–130. *See also* Shibe Park.

Coombs, Jack, 41

Corcoran, Tim, 158

Corrales, Pat, 154, 156

Corridon, Frank, 24

Coveleski, Harry, 24–25

Covington, Wes, 115

Cowley, Joe, 161

Cox, William B., 76, 82–83

Cravath, Gavvy, 15, 31–38, 41, 46–47

Cross, Monte, 18

Culp, Ray, 115, 118–119

Dahlgren, Babe, 82

Dalrymple, Clay, 120, 122

Dark, Alvin, 112

Daulton, Darren, 166, 168–169, 171, 173, 175–178

Davis, Curt, 67–69, 75

Davis, Spud, 57, 63–64, 66, 73

Delahanty, Ed, 10–12, 16–19, 143

Demaree, Al, 34

Demeter, Don, 113–115

Denny, John, 147, 156–158

Dernier, Bob, 7, 153–154, 163

Detroit Tigers, 82, 98–99, 102, 128, 147, 158, 161

Diaz, Bo, 154, 157, 168

Dillhoefer, William "Pickles," 38–39

DiMaggio, Joe, 94

DiMaggio, Vince, 84

Dooin, Charles "Red," 28, 30, 33–34, 43

Doolan, Mickey, 23, 33

Donahue, Red, 16

Donovan, "Wild" Bill, 47

Drew, J. D., 179

Drews, Karl, 98

Duffy, Hugh, 21–22, 24

Duggleby, Bill, 18–19

Duncan, Mariano, 176

Dykstra, Lenny, 166–169, 171–178, 180

Eisenreich, Jim, 166, 172–174, 176–178

Elia, Lee, 161–162

Elliott, Jumbo, 63, 75

Ennis, Del, 77, 85–90, 94–95, 98–99, 102

Etten, Nick, 79–80

Farrell, Turk, 104, 106, 112, 120

Feliz, Pedro, 200

Felske, John, 159, 161

Ferguson, Bob, 8–9

Ferguson, Charlie, 11

Fernandez, Chico, 104

Finn, Neal "Mickey," 66

Fitzsimmons, Freddie, 81–82, 84

Fletcher, Art, 44, 46, 50–52

Flick, Elmer, 12, 16, 18

Florida Marlins, 171, 176, 180, 199, 201

Foxx, Jimmie, 81, 84

Franco, Julio, 146

Francona, Terry, 166–167, 178–179, 186

Fraser, Chick, 16, 19, 21

Freese, Gene, 107

Fregosi, Jim, 166, 169, 172, 176, 178

Frisch, Frankie, 51

Frye, Charlie, 78

Fryman, Woody, 122

Gamble, Oscar, 126

Gant, Ron, 181

Garber, Gene, 135, 138–140

Giles, Bill, 160–161

Gillick, Pat, 185, 200, 203

Glanville, Doug, 180–181, 186, 188

Glavine, Tom, 199

Gleason, Kid, 11

Gomez, Chile, 68

Gonzalez, Tony, 114–115, 120, 122

Gordon, Tom, 196

Grace, Mike, 178

Green, Dallas, 115, 127, 142, 149–150, 153

Green, Tyler, 177

Greene, Tommy, 166, 169, 172–174, 176

Grissom, Lee, 79

Groat, Dick, 119–120

Gross, Greg, 158, 161–162

Gross, Kevin, 159, 161

Halladay, Roy, 207–214

Hamels, Cole, 198, 200–203, 207–208, 210, 212–214

Hamilton, Jack, 114

Hamilton, Billy, 9

Hamner, Granny, 77, 84, 87, 95, 99–100

Hamner, Garvin, 84

Harper, George, 51–52

Harris, Bucky, 76, 82

Haslin, Mickey, 68

Hayes, Charlie, 177

Hayes, Von, 158–159, 163, 168

Hebner, Richie, 138

Heintzelman, Ken, 88
Henline, Butch, 49–50
Hernandez, Willie, 147, 156, 158
Herrera, Pancho, 112
Higbe, Kirby, 73, 78–79
Hoerner, Joe, 128
Holke, Walter, 51
Hollins, Dave, 171, 173
Hornsby, Rogers, 48
Houston Astros (a.k.a. Colt .45s), 110,
     114, 149–150, 155, 193, 195, 201
Howard, Ryan, 184–185, 194, 196–201,
     203–205, 207, 210, 213
Hubbell, Bill, 46, 49–51
Hurst, Don, 45, 56–57, 60, 63–64

Ibanez, Raul, 204
Incaviglia, Pete, 172, 178

Jackson, Danny, 166, 171, 176, 182
Jackson, Larry, 111, 119, 122
Jackson, Michael, 161
Jackson, "Shoeless" Joe, 41
James, Chris, 162–163
Jeffries, Greg, 177
Jeltz, Steve, 162
Jenkins, Ferguson, 7, 60, 111, 118–119
Jenkins, Geoff, 203
Johnson, Davey, 138, 140
Johnson, Deron, 129, 131
Johnson, Syl, 68, 73
Johnstone, Jay, 136–137, 140
Jones, Doug, 176
Jones, Willie, 96, 99–100, 106
Jorgens, Orville, 68
Judd, Oscar, 86

Kaat, Jim, 138–139
Kalas, Harry, 97, 129–130, 158, 161,
     174, 190, 192, 195, 204
Kansas City Athletics, 26, 44, 76
Kansas City Royals, 148, 151

Karl, Andy, 85
Kazanski, Ted, 99, 103
Keister, Bill, 19
Kelly, George, 51
Kendrick, Kyle, 208
Kennedy, John, 77, 104
Killefer, Bill, 32–33, 38
Klein, Chuck, 45, 56–57, 59–66,
     69–71, 73, 78, 119, 143, 173
Knabe, Otto, 33
Knight, Jack, 54
Knowles, Darold, 119
Konetchy, Ed, 47
Konstanty, Jim, 93–96, 99
Koosman, Jerry, 158
Koufax, Sandy, 116, 119
Kruk, John, 163, 166, 169, 171–173,
     176, 183

Lajoie, Nap, 12, 14, 16–18, 26
Landis, Kenesaw Mountain, 51, 66,
     76, 82, 84
Leach, Freddy, 54–56
Lee, Cliff, 49–50, 185, 204–206,
     209–210, 212–214
Lee, Travis, 189
LeMaster, Wayne, 70
Leonard, Dutch, 86–87
Leyva, Nick, 163, 169
Lidge, Brad, 185, 200–203, 205–206,
     212
Lidle, Cory, 189, 196
Lieber, Jon, 194
Lieberthal, Mike, 179, 181, 185–186,
     190–191, 194
Litwhiler, Danny, 78, 80–81
Lobert, Hans, 30–34, 71, 80
Lock, Don, 120
Locke, William H., 31–32
Lofton, Kenny, 194
Lonborg, Jim, 132–133, 135–136
Lopata, Stan, 95, 102–103

Los Angeles Angels, 87
Los Angeles Dodgers, 6, 107, 114–115,
     119, 127, 138–139, 141, 156–157,
     185, 202, 205–206, 212. See also
     Brooklyn Dodgers.
Lucchesi, Frank, 126, 128, 131
Luderus, Fred, 30–32, 35, 37, 41
Luzinski, Greg, 126–127, 131–136,
     138, 140–141, 150, 152, 192

Maddox, Garry, 127, 134, 136, 138,
     140–141, 148–150, 156–157, 160,
     173
Madison, Ryan, 212
Mack, Connie, 14, 17–18, 26, 28, 71,
     102, 192
Magee, Sherry, 15, 21–25, 27–28,
     30–34, 42
Mahaffey, Art, 113–114, 118
Mallon, Les, 63
Mantle, Mickey, 93
Manuel, Charlie, 193–196, 201, 204,
     207, 211, 214
Martin, Hersh, 71
Martinez, Pedro, 204–205
Matthews, Gary, 152–154, 156–157
Mauch, Gene, 110–117, 122
May, Pinkie 78
Mayer, Erskine, 33–34, 37
Mays, Willie, 77, 93, 106
McBride, Bake, 138, 141, 152, 164
McCarver, Tim, 126, 128, 138
McCormick, Frank, 85
McDowell, Roger, 163
McGraw, Tug, 127, 135, 137–138,
     140–142, 146, 148–151, 156, 191
McInnes, Stuffy, 44, 55
McQuillan, George, 24–25, 27–28, 30
Meadows, Lee, 41, 46, 49
Mesa, Jose, 190–191
Melton, Rube, 80
Meusel, Irish, 41, 46–47, 163

Meyer, Jack, 106, 112
Meyer, Russ, 88, 98
Milton, Eric, 193
Milwaukee Brewers, 105, 113, 185, 194, 196, 201–202
Milwood, Kevin, 184, 191, 193
Mokan, Johnny, 45, 54
Montanez, Willie, 129, 131, 133–134, 144
Montgomery, David, 179
Montreal Expos, 111, 150, 169, 191
Moore, Earl, 27–28
Moore, Johnny, 67–69
Moore, Terry, 100, 102
Moran, Pat, 15, 33–35, 38, 40–41
Morandini, Mickey, 171, 174, 177–178, 186
Morgan, Joe, 112, 135, 150, 156–158
Moyer, Jamie, 198, 200–201, 208
Mulcahy, Hugh "Losing Pitcher," 70–71, 73, 78–79
Mulholland, Terry, 166, 168–169, 171–172, 174, 176, 178
Murphy, Dale, 168
Murray, Billy, 24–25, 27
Myers, Brett, 191, 196, 200–202

New York Giants, 22–23, 25, 31–32, 34, 38, 41, 44–47, 51–52, 64, 68, 77, 104, 163–164
New York Mets, 110, 114, 125, 132, 148, 159–160, 174, 179, 185, 196, 198–199, 201, 208
New York Yankees, 47, 79, 92–96, 102, 115, 179, 185, 196, 204, 206, 210
Northey, Ron, 83–84, 86
Nugent, Gerald P. "Gerry," 63, 68, 73, 78, 80, 82

Oakland Athletics, 26, 147
Oates, Johnny, 134
O'Connell, Jimmy, 51

O'Doul, Lefty, 45, 56–57, 61–63
O'Neill, Steve, 93, 98–100
Oswalt, Roy, 208, 210, 212
Owens, Jim, 107, 112
Owens, Paul, 131, 138–140, 156, 159
Ozark, Danny, 127, 132, 136–137, 139, 141–142, 149

Padilla, Vicente, 190–191, 193
Papelbon, Jonathan, 214
Parrish, Lance, 161–162
Paskert, Dode, 30–31
Passeau, Claude, 69–71, 73, 78
Pence, Hunter, 210
Pennock, Herb, 83–86
Perez, Tony, 156, 158
Philadelphia Athletics, 9, 11, 14, 16–17, 19, 20, 22, 24, 26–27, 28, 35, 41, 48, 55, 70–72, 76, 81, 102. See also Kansas City Athletics and Oakland Athletics
Philadelphia Eagles, 72
Pierre, Juan, 213, 215
Pittinger, Charlie "Togie," 22
Pittsburgh Pirates, 14, 16, 49, 52, 63, 100, 112, 122, 128, 133–134, 137–138, 140, 149, 159, 161, 163, 184, 191
Post, Wally, 107
Potter, Jimmy, 19, 21–22, 27
Prendergast, Mike, 38–40
Prothro, James "Doc," 61, 73, 78–79
Providence Grays, 9, 11

Quantrill, Paul, 177
Quinn, John, 107, 114, 119

Raffensberger, Ken, 83, 86
Rapp, Goldie, 47
Rawley, Shane, 159, 161
Reach, Al, 8–9, 19
Ready, Randy, 163, 169

Recreation Park, 13
Reed, Ron, 127, 138, 140–141
Relaford, Desi, 180
Repulski, Rip, 104
Ring, Jimmy, 49–52, 56
Ripken, Cal, 157
Rivera, Ben, 172
Rixey, Eppa, 15, 36–38, 40, 46, 119
Roberts, Robin, 77, 88–89, 92–96, 98–107, 112–114, 192
Robinson, Jackie, 56, 77, 86–87, 94, 96, 104, 132
Rogers, John, 8–9, 17, 19
Rojas, Cookie, 118, 122
Rolen, Scott, 166–167, 178–181, 186–187, 189–190
Rollins, Jimmy, 173, 184–186, 188–191, 193–196, 198–199, 201, 204–205, 211–214, 216
Rose, Pete, 7, 127, 140, 142–143, 151–153, 156, 158
Roth, Alice, 104
Rowand, Aaron, 185, 199
Rowe, Schoolboy, 82, 86–88
Ruiz, Carlos, 198, 200, 203, 205, 208–209, 213–214
Ruth, Babe, 9, 35–36, 44, 46–47, 55, 57, 160
Ruthven, Dick, 140, 142, 150
Ryan, Mike, 122, 128

Saam, Byrum, 110
Samuel, Juan, 158–163, 174
San Diego Padres, 111, 174, 181, 188
San Francisco Giants, 112–113, 150, 155, 185, 194, 208
Sandberg, Ryne, 7, 60, 146, 153, 158, 214
Sanford, Jack, 104, 106
Santiago, Benito, 178
Sawyer, Eddie, 77, 87–88, 93, 95–96, 98–99, 106, 110, 112

Schanz, Charley, 81, 83–84

Schilling, Curt, 166–167, 171–172, 174, 177–181, 186

Schmidt, Mike, 6–7, 85, 126–127, 129, 132, 134–136, 138, 140–143, 148, 150, 152, 156, 158–163, 165, 177, 184, 189, 191–192, 196

Seaton, Tom, 32–33

Selma, Dick, 128–129, 131

Seminick, Andy, 77, 88, 94

Shettsline, Billy, 21–22

Shibe Park, 27–28, 44, 48, 55, 60, 66, 71–72, 80, 85–86, 88, 92, 94, 98, 104. *See also* Connie Mack Stadium.

Short, Chris, 111, 116–120, 122–123, 128–129

Shotton, Burt, 44, 55–57, 60, 62, 64, 66–67

Simmons, Curt, 77, 87, 93–96, 98–100, 108

Sisler, Dick, 92, 94–95, 97, 116

Skinner, Bob, 111, 122–123

Slocumb, Heathcliff, 177

Smith, Mayo, 100, 102–103, 106

Snider, Duke, 93

Sparks, Tully, 23, 27

St. Louis Cardinals, 22, 56–57, 64, 66, 70, 81, 83, 87, 99, 116–117, 120, 122, 126, 154–156, 162, 167, 173, 190, 196, 201, 204, 207, 210–212

Stone, Jeff, 158

Stuart, Dick, 118

Stengel, Casey, 46

Stone, Jeff, 159

Sweetland, Les, 56–57

Tampa Bay Devil Rays, 185, 189, 200, 202–203

Taylor, Tony, 112–113, 115, 122, 128, 137

Tekulve, Kent, 159, 161

Texas Rangers, 194

Thomas, Lee, 147, 162–163, 166, 169, 171, 179

Thomas, Roy, 19, 22–23

Thome, Jim, 184–185, 190–191, 193–194, 199

Thompson, Fresco, 44, 55, 57

Thompson, Milt, 161, 172–173

Thon, Dickie, 163

Titus, "Silent" John, 21–22

Toronto Blue Jays, 166–167, 172, 174

Trillo, Manny, 127, 142, 150–151, 154

Twitchell, Wayne, 132–133

Valenzuela, Fernando, 176

Verban, Emil, 85–86

Veterans Stadium, 6–7, 48, 72, 93, 126–130, 143, 148, 150, 157, 160, 163, 166, 171–172, 174, 178, 180, 184, 188, 191–192

Victorino, Shane, 201–202, 205, 213–214, 217

Virgil, Ozzie, 159

Vukovich, George, 152–153

Vukovich, John, 162

Urbina, Ugueth, 194

Unser, Del, 132, 142, 150–151

Utley, Chase, 185, 194, 196–201, 203–204, 206–208, 211, 213

Wade, Ed, 179, 181, 185

Wagner, Billy, 193–195

Wagner, Honus, 16, 24

Waitkus, Eddie, 88–89, 94

Walker, Harry, 86, 97

Walters, Bucky, 67, 69–71

Washington Nationals, 195, 204, 207–208, 213

Washington Senators, 11, 18, 82, 86

Watson, John "Mule," 40

Weintraub, Phil, 71

Werth, Jayson, 200–201, 204–205, 207–208

West, David, 172, 175, 177

White, Bill, 119–120, 122

Whitney, Arthur "Pinky," 56–57, 61–62, 69–70

Whitted, Possum, 34, 38

Wilhelm, Kaiser, 44, 47, 49–50

Williams, Cy, 44, 46–52, 55

Williams, Mitch, 166, 169, 172, 174–176

Willoughby, Claude, 57

Wilson, Glenn, 147, 158–159

Wilson, Jimmie, 52, 54, 60–61, 66–68, 71, 75

Wine, Bobby, 114–115, 120

Wise, Rick, 120, 122–123, 126, 128–129, 131

Wolf, Randy, 181, 185–186, 188, 190–191, 193

Woodward, Woody, 162

Worrell, Tim, 193

Wright, Harry, 9–10

Wrightstone, Russ, 51, 54–55

Youngs, Ross, 51

Zimmer, Chief, 19